IMAGES
of America

IJAMS NATURE CENTER

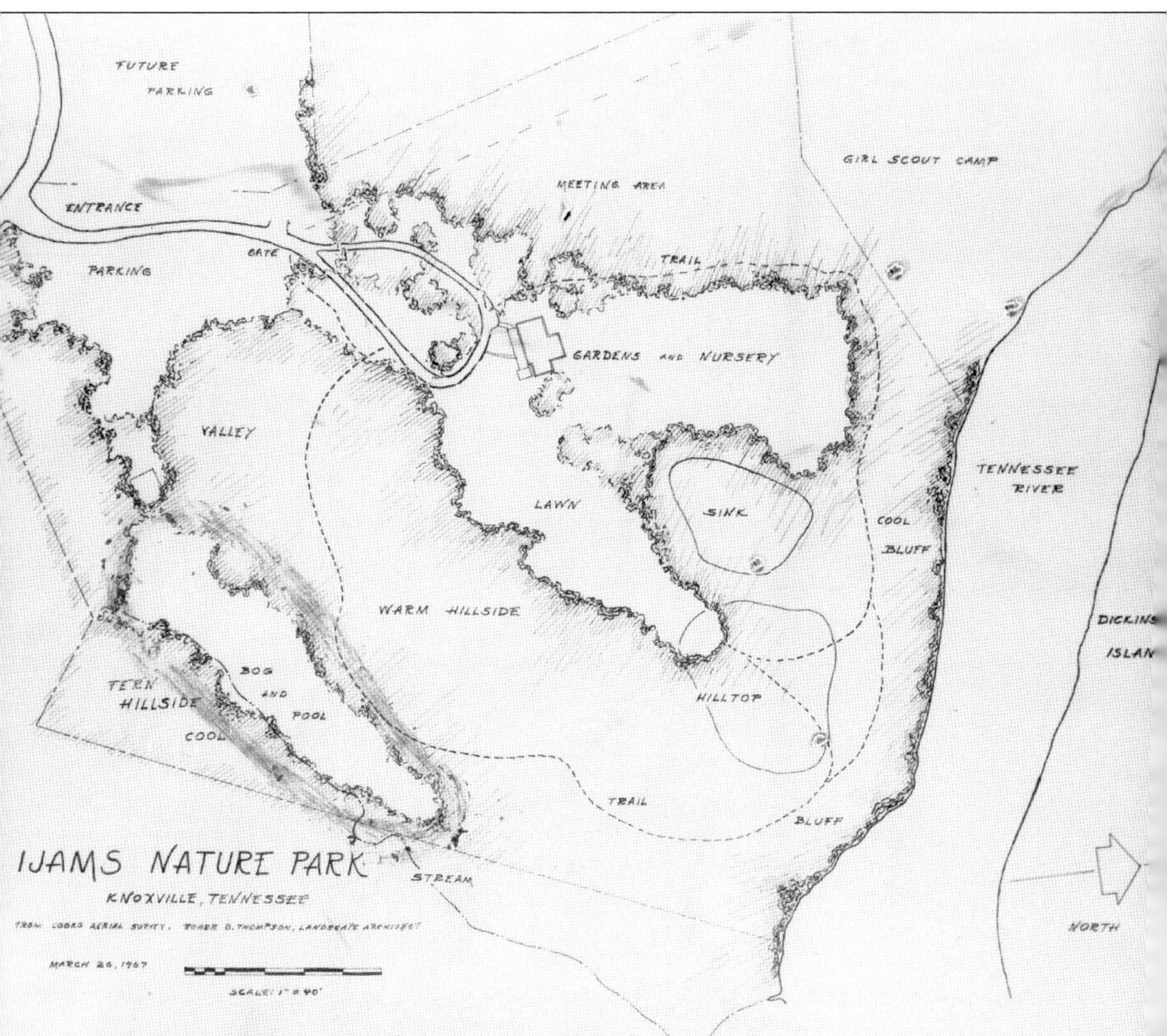

Roger B. Thompson, from the University of Tennessee horticulture department, was hired as the consulting landscape architect in 1964 to support the overall conservation plan for the proposed Ijams Nature Park. This map was drawn using an aerial survey. Based on 50 years of development and management by Harry and Alice Ijams, Thompson stated, "The park now contains plants which display the whole story of natural growth, degeneration, and renewal, and areas of many varying degrees of sunlight, moisture, slope, competition, etc." The city of Knoxville's new nature park was very special indeed. (*Knoxville News Sentinel.*)

On the Cover: Three of the Ijams daughters pose for the camera by a small pond at the Ijams Bird Sanctuary in July 1923. Accomplished naturalists and Girl Scouts, the girls were raised in a natural setting unique among American backyards. The landscape would later become a public nature park for all of Knoxville to enjoy. From left to right are Martha, Elizabeth, and Mary Ijams. (Ijams family collection.)

IMAGES
of America

IJAMS NATURE CENTER

Paul James

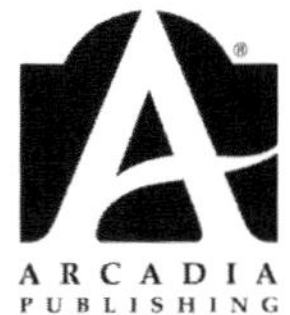

ISBN 978-0-7385-8579-6

Published by Arcadia Publishing
Charleston, South Carolina

Printed in the United States of America

Library of Congress Control Number: 2009940330

For all general information contact Arcadia Publishing at:
Telephone 843-853-2070
Fax 843-853-0044
E-mail sales@arcadiapublishing.com
For customer service and orders:
Toll-Free 1-888-313-2665

Visit us on the Internet at www.arcadiapublishing.com

Dedicated to the memory of the original architects of the Ijams legacy: H. P., Alice, Elizabeth, Jo, Mary, and Martha Ijams.

Contents

ACKNOWLEDGMENTS

This book would only be an idea without the support and generosity of the Ijams grandchildren, George Kern, Martha Kern, and Mary Gallant, who provided full access to the Ijams family photography archives, most of which had not seen the light of day for many years. Thank you so much for your time, patience, and friendship.

Special thanks goes to Steve Cotham, manager of East Tennessee History Center's Calvin M. McClung Historical Collection, who set me on the right path and contributed images; Maggie Bullwinkel, editor with Arcadia Publishing, for enthusiasm and unwavering support for the project; Paul Efird, *Knoxville News Sentinel*, for archive scans; Annette Hartigan, archivist with the Great Smoky Mountains National Park, for sharing valuable time and resources; Norma Lowe, volunteer with the Girl Scout Council of the Southern Appalachians, for help navigating archive material; Lynn Faust, for turning a brief mountaintop encounter into a new friendship with descendants of Col. W. B. Townsend and Mabel Ijams; Larry Franklin and his dear wife, Cissie, who also shared rare photographs; Sally Judiscak and Marielle Robertson for editing assistance; and Jack Neely for research assistance, editing, and expanding my historical horizons.

Thanks also to the following people who greatly enhanced this book by sharing photographs and memories or helping with identifications: Stephen Lyn Bales, Robert Bell, Edna Bell, Peg Beute, Jim Campbell, Marcia Davis, Mary Farmer, Kathleen Hancock, Lynn Montgomery, Alan Mealka, Harry Moore, Pam Petko-Seus, Nancy Tanner, Jane Williams, James E. Thompson, Thompson Photo Products, and Tennessee Ornithological Society.

Finally, thanks to Julie and Isabel James for sparing family time for me to bring this project to fruition.

Unless noted otherwise, all photographs are used courtesy of the Ijams family collection.

INTRODUCTION

When I look at your charming little home in the woods, I wonder why people build mansions. With its walls faced with slabs of trees, vine-covered to a great height, it fits into the wood so perfectly that it seems a part of the lovely landscape, and not an intrusion.

—Anonymous, *Knoxville News Sentinel*

The anonymous editor responsible for the "Ask Gen. Knox" column in the *Knoxville News Sentinel* wrote the above words about the Ijams family house some time in the 1930s. The same can be said about Ijams Nature Center and how it fits perfectly into the local landscape. For over the course of a century, a small plot of land on the outskirts of Knoxville has quietly had a profound impact on the lives of countless people and has developed a considerable sense of place. The property, abundant with native wildflowers and birdlife, has always welcomed folk seeking a connection with the earth or simply wishing to take a stroll through the woods. Throughout the early years, the Ijams family developed the original 20 acres into a semi-private natural showplace, sharing it with local garden clubs and birding groups who identified with it as a rallying point for horticultural activities, annual bird counts, and nature study. Harry and Alice Ijams were also in great demand, giving talks across town, leading nature walks, hosting flower workshops, or helping Girl and Boy Scouts earn their badges. Schoolchildren consistently visited the wildlife sanctuary for decades, with Fountain City Elementary School making a trip to Ijams in the early 1940s and others probably before then.

A century later, the green movement mirrors the beliefs and philosophies of the Ijams family. Harry Ijams's passion and expertise as Knoxville's first proper ornithologist spearheaded a birding movement throughout the region, which echoed across the state. Alice Ijams, with her philosophy of conservation and preservation, similarly inspired the creation of a horticultural movement, conceived numerous garden clubs, and managed a 12-year stint of educational exhibits at the Tennessee Valley Agricultural and Industry Fair. Despite rapid changes in the world today, many of the family's age-old concepts still apply to caring for the earth in a sustainable way.

Looking back, the Ijams place would now be considered a near-perfect model of how to live a sustainable life in harmony with nature. Harry and Alice Ijams used the natural features and resources of the land to cultivate wildflower meadows, propagate flowers, grow vegetables, and develop habitats for birds and other native wildlife. They also created rock gardens, overlooks, small lily ponds, and larger ponds for their daughters to swim in and play around. Many of these features, such as the Lotus Pond and a hillside of Lenten roses planted by Alice Ijams, can still be enjoyed along the Discovery Trail at Ijams Nature Center today.

In effect, the Ijams daughters—Elizabeth, Jo, Mary, and Martha, all talented naturalists and ornithologists in their own right—were the first students to be educated on the property. The daughters' own environmental heirs include the thousands of schoolchildren and Scouts that came after them on field trips and nature walks to experience the magic of the woods and the natural landscapes often taken for granted throughout East Tennessee.

Over the years, Ijams Nature Center has grown into a truly multidimensional place. The topography of the original home site now seamlessly segues into extensive rolling woodland trails, incorporating a charming boardwalk on the Tennessee River. Across Island Home Avenue, the imposing marble cliffs of Mead's Quarry reflect in crystal-clear waters. All of these natural features deflect the notion of a busy downtown center just 3 miles away, with only the hum of traffic and small airplane chatter from the nearby airport up above.

Very few cities enjoy a wildlife sanctuary accessible so close to a downtown area, and with continued greenway connections, Ijams will one day soon be a destination easily reached by everyone from all sectors of Knoxville by vehicle, bicycle, or on foot. Ijams Nature Center has often been called the jewel in the crown of Knoxville parks. Such a heady title is justified, since it perfectly complements the assortment of quality neighborhood parks, expansive natural areas such as Seven Islands Wildlife Refuge, and the Great Smoky Mountains National Park itself.

Although not a definitive history, this book attempts to capture the early years of the Ijams family, local ornithologists, and outdoor enthusiasts, as well as the development of the wildlife sanctuary and the ongoing environmental legacy that still thrives more than a century later. It is the story of how members of local garden clubs and officials with the City of Knoxville rallied to acquire and turn the property into a public nature park for all people. In addition, it is a glimpse of how the Ijams family and the Townsends came together to create a Girl Scout heritage in the Great Smoky Mountains, and how the first official campsite on Mount LeConte was created by dedicated Knoxville environmentalists striving to protect the mountains and create a national park.

Also featured are visual accounts of nearby quarry sites, which were thriving industrial hubs at the time that Harry and Alice Ijams set up home next door in 1910, extracting pink Tennessee marble used in local buildings and in monuments in the nation's capital and New York. These images are in stark contrast to the tranquil photographs of the Island Home Bird Sanctuary, and yet both were destined to converge many decades later into a public wildlife sanctuary that is Knoxville's gift to everyone.

One

THE IJAMS FAMILY

Joseph H. Ijams, hired as the principal of the Tennessee Deaf and Dumb Asylum, brought the Ijams name to Knoxville, Tennessee, in 1866. The asylum was in a state of neglect after being used as a military hospital during the Civil War, and Joseph Ijams helped turn the school around before his untimely death in 1882. Joseph and Mary Ijams had two daughters and three sons—Dr. Howard A. Ijams was the first quarterback for the Tennessee Volunteers football team, Edwin was superintendent for the Little River Lumber Company, and Harry was a gifted artist who became Knoxville's first ornithologist and created a legacy of conservation and nature study that still persists throughout the region today.

Harry Ijams, widely known as H. P., was a young commercial artist when he married Alice Yoe in 1905. With an avid appetite for the outdoors, H. P. and Alice hiked throughout the Smoky Mountains on their honeymoon, winding up at a memorable spot that later became Elkmont. H. P. had prepared for the trip by hiking from Knoxville to Asheville at a time when road and trail markers barely existed. A future wedding anniversary proved just as adventurous—a canoe trip down the Tennessee River from Knoxville to Chattanooga. The expedition took seven days, with the couple battling heavy rains for much of the journey. The intrepid explorers had the foresight to mail fresh clothes on ahead, which highlighted the couple's creative and practical nature.

After the birth of their first daughter, Elizabeth, H. P. and Alice purchased a 20-acre property in 1910 on the outskirts of town. The couple moved their one-story house from Sevierville Pike to Island Home Pike, which was once part of wealthy Massachusetts-born businessman Perez Dickinson's Island Home estate along the Tennessee River. By the end of the World War I, three more daughters—Josephine, Mary, and Martha—were born at the new house, which H. P. expanded to accommodate the growing family. All of the Ijams daughters would follow in their parents' footsteps, adopting similar passions for wildlife, bird-watching, and outdoor exploration throughout their own lives.

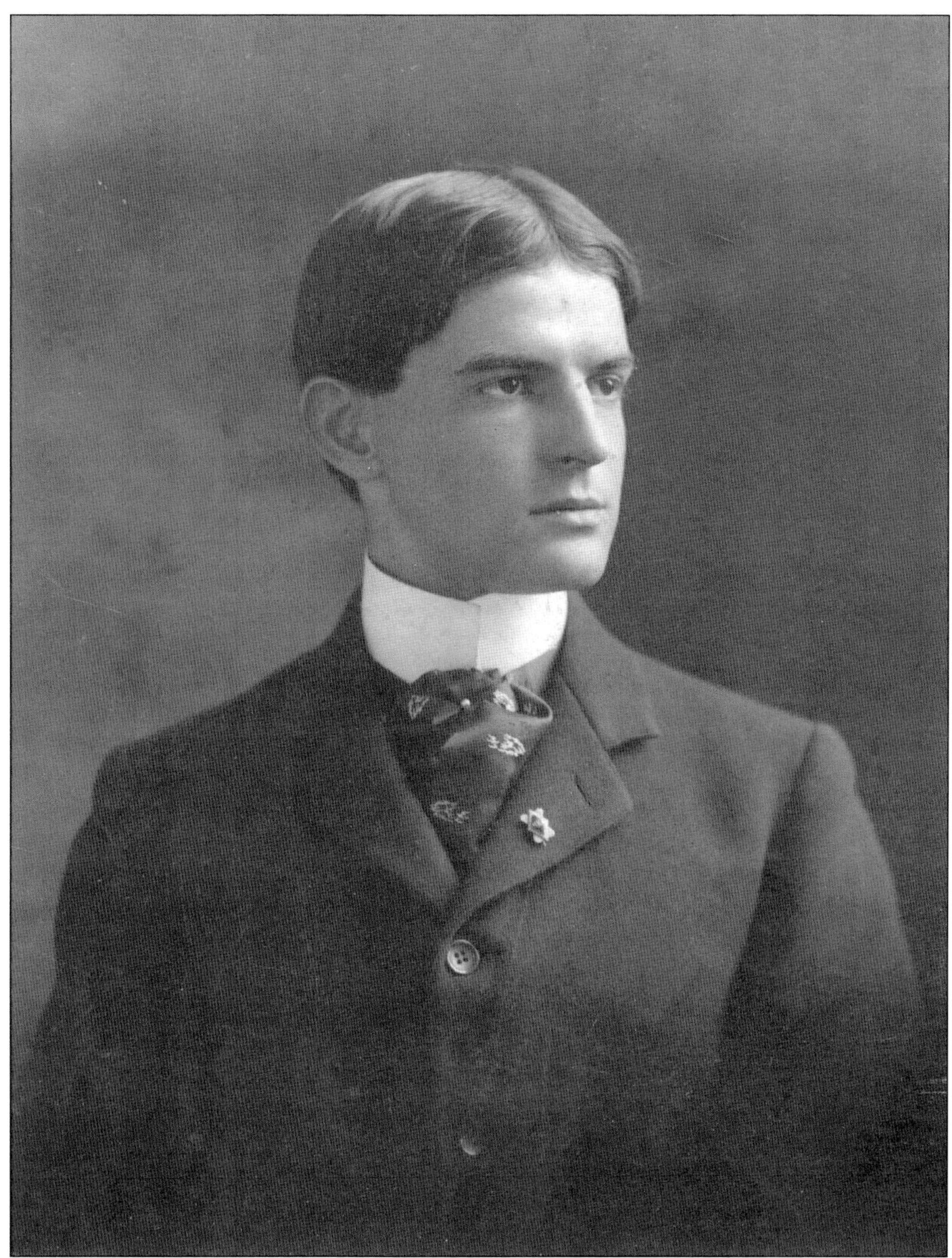

Born in Knoxville in 1876, Harry Pearle Ijams, known widely as H. P., attended public schools and the University of Tennessee before studying at the Cincinnati School of Art. By 1901, H. P. was working as a manager at the Knoxville Engraving Company, and he later became a commercial artist with the architect and engraving company Gredig and Ijams. From the 1920s until his retirement in the early 1950s, H. P. was a resident illustrator for the *Knoxville News Sentinel* and also worked as a freelance artist.

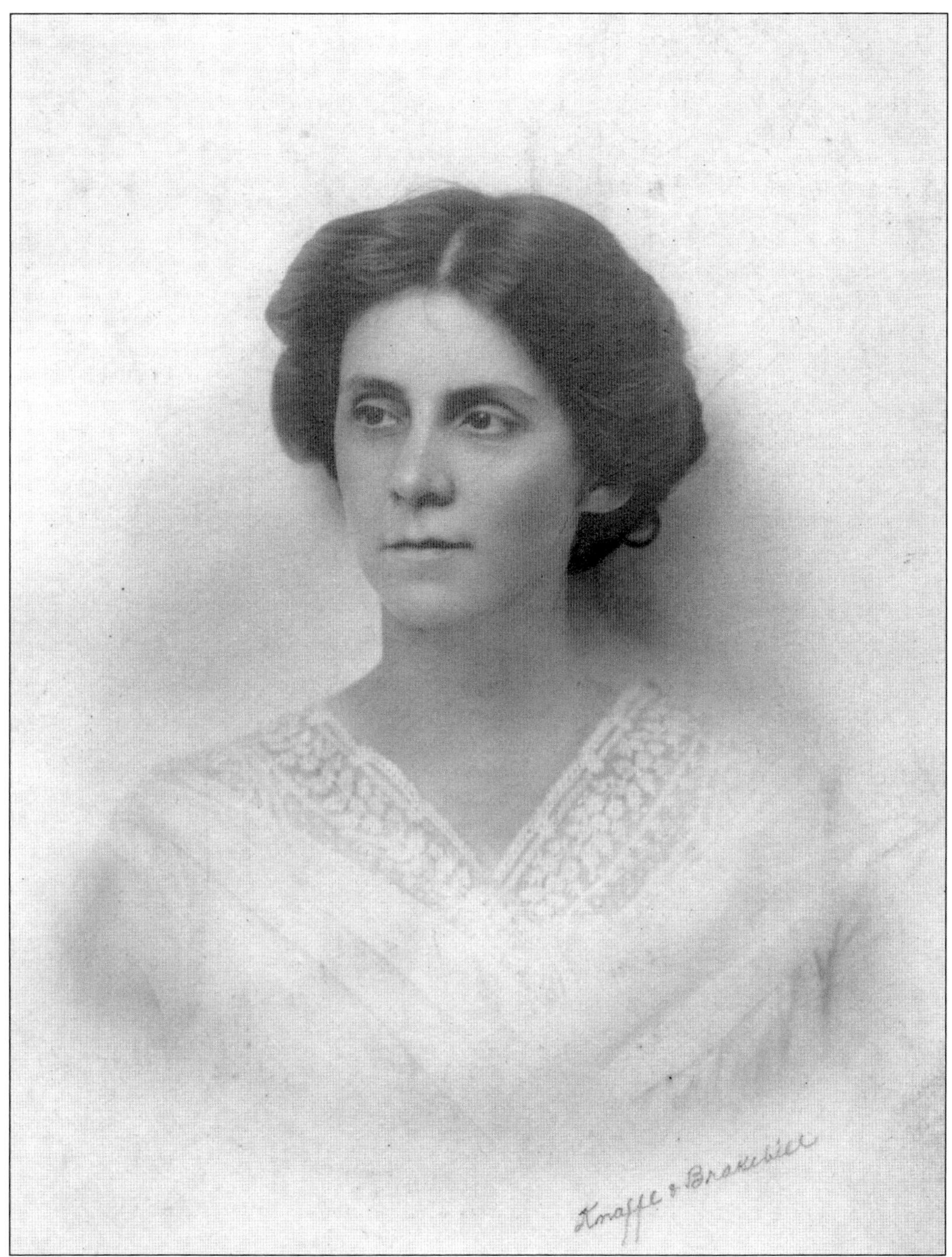

This portrait of Alice Yoe as a young woman was taken around the time she married Harry Ijams in 1905. Born in Jefferson City, Tennessee, in 1880, Alice became Knoxville's leading horticulturalist, and she was widely known as a "walking encyclopedia of garden clubs." An expert flower arranger, Alice conducted Knoxville's first flower arrangement class in 1935 and was fondly remembered by the Church Street Methodist Church for faithfully supplying fresh flowers from her garden every Sunday.

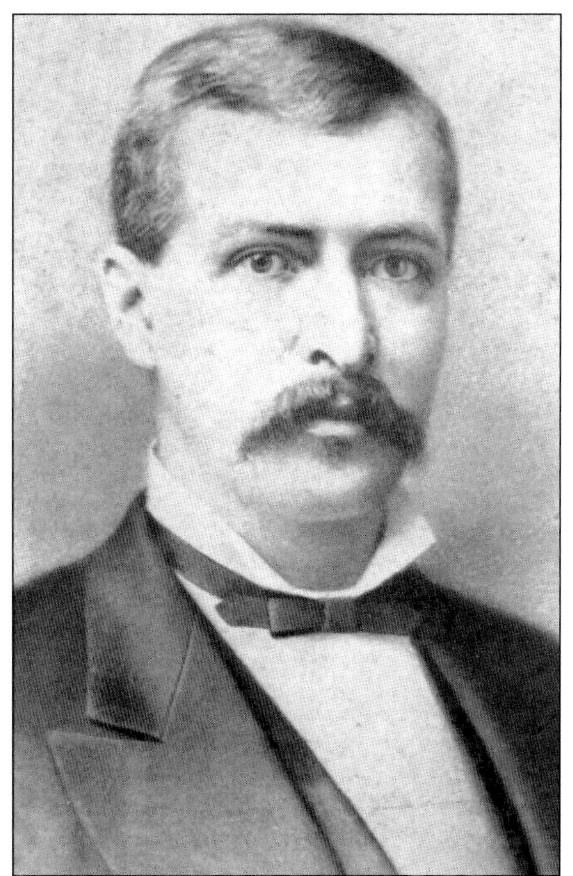

Joseph H. Ijams was hired as principal of the Tennessee Deaf and Dumb Asylum in 1866 to rebuild the facility after it was used as a military hospital during the Civil War. Previously a teacher at the National Deaf-Mute College in Washington, D.C., Joseph was regarded as "the finest deaf-mute teacher in the country." His tenure was cut short when he died suddenly on Christmas Eve in 1882, leaving a widow, Mary, and five children, including young Harry Ijams. (Tennessee School for the Deaf.)

The Tennessee Deaf and Dumb Asylum, later renamed the Tennessee School for the Deaf, was originally located downtown at the corner of Broadway Street and Western Avenue. The asylum operated at that location until 1924, when it moved to the Perez Dickinson estate along the Tennessee River in South Knoxville. The former downtown location subsequently became the site of Knoxville City Hall for many years. It is coincidental that the deaf school's present location is adjacent to Ijams Nature Center. (Tennessee School for the Deaf.)

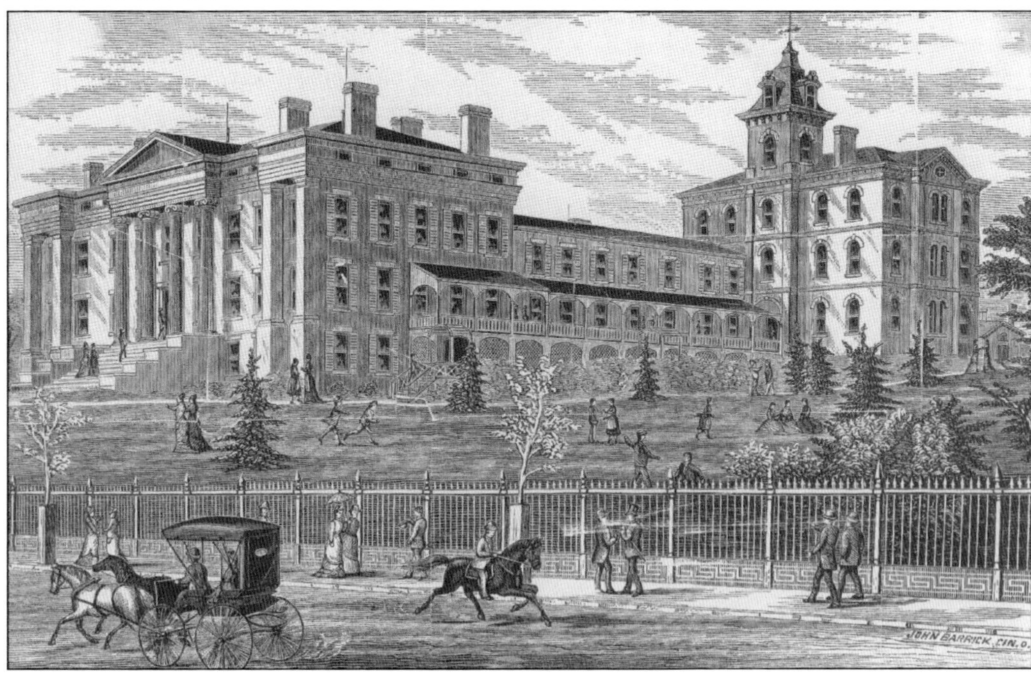

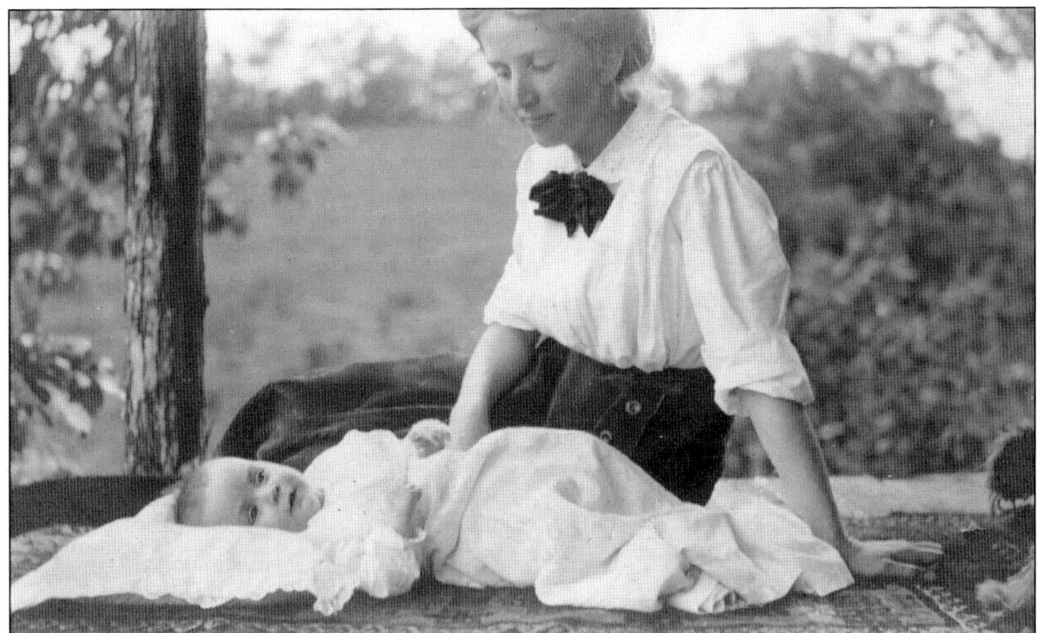

After their marriage, H. P. and Alice Ijams lived for a brief time in Florida before moving back to Knoxville for the birth of their first child, Elizabeth, in 1909. The same year, H. P. was active in community life, including being a board member of a progressive organization, the Recreation Polytechnic Guild, which "intended to improve the lot of working people" by offering a variety of evening lessons including music, medicine, and drawing.

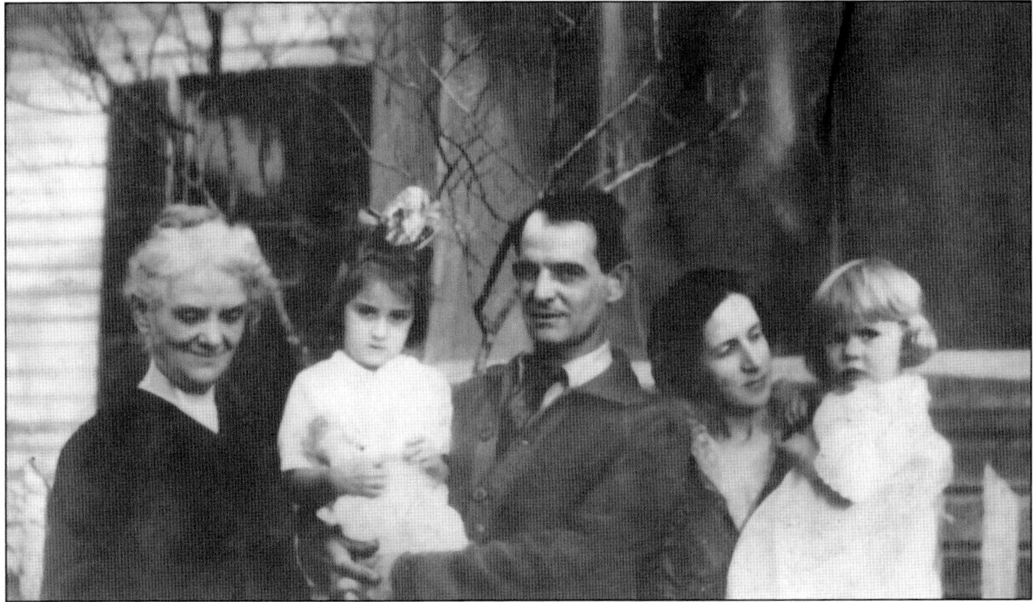

This photograph is rare portrait of the Ijams family around 1915. From left to right are H. P.'s mother, Mary Aiken Ijams, Elizabeth, Harry, Alice, and Josephine. H. P.'s mother and father had been childhood playmates in Rushville, Ohio, before reuniting much later and marrying in Knoxville in 1868. After her husband passed away, Mary Aiken Ijams continued to work as a teacher at the Tennessee Deaf and Dumb Asylum.

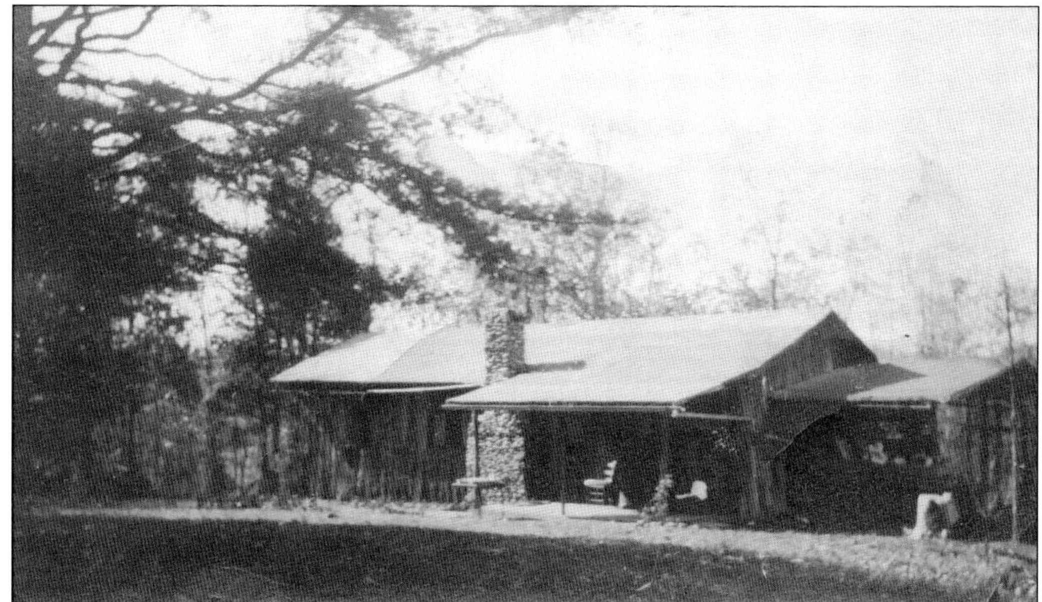

Before purchasing a 20-acre property on Island Home Pike in 1910, H. P. and Alice Ijams lived on a small farm on Sevierville Pike. They took the house with them, which at the time was more like a small log cabin. As the family grew, H. P. and a local carpenter added onto it and, in 1924, added a second story with sleeping porches for their four daughters.

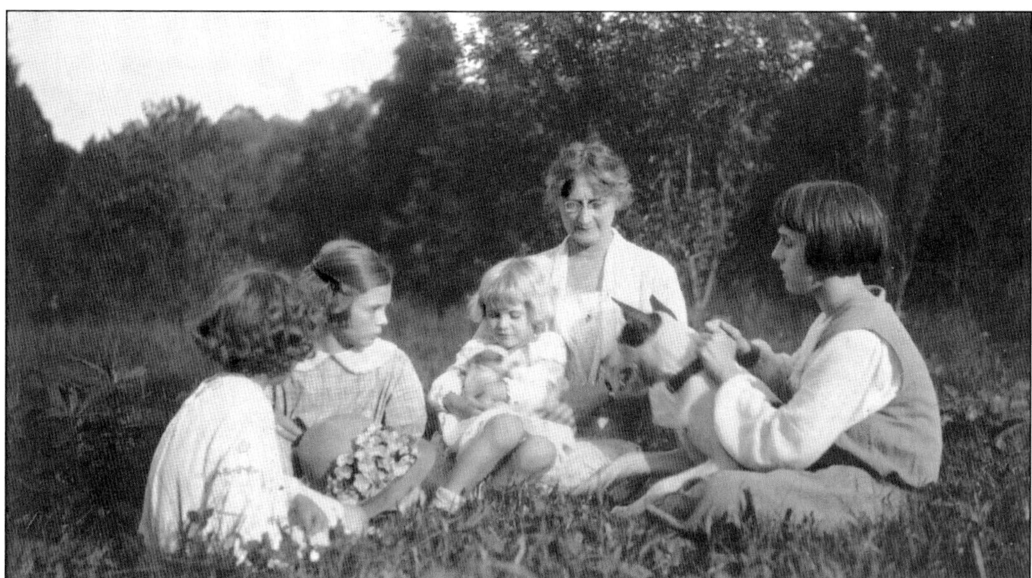

The four Ijams daughters enjoyed the natural splendor of the outdoors while they grew up on the family farm on Island Home Pike. From left to right are Mary, Jo, Martha, May Mamma (Alice Ijams's older sister), and Elizabeth. Dogs were a permanent fixture at the Ijams place. Here, Martha holds a puppy while Elizabeth pets the family dog, Bruno.

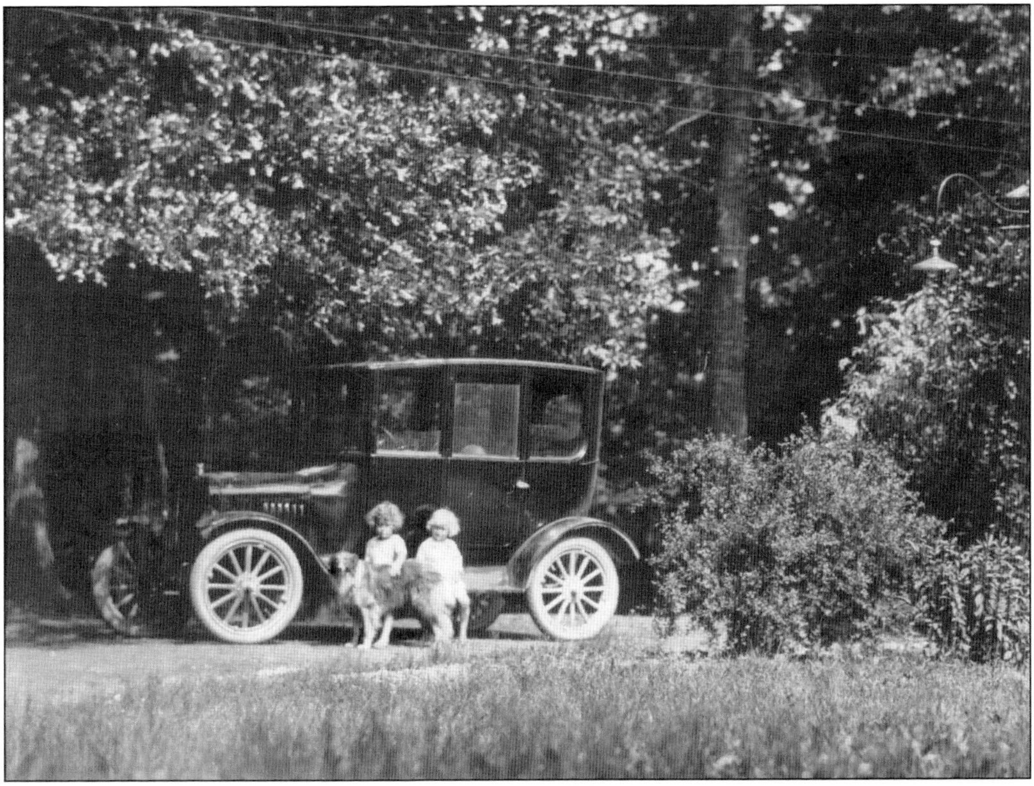

The nearest streetcar was almost a mile away, and given the Ijams family's fondness for Smoky Mountain expeditions, a vehicle was probably considered a necessity. Here Mary and Martha Ijams rest on the family automobile, which Alice Ijams would load up with flowers to sell directly to the public in the downtown Market Square Hall as well as to local florists.

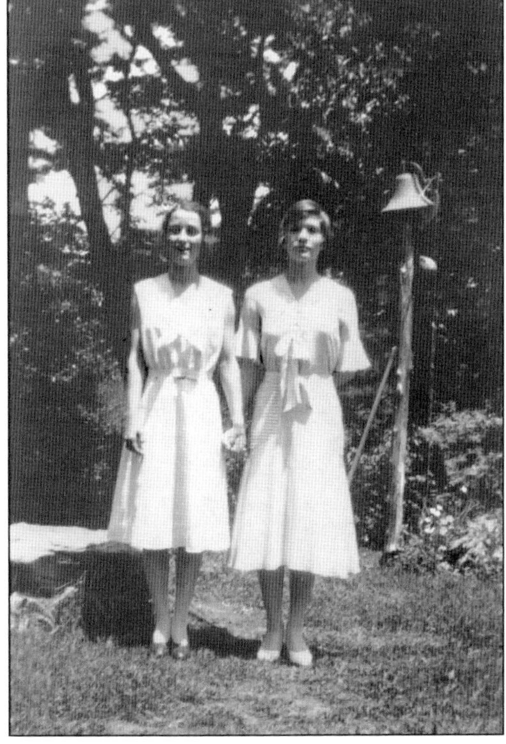

The two eldest Ijams daughters, Elizabeth (left) and Josephine, pose by the outdoor bell, which would become a permanent feature over the years at the Ijams place. Elizabeth's first name was actually Alice, named after her mother, while Josephine was named after her grandfather, Joseph H. Ijams.

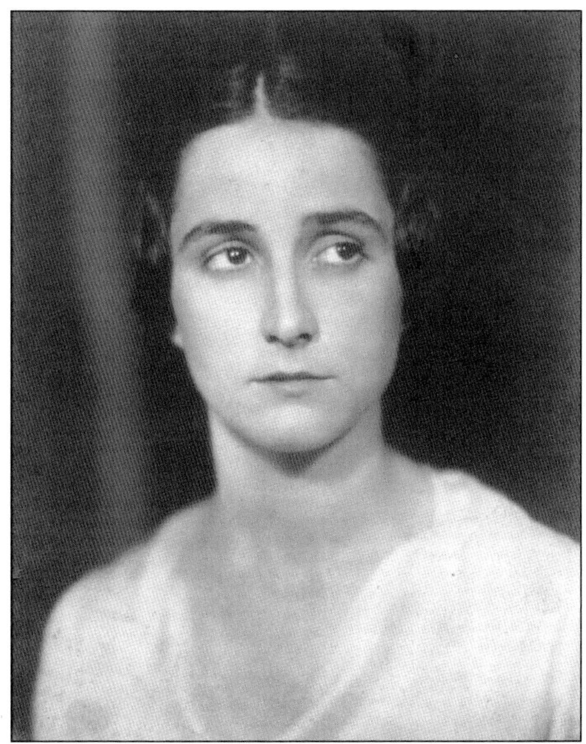

Elizabeth Ijams was the eldest of the Ijams daughters. While a student at the University of Tennessee, she was hired as the director of Knoxville Girl Scouts, and she went on to spend her entire career with the organization.

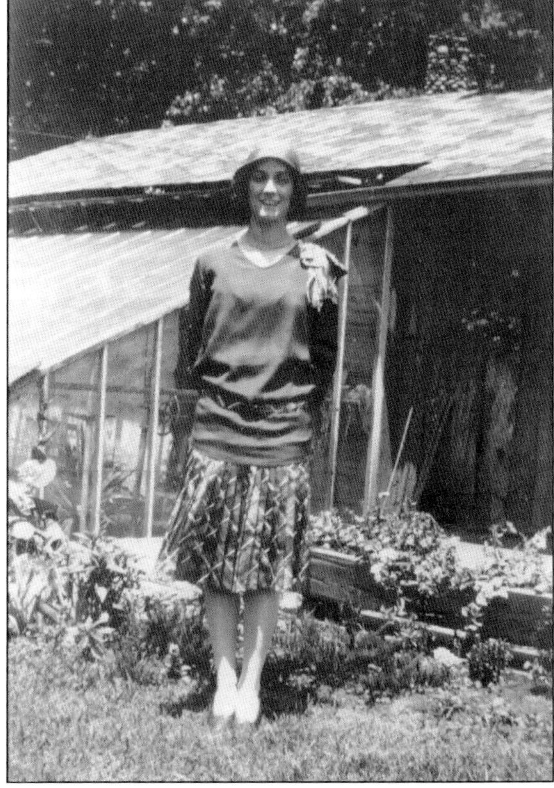

Elizabeth Ijams earned her nickname, Izzy, from schoolteachers who were confused even back then about how to pronounce the Ijams name. Northern schoolteachers pronounced the name "idge-ums" while teachers from the South pronounced it "eye-jams." The northern mentality at Knoxville High School prevailed, and Elizabeth was forever known as "Izzy Idge-ums." The correct way to pronounce the name is to rhyme with "times."

Elizabeth Ijams shivers in the snow at Newfound Gap. The first junior member of the East Tennessee Ornithologist Society when it formed in 1924, Elizabeth was likely joining birders on a Christmas bird count in the Smokies.

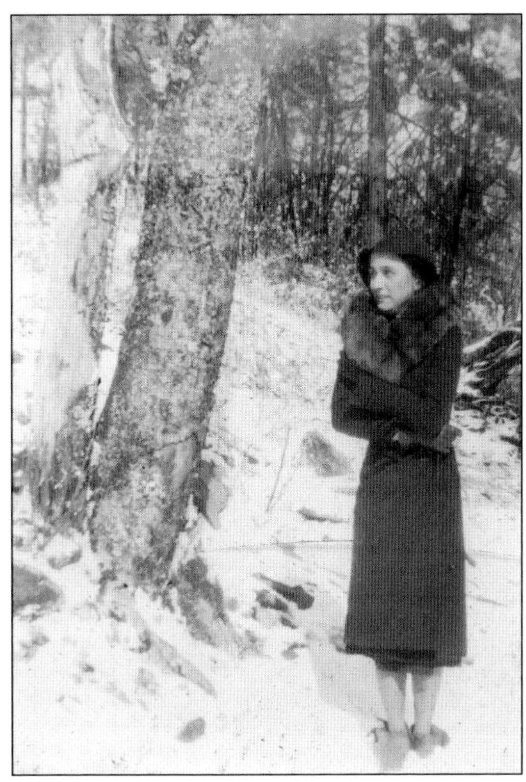

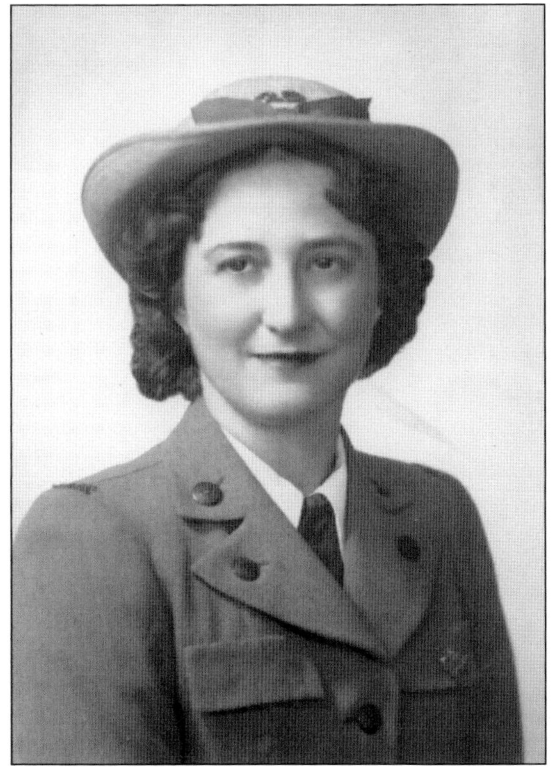

As director of Knoxville Girl Scouts, Elizabeth Ijams attended the Edith Macy Training Camp for Girl Scout leaders at Briarcliff Manor, New York, in 1930. The training and subsequent experience as camp director at Camp Margaret Townsend in the Smokies led to senior positions across the nation during her long career in the Girl Scouts.

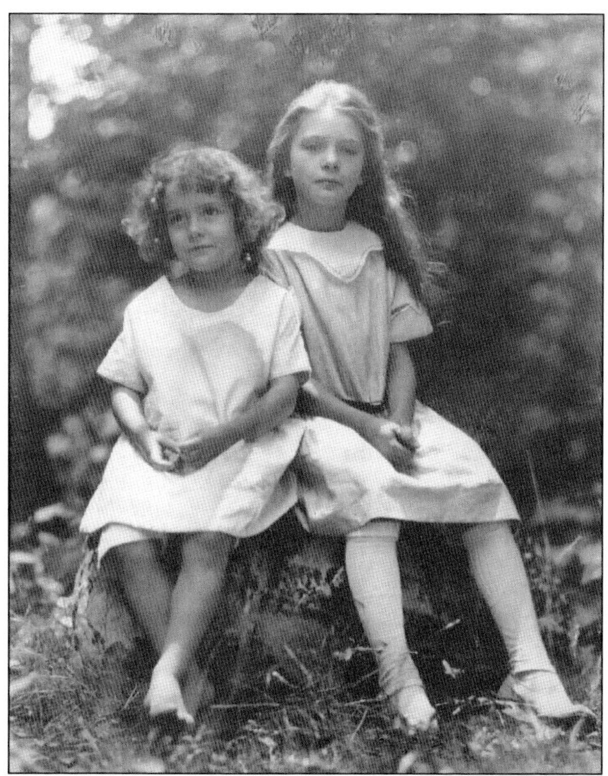

Mary (left) and Jo Ijams pose on a large rock that was a popular bench for the young children during the early 1920s. Jo was the first of the Ijams daughters to be born at the new family home on Island Home Pike in 1912. Like her sisters, she enjoyed a rural childhood but with the conveniences that nearby downtown Knoxville had to offer.

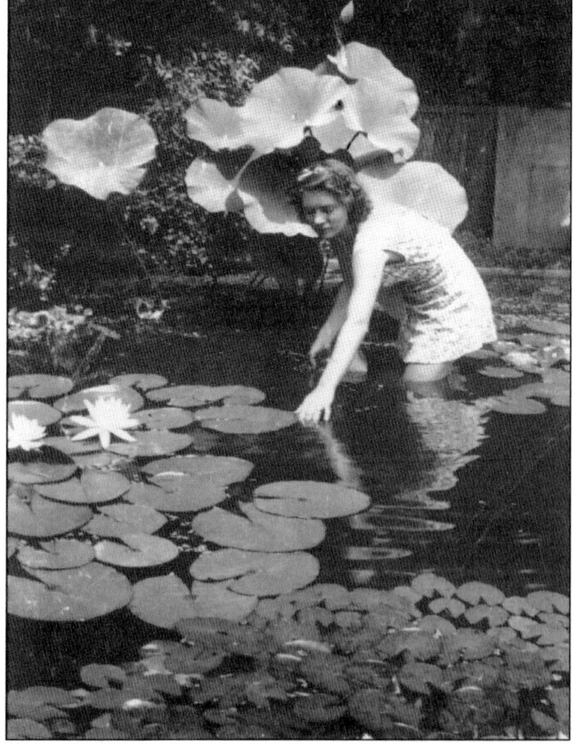

Jo Ijams wades through the lily pond, a classic feature of the Ijamses' front porch, which remained for many years after the property became a public nature center. The foundation of the pond still exists underneath the Miller Education Building at the Ijams home site today. As a young girl, Jo was a gifted Girl Scout, a member of the YMCA and University of Tennessee swim teams, and a summer camp director.

After graduating from the University of Tennessee, Jo worked for the *Knoxville News Sentinel* as a switchboard operator. She later worked for the Standard Knitting Mill before marrying Albert George Kern Jr. in 1949.

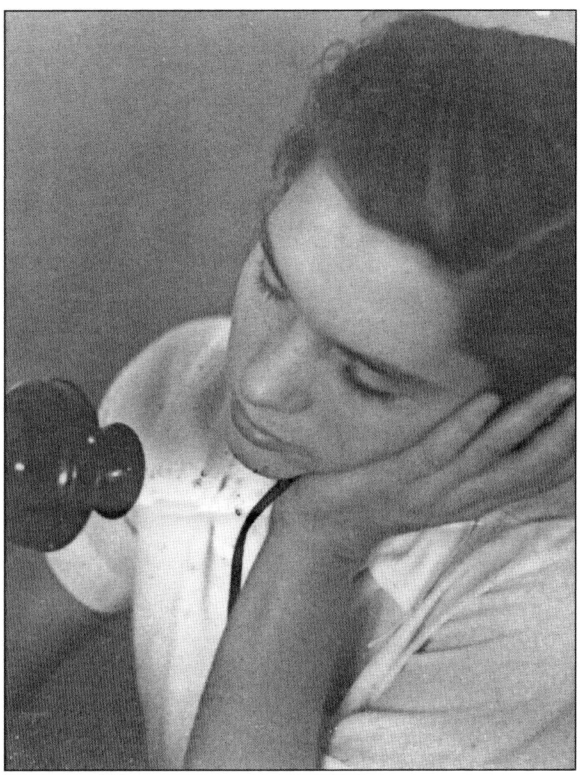

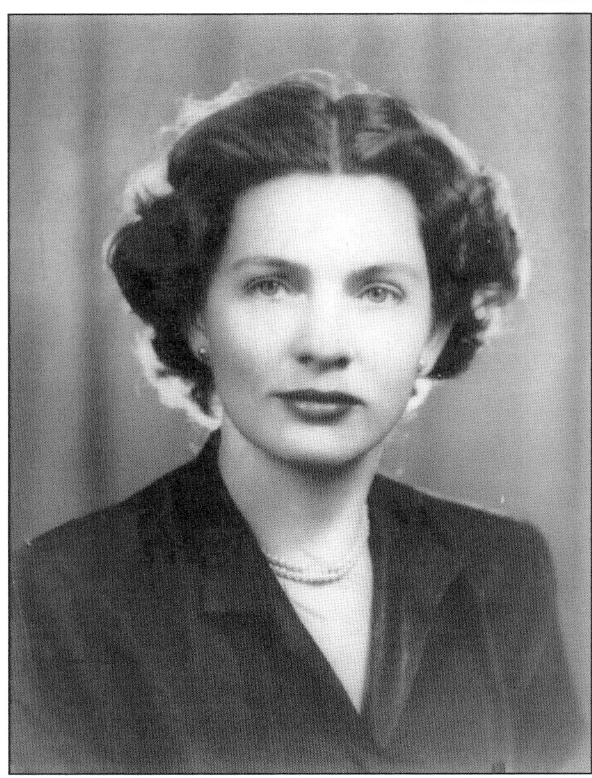

In the 1950s and 1960s, Jo Ijams Kern was conservation chairman for the Knoxville Garden Club. A tireless advocate for state parks, she attended numerous conservation workshops with Knoxville teachers at Fall Creek Falls State Park. Jo and her husband also worked hard with the Trust for Public Land to create House Mountain State Park near Knoxville, and she served as a board member of Ijams Nature Center before she died in 1990.

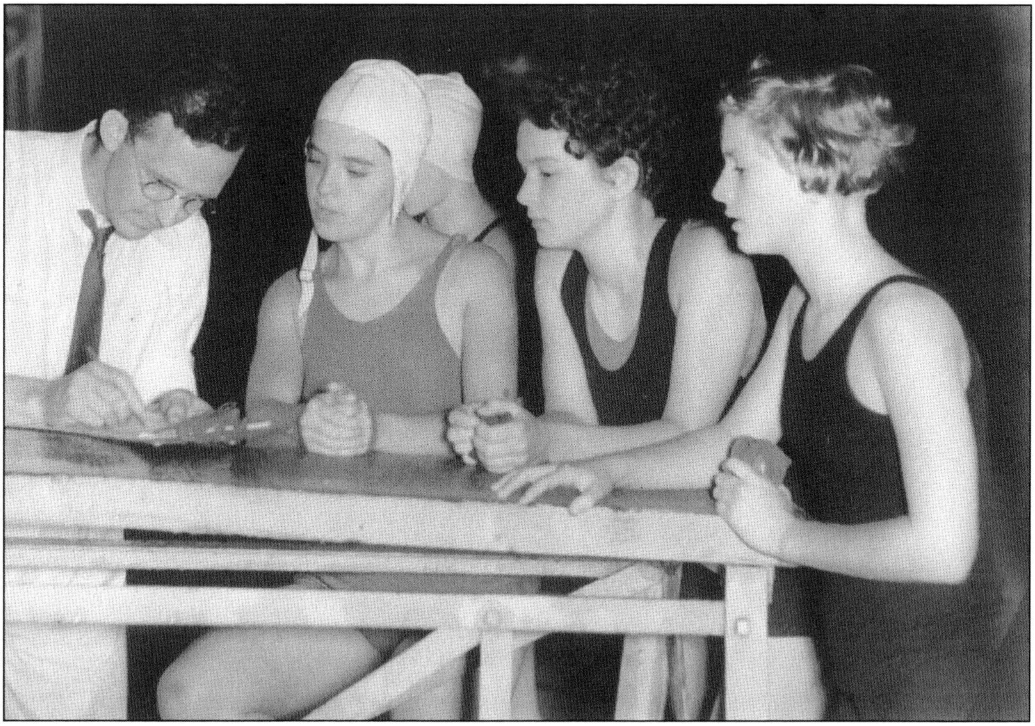

Jo, Mary, and Martha Ijams were all proficient swimmers and members of the Knoxville Girls Swim Team. When they weren't swimming in Lake Avis on the Ijams Farm, the Ijams girls frequently practiced at Whittle Springs pool in East Knoxville. This photograph appeared in the *Knoxville News Sentinel* on August 17, 1932, the day that the swim team headed to the Mid-Atlantic Swimming Championship in Charlotte, North Carolina, where Mary collected three medals. George Barber, head of the YMCA physical department, studies swim times with three of the junior swimmers: Bootie Wehunt (left), Mary Ijams (center), and Martha Ijams. (*Knoxville News Sentinel.*)

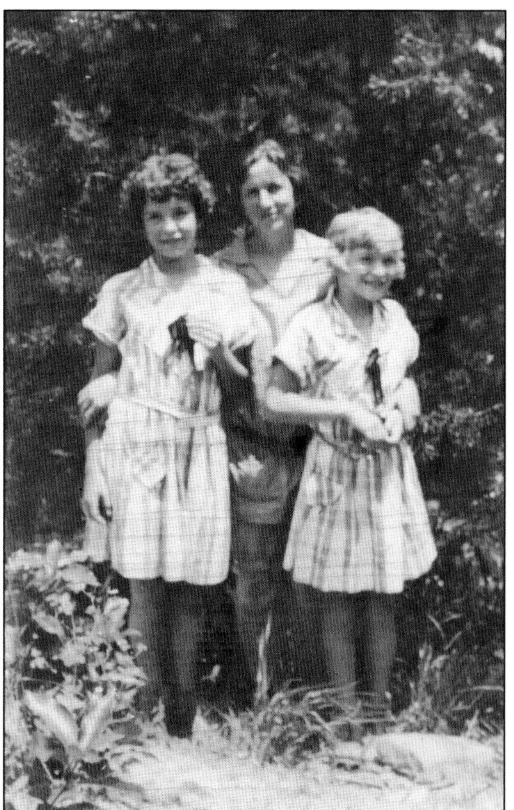

Alice Ijams, here with Mary (left) and Martha, raised her girls to appreciate and enjoy nature. Almost a century later, the same philosophy forms the core of Ijams Nature Center's First Child in the Woods program—a unique educational series that introduces young children to the wonders of nature and earth science.

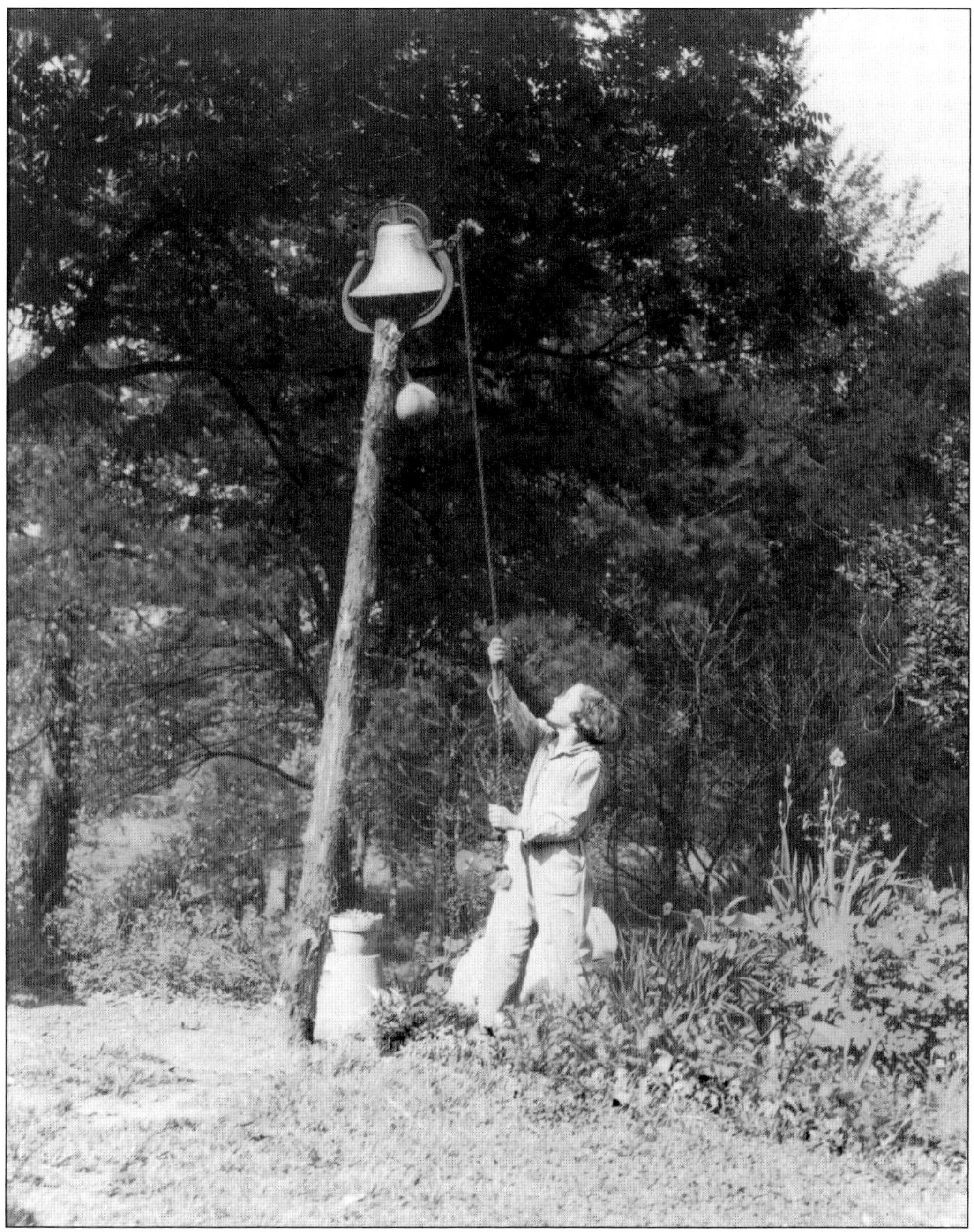

Mary Ijams, born in 1916, rings the bell outside the Ijams house. Mary was considered a "true Girl Scout in every way" and was only a few badges short of becoming a Golden Eaglet upon her untimely death in an automobile accident at the age of 16. On August 22, 1932, Mary and Elizabeth Ijams were driving to Beach Haven near Banner Elk, North Carolina, to collect their sister Jo when their car overturned on the highway east of Rutledge, Tennessee. Although Elizabeth suffered only minor injuries, Mary died instantly. Only a few weeks before, Mary had won the annual Girl Scout swimming competition at Camp Margaret Townsend in the Smokies.

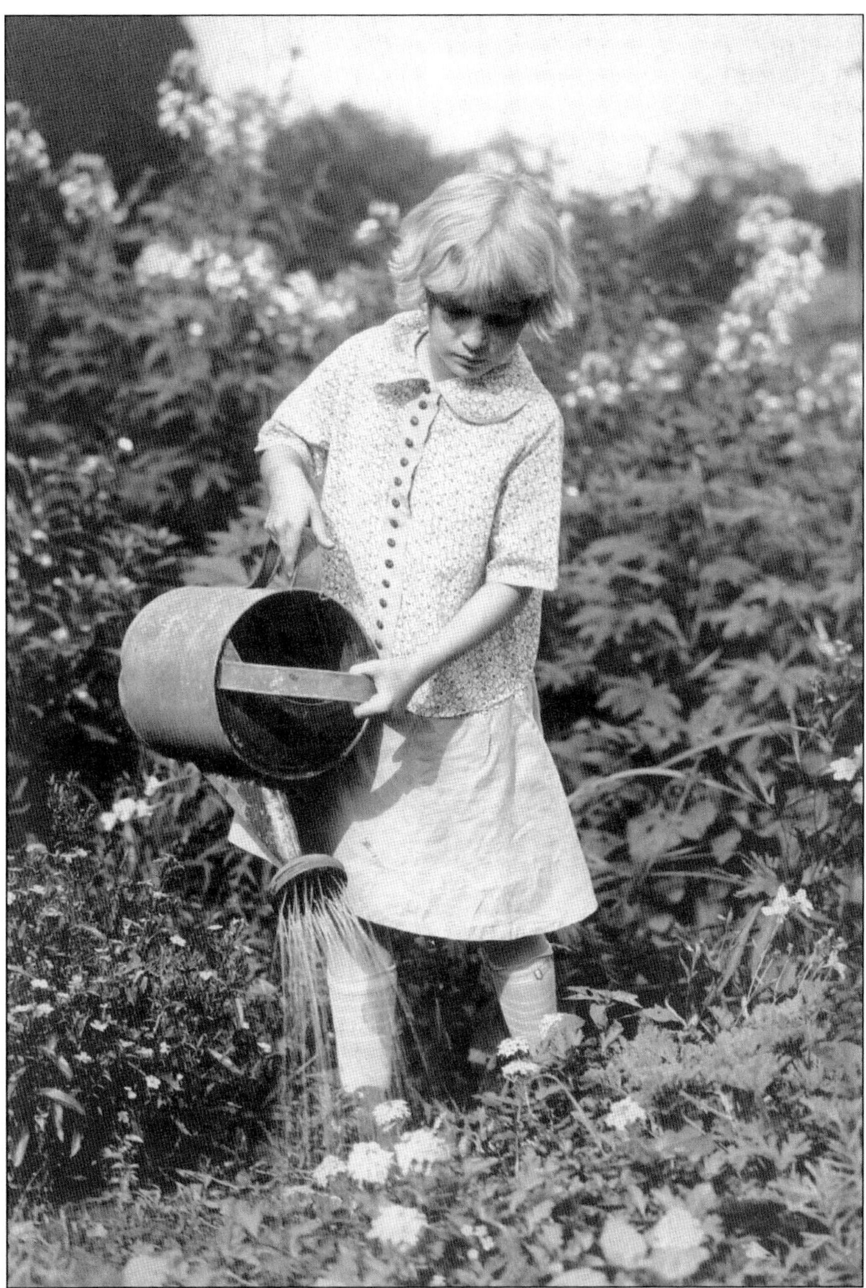

Martha Ijams, born in 1918, was the youngest of the Ijams daughters, and like her mother, she was a lifelong devotee to gardening and cooking. Martha graduated from the University of Tennessee with a bachelor's degree in home economics and a masters in early child development. Martha is fondly remembered as a teacher of home economics at Maryville High School, where she taught for more than 20 years. This photograph of Martha tending to her mother's flowers would have been taken around the late 1920s. Wildlife and animals remained a constant part of Martha's life, and with her husband, Dr. Frank Lovingood, she became renowned locally for breeding prized beagles and American saddle horses (now known as American saddlebreds) in Blount County. Martha died in 2004.

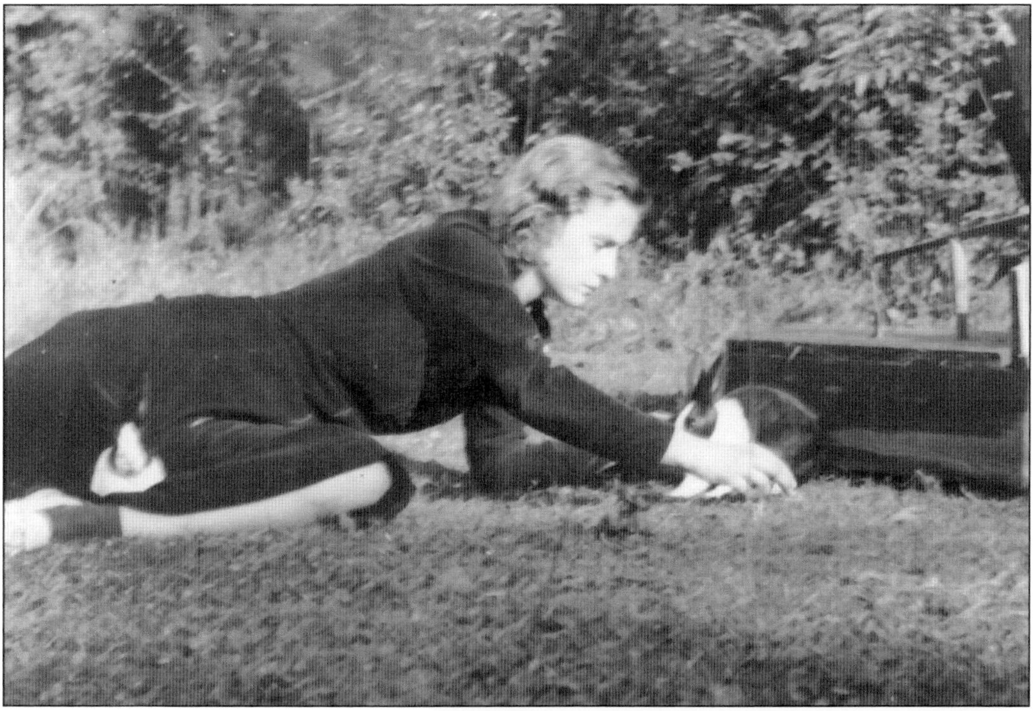

Martha Ijams, like her sisters, absorbed her parents' passions and loved to watch and study birds as well as discover and appreciate the beauty of East Tennessee's native wildlife.

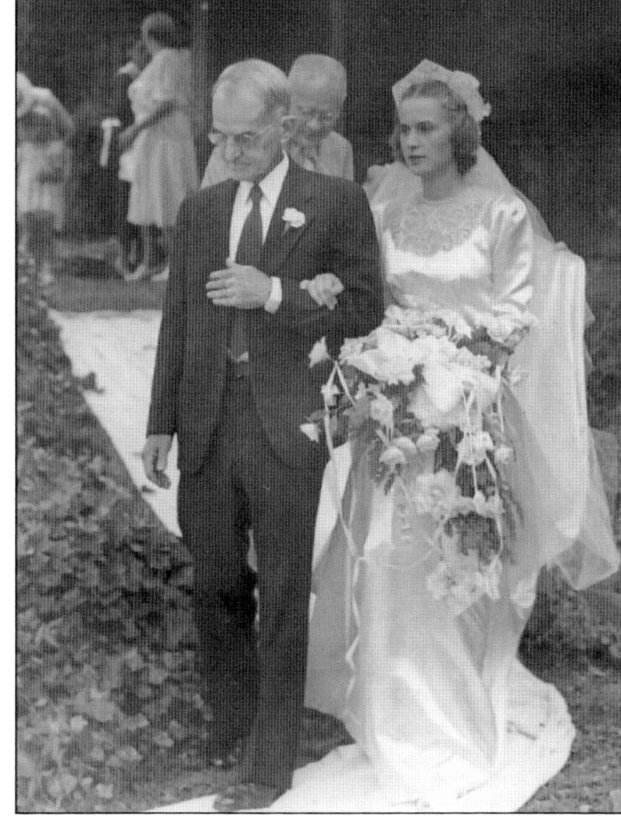

Ijams has been a popular destination for wedding ceremonies, and one of the first was Martha Ijams's own ceremony in 1943, when she married Dr. Frank Lovingood. Here, H. P. accompanies Martha down a natural aisle from the house to the lawn. Behind them is Knoxville florist, ornithologist, and hiker Brockway Crouch, who supplied the flowers for the special occasion.

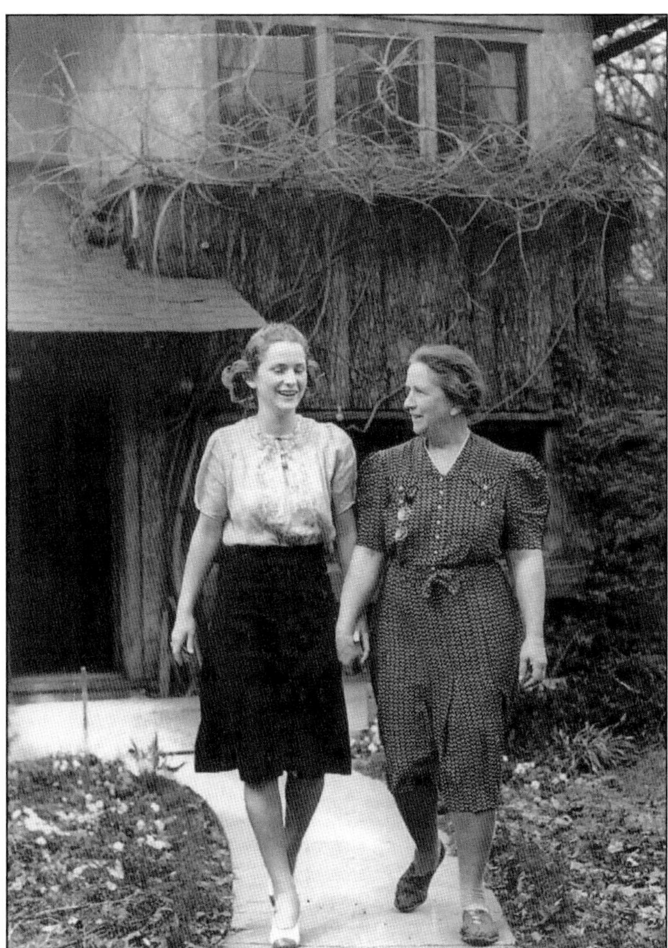

Martha and Alice Ijams enjoy a family moment in front of the Ijams home. The photograph was taken in the early 1940s, when Martha was a senior at the University of Tennessee and Alice was fully immersed in her volunteer role as manager of women's exhibits at the Tennessee Valley Agricultural and Industry Fair.

In the center of this photograph is one of Alice Ijams's sisters, Della Yoe. A well-known Knoxvillian, Della penned *These Are Our Lives*, a documentary about Depression-era poverty in America, and acted as publicity agent for the Charles Coburn Players. Alice and Della's father, John Williams Yoe, was also renowned in his day after serving in the Confederate army and later becoming a lawyer and mayor of West Knoxville. From left to right are Jo, Elizabeth, Della Yoe, Alice, and H. P. Ijams.

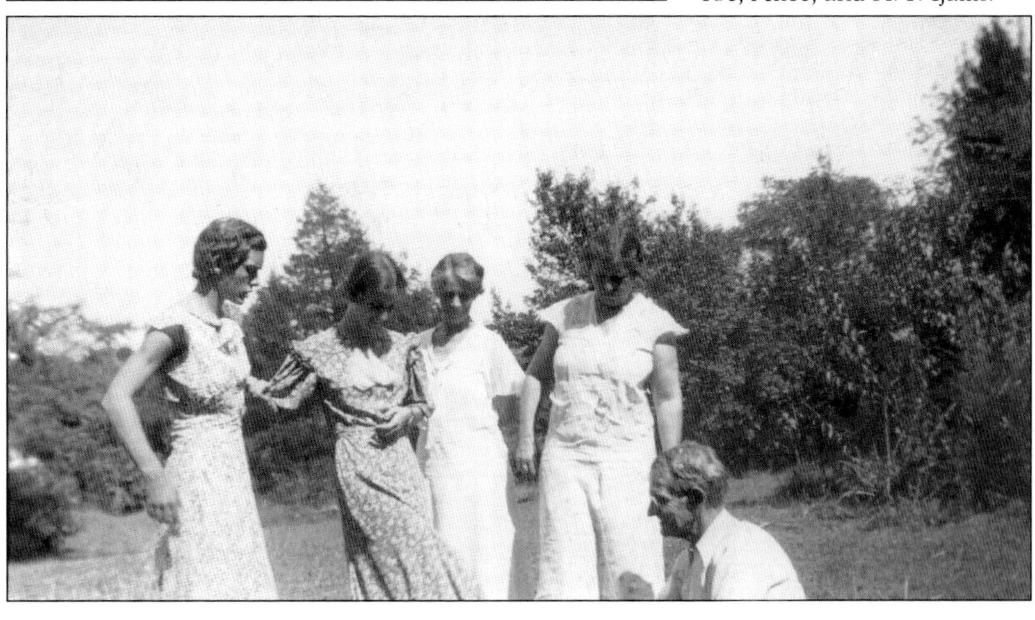

Here is H. P. Ijams in a relaxed mood with a pet fox terrier. At this age, H. P. had been a devoted ornithologist and naturalist for most of his life. As a boy, his interest in wildlife had been awakened after stealing eggs from a bird's nest for a collector. Oology, the study of bird's eggs, was a popular naturalist activity during the 19th and early 20th centuries and contributed much to the foundation of natural history knowledge that exists today.

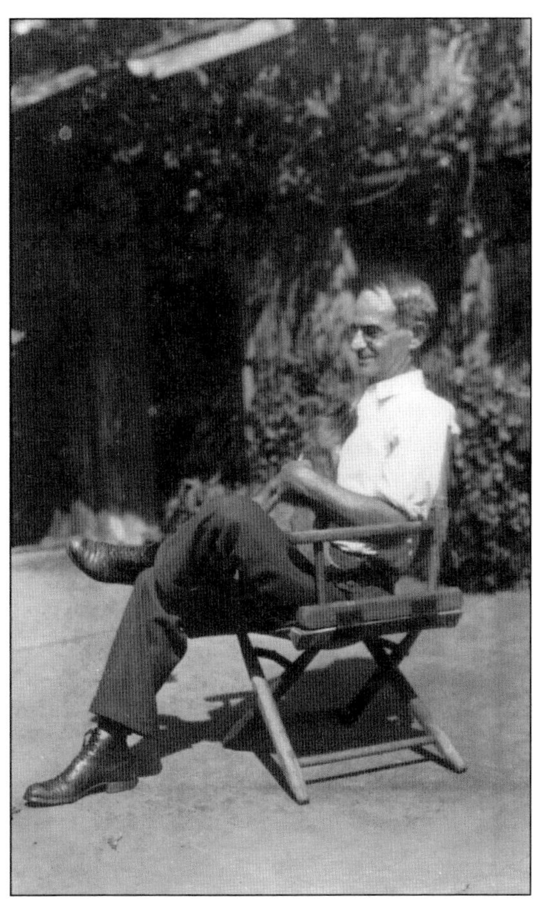

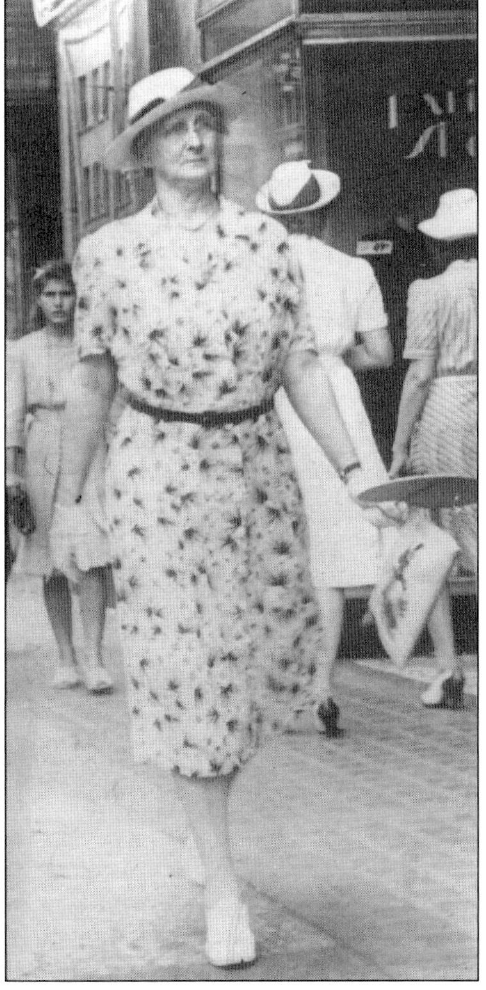

Throughout the 1930s and 1940s, Alice Ijams managed the women's exhibits and "florticultural" displays at the popular Tennessee Valley Agriculture and Industry Fair. Alice's talents were in much demand. She was also a council member and commissioner for the Knoxville Girl Scouts and secretary of Knoxville High School and was always busy with her garden club activities.

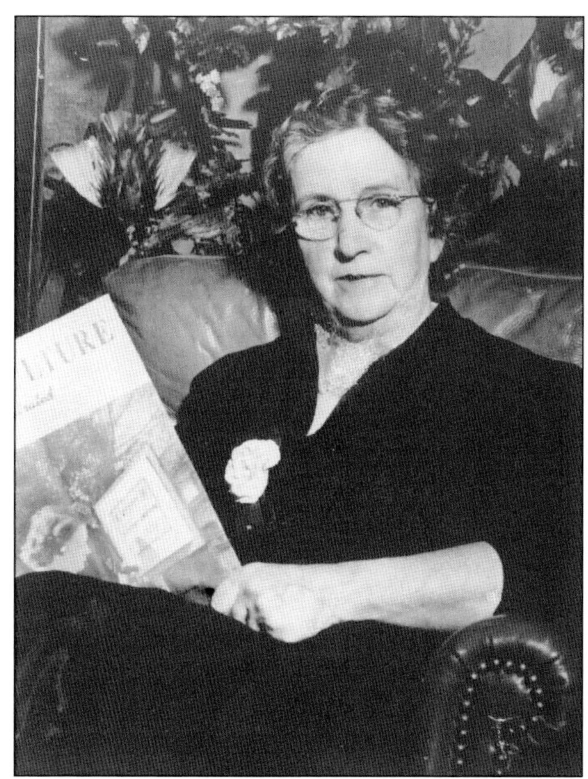

Later in life, Alice Ijams was widely known as Knoxville's "First Lady of Garden Clubs." A charter member of the Knoxville Garden Club, Alice Ijams became its president for two years, 1944–1946. With a philosophy of conservation and preservation, Alice also inspired the creation of numerous local garden clubs and served as president of the Knox County Council of Garden Clubs from 1946 to 1948. In 1945, the Knoxville Girl Scouts Council awarded both Alice and H. P. Ijams thanks badges for exceptional service. Alice passed away in 1964.

As one of Knoxville's most respected citizens, H. P. was considered world wise, well-read, and was said to have conversed on any subject "like a true diplomat." Although he did not invest heavily in the stock market himself, he was frequently sought out by friends for financial advice. H. P. passed away in 1954 and left behind an enduring environmental legacy that continues to this day.

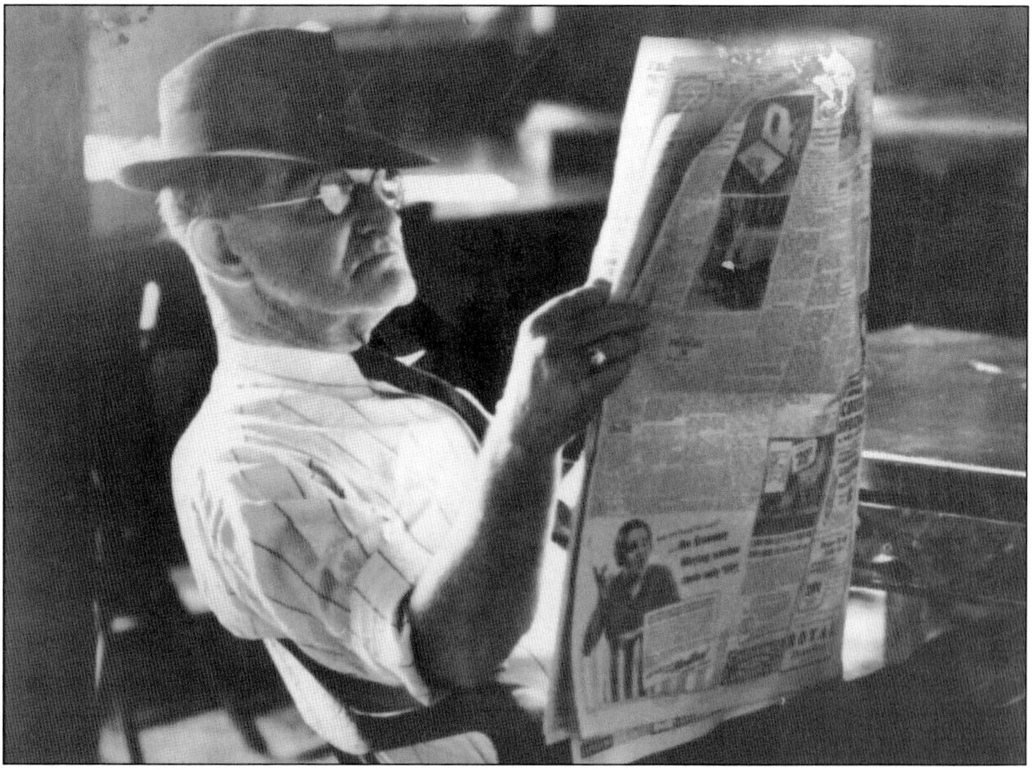

Two

House and Garden of Long Shadows

As the Ijams daughters grew up, the mainstay of their childhoods was the Ijams farm, which H. P. Ijams was developing by this time into a mature, natural showplace. Another story was added to the house, including a lean-to greenhouse covered in vines and gourds, and in front, a small lily pond added a touch of grace to the rustic abode. The Ijams family lived outdoors practically every waking moment, only going indoors during inclement weather and to sleep. Mealtimes were announced by ringing the garden bell, which ushered in the children and H. P., who was usually off on the grounds somewhere checking his bird boxes. In a 1952 article for the *Volunteer Gardener*, Alice Ijams recalled the era perfectly:

> I devote the major portion of my time to gardening, my prime interest being growing flowers—with vegetables secondary, but not neglected. Landscaping these 17 acres was quite an accomplishment on the part of my husband. The land slopes gently toward the river and lies fairly flat and smooth in front of the house, a rustic two-story residence fitting picturesquely into the landscape. The outer edges are densely grown with a variety of shrubs and trees, from which long shadows extend both early morning and late afternoon. Although we never considered giving our modest little place a name, if we had so dignified it, my choice would have been Long Shadows.

In the early days, the Ijams girls were content to play in the hay barn or take rides on a donkey they kept. Jo Ijams's family newsletter, produced between 1922 and 1926, documented their many outdoor pursuits, including the construction of a spring-fed pond named Lake Avis. H. P. preferred his girls not to swim in the sluice on the Tennessee River, so he built a pond where the girls could swim or canoe. In the 1930s, after the girls had grown, Alice planted Egyptian lotus (water lily) on the pond, which covered the entire surface. The fabulous sight was a local sensation, and people from across town would take the streetcar to the Ijams place just to see the gorgeous lotus blooms.

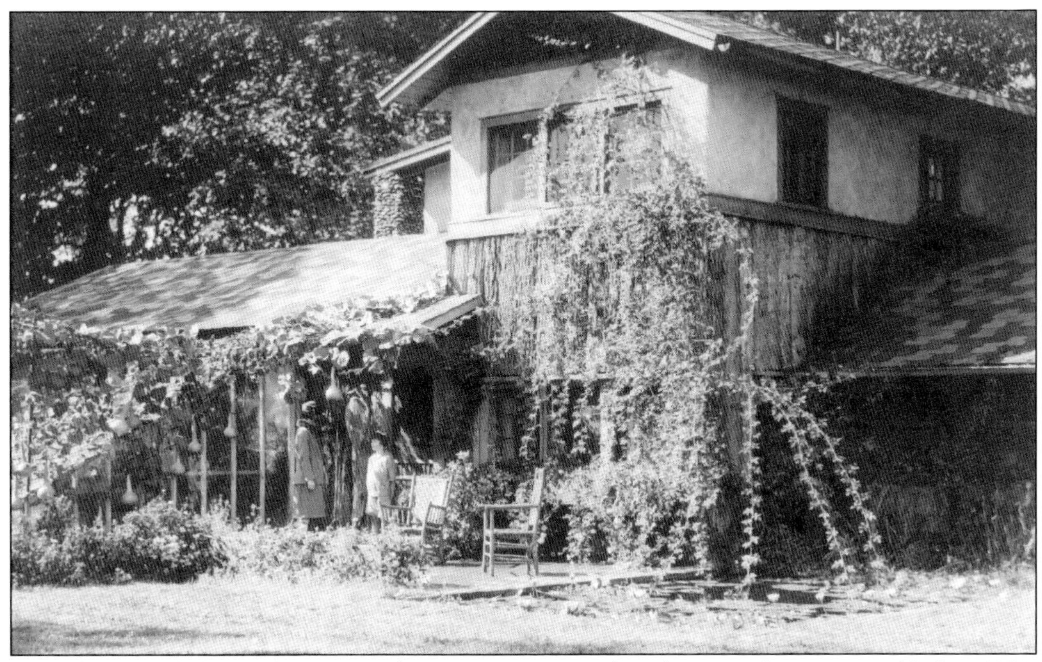

This photograph shows the Ijamses' house in its prime after the second story was added in 1924. H. P. Ijams designed the newer version himself and was aided by only one hired carpenter. The Miller Education Building that now stands in its place was designed by architect Bill Barth to capture the essence of the original house.

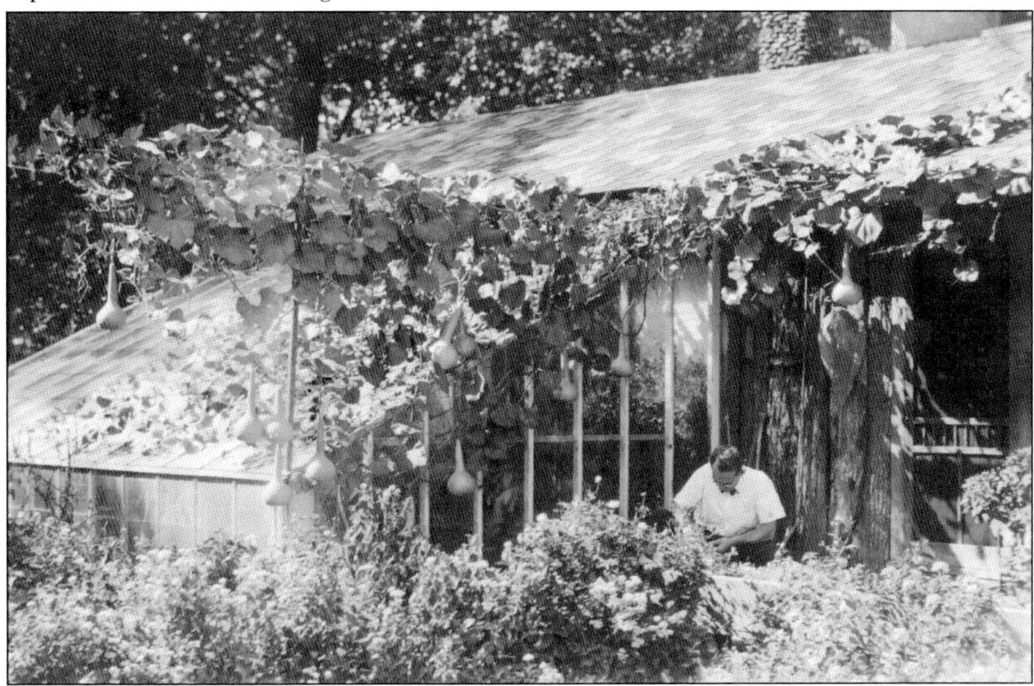

Vines and gourds adorned the lean-to greenhouse and front porch at the Ijams home during the 1920s. H. P. Ijams is seen here wearing a bow tie, not traditional attire for the consummate naturalist, although shirts and ties were commonly worn in those days for most endeavors.

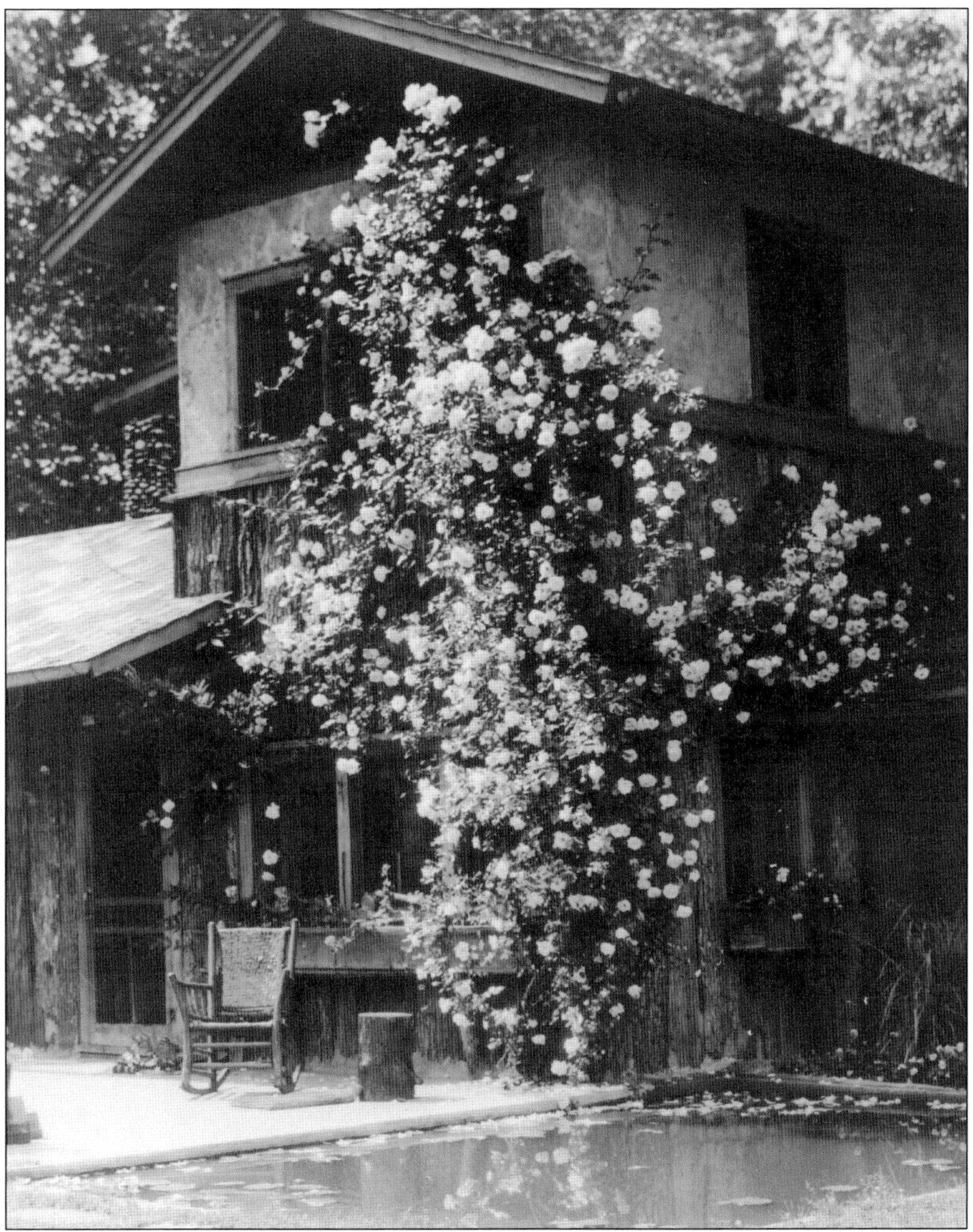

A rosebush in bloom perfectly showcased the front of the Ijamses' house in this photograph that accompanied Alice Ijams's article in the *Volunteer Gardener* in 1952. Alice wrote, "Having always been outdoor people, we devoted very little time to planning the simple little house we still occupy. Our plan consists of screened porches on both floors and a dining alcove facing the garden and overlooking the lily ponds, fruit trees, and three terraced rock walls. The upper half of the house is plastered and the lower story covered with bark slabs from trees cut on the grounds. We have all the room that any busy horticulturalist would care to keep since the nestlings have flown and we are now alone."

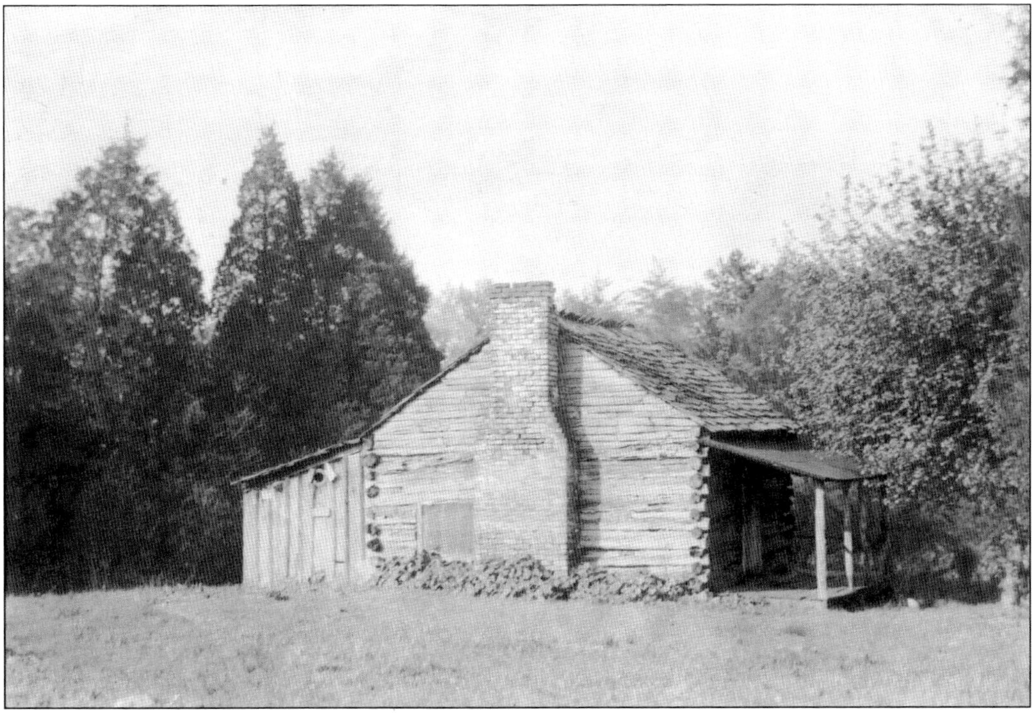

When Harry Ijams purchased the farm in 1910, an unusual condition was part of the sale. It was stipulated that Ms. Giffin and Ms. Johnson, an elderly pair of ladies who lived in an old cabin on the property, could live in it for the rest of their lives, at which time ownership would revert to the Ijams family. The rustic cabin was originally situated at the far edge of the home site lawn.

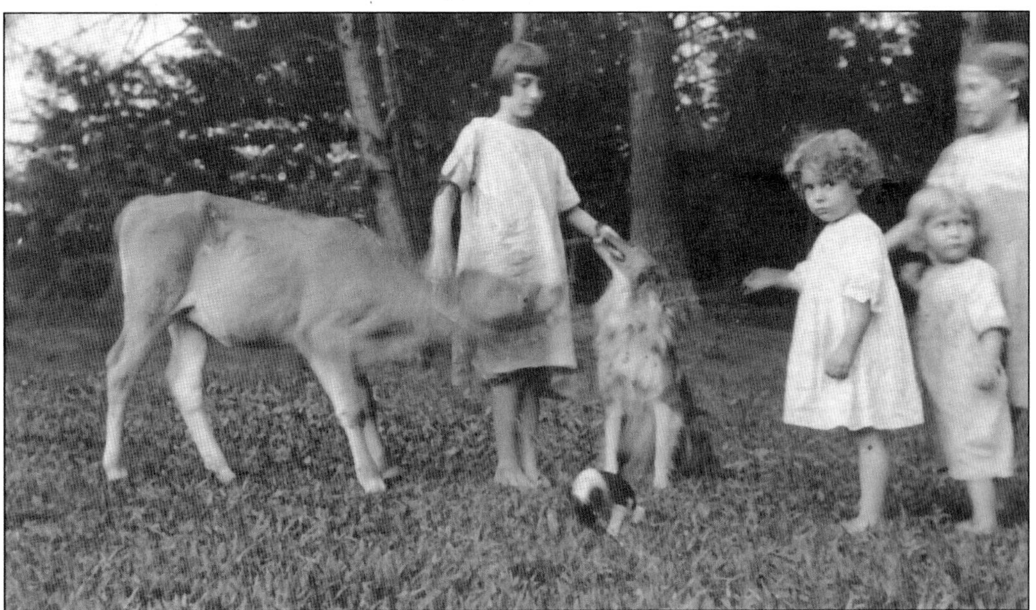

On the farm, a milk cow, donkey, hayloft, and barn provided a rustic childhood for the Ijams children, who, like many youngsters of the day, went barefoot. Jo Ijams once said, "We didn't get civilized until we went to town."

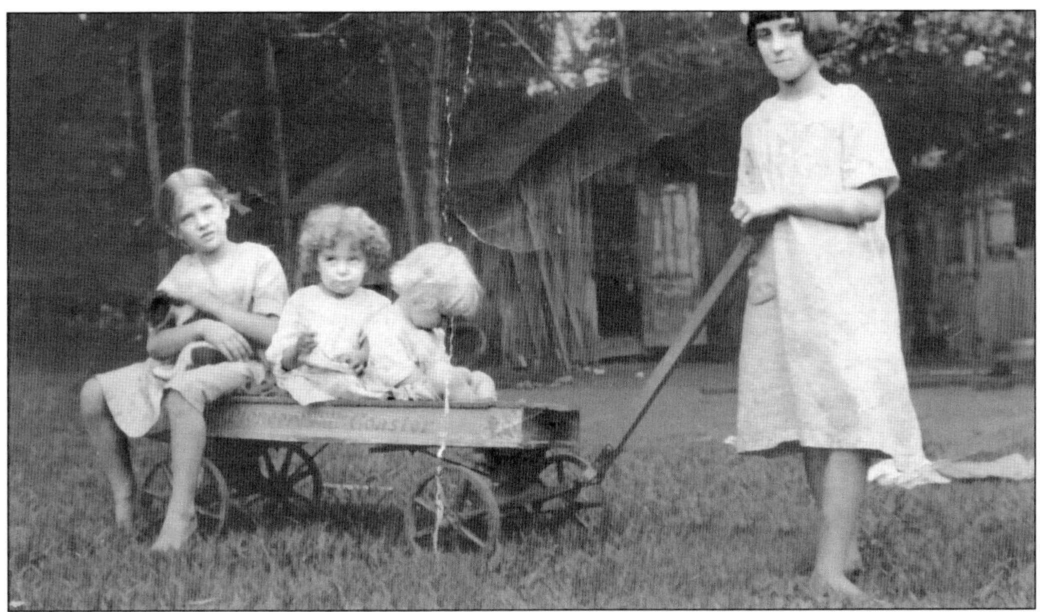

Elizabeth Ijams leads the girls around the farm in a Pioneer Artillery Wheel Coaster wagon. In the background, H. P. Ijams's various tool sheds and outbuildings can be seen.

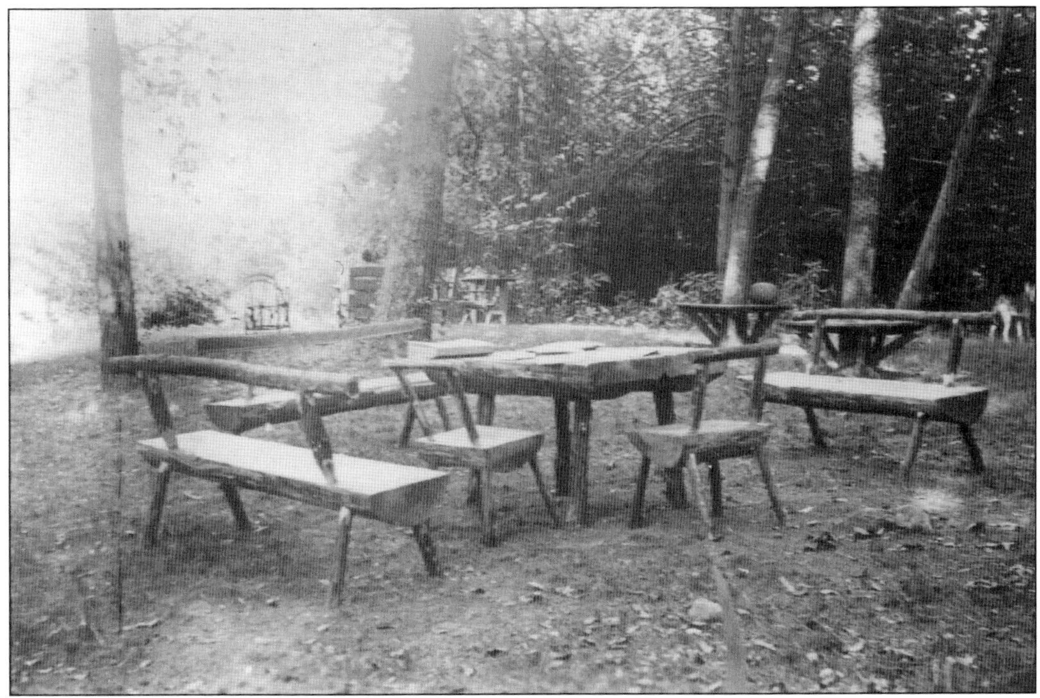

Owen Tharp, a worker in Alice Ijams's greenhouses, carved this suite of outdoor dining furniture from a single chestnut tree using an old-fashioned implement called an adze.

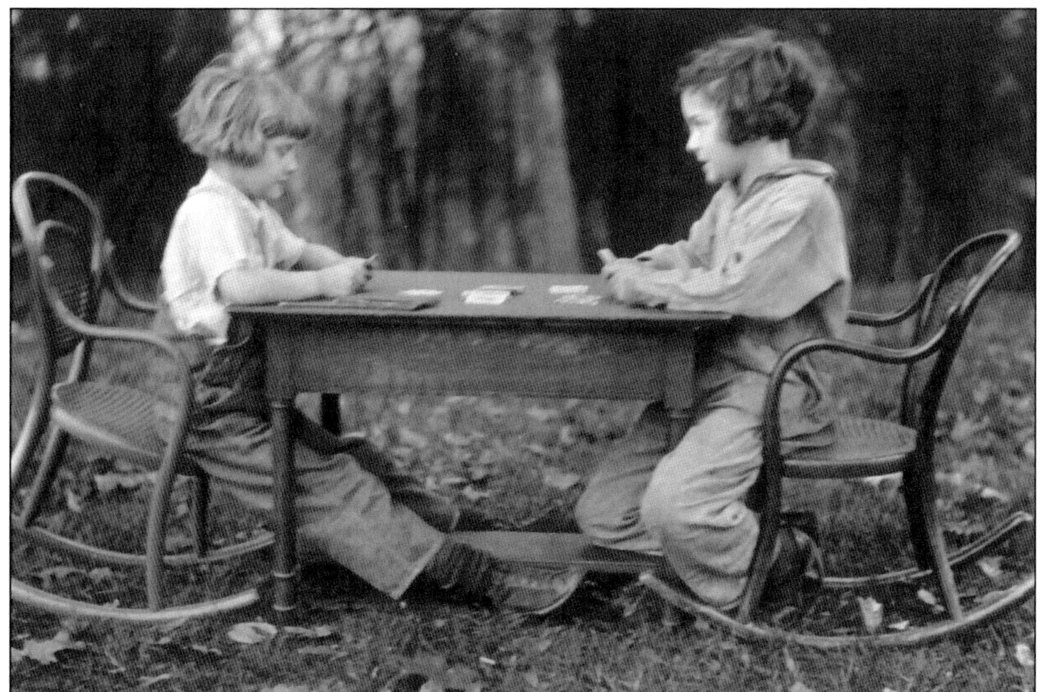

A perfectly composed photograph of Martha (left) and Mary Ijams playing cards outdoors on the Ijams farm is captured by Russell Harrison. Although not widely known as a professional photographer, Harrison's photographs of natural and landscape subjects were often extraordinary.

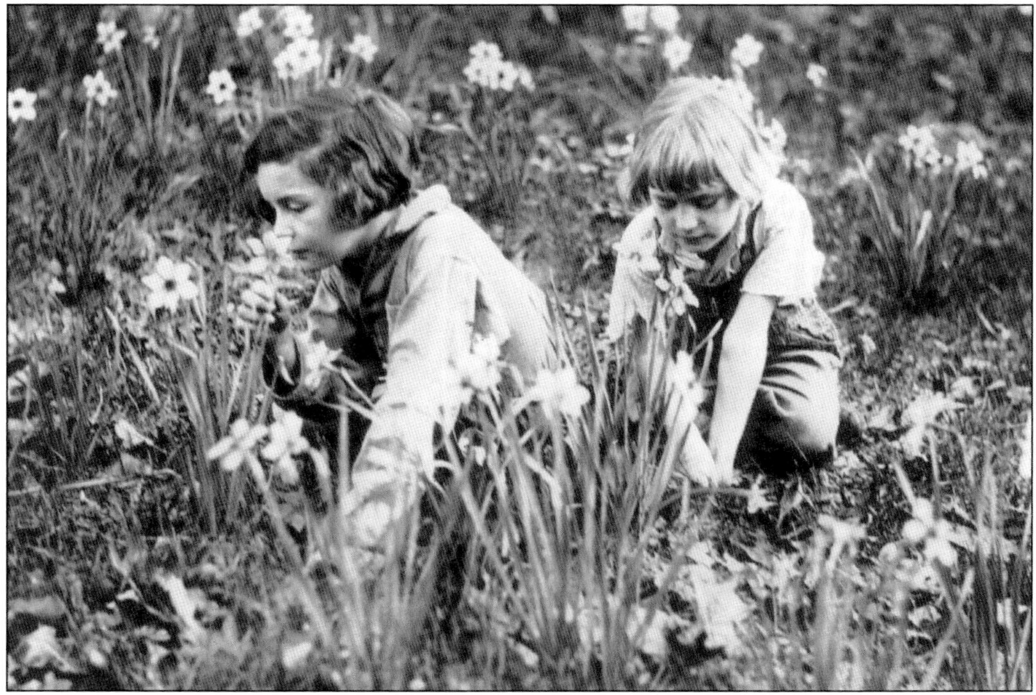

Russell Harrison again captured the carefree days of Mary (left) and Martha Ijams's childhood growing up on a rustic farm on the outskirts of Knoxville around 1926.

Jo Ijams poses with Brockway Crouch's tame raccoon at the Ijams farm around 1925. Crouch, a fellow ornithologist and active member of the Smoky Mountain Hiking Club, often brought the raccoon to the Ijams farm, where it played with the Ijams girls on a sandbar along the Tennessee River. The raccoon even accompanied Crouch when he went canoeing.

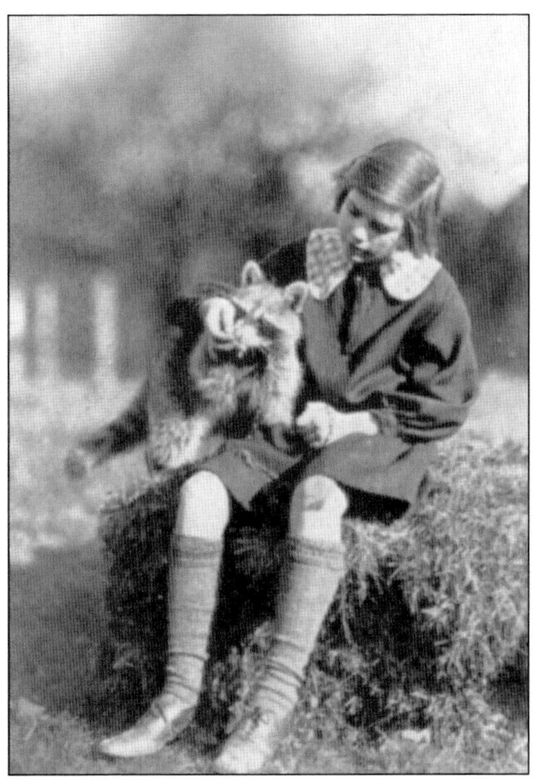

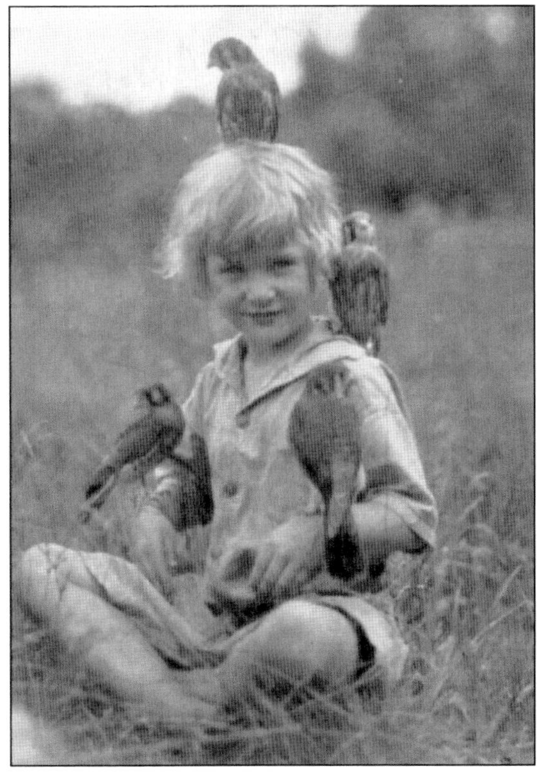

Martha Ijams poses with sparrow hawks, now better known as American kestrels, which had been raised by her father. This photograph taken by Russell Harrison appeared in the *New York Times* in 1925.

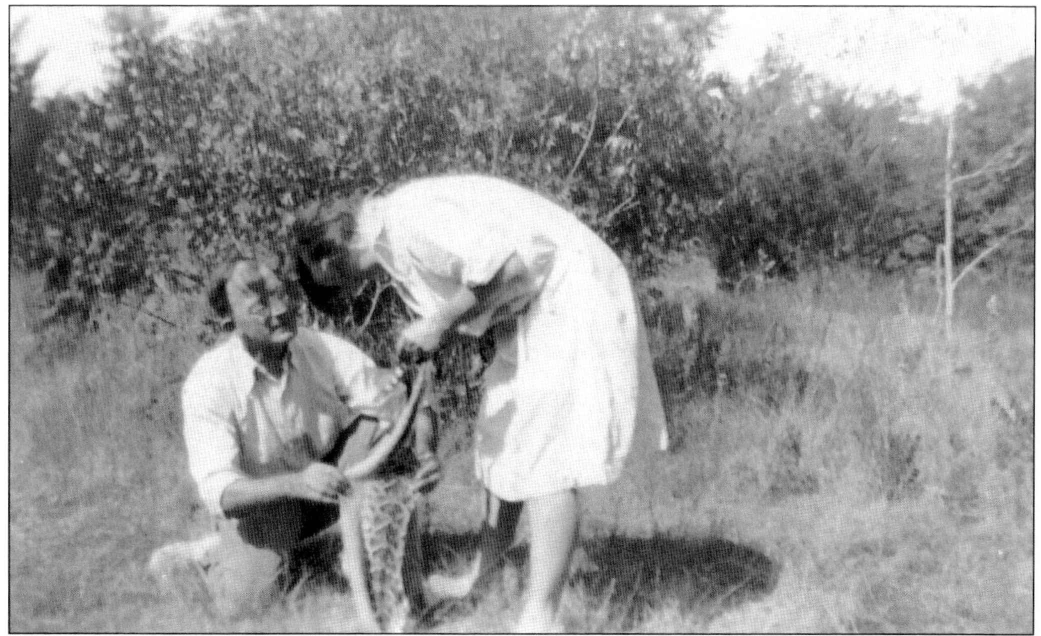

H. P. and Alice Ijams were experts in all facets of outdoor life. Here they are skinning a rattlesnake, which was probably found dead on the property. Since nothing was wasted at the Ijamses' place, it was likely skinned to serve as an educational specimen.

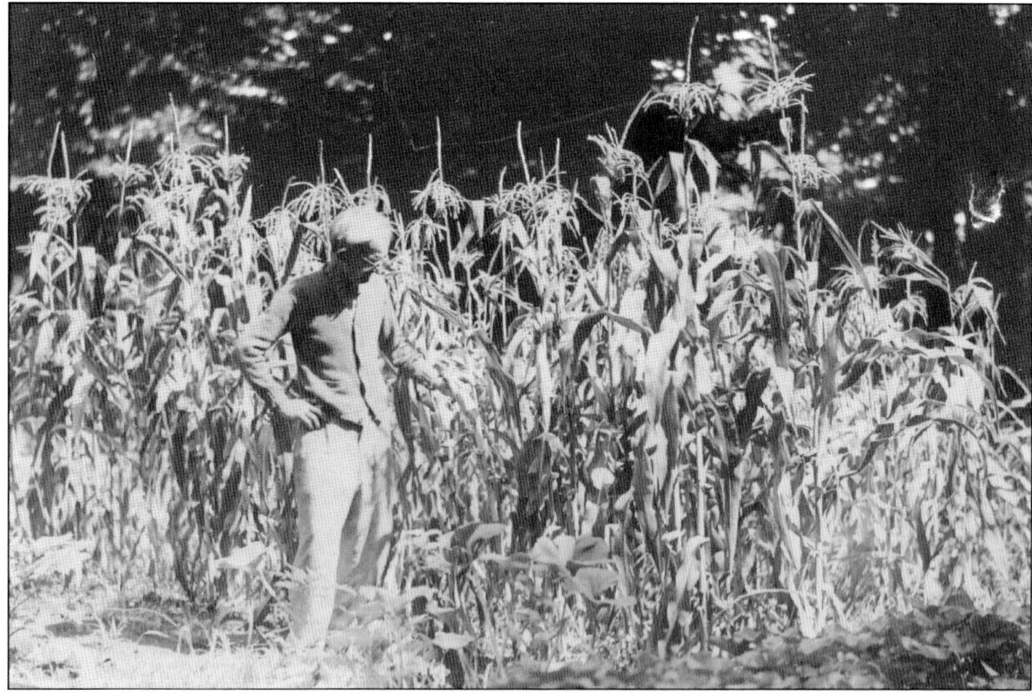

H. P. Ijams tends to his corn in the field behind the Ijams house. Since the property became a public nature center in the 1960s, Ijams Nature Center has rarely been associated with agricultural use. Yet during those early years, the Ijams family was practically self-sustaining, with every aspect of the property servicing family needs or enhancing wildlife habitat.

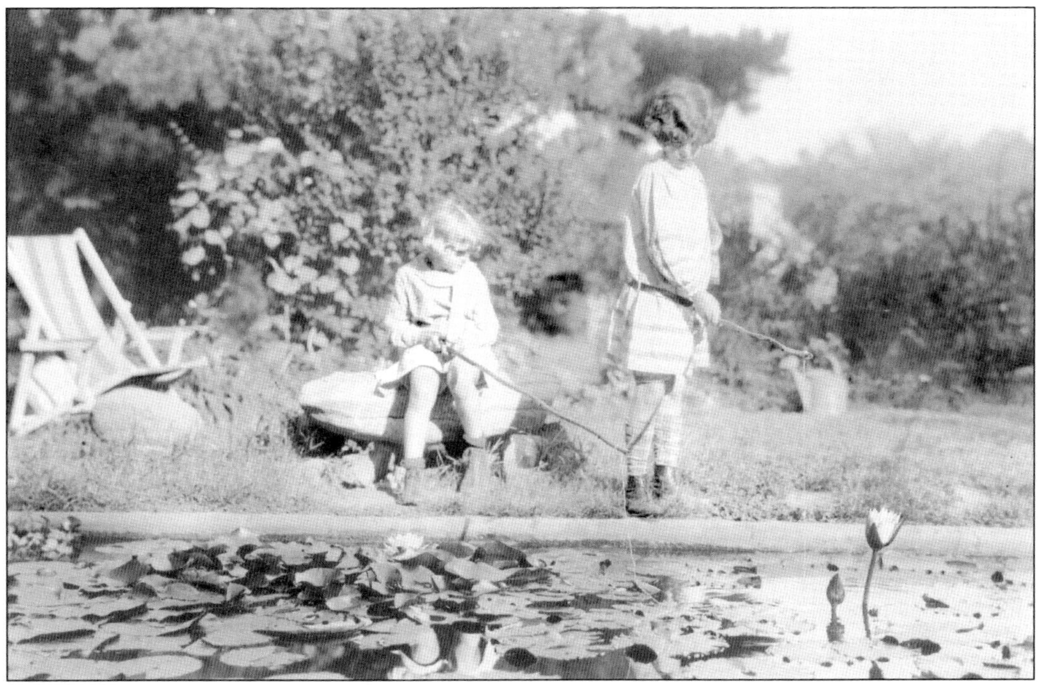

Martha (left) and Mary, using homemade fishing rods, try their luck in the lily pond in front of the Ijams house during the mid-1920s.

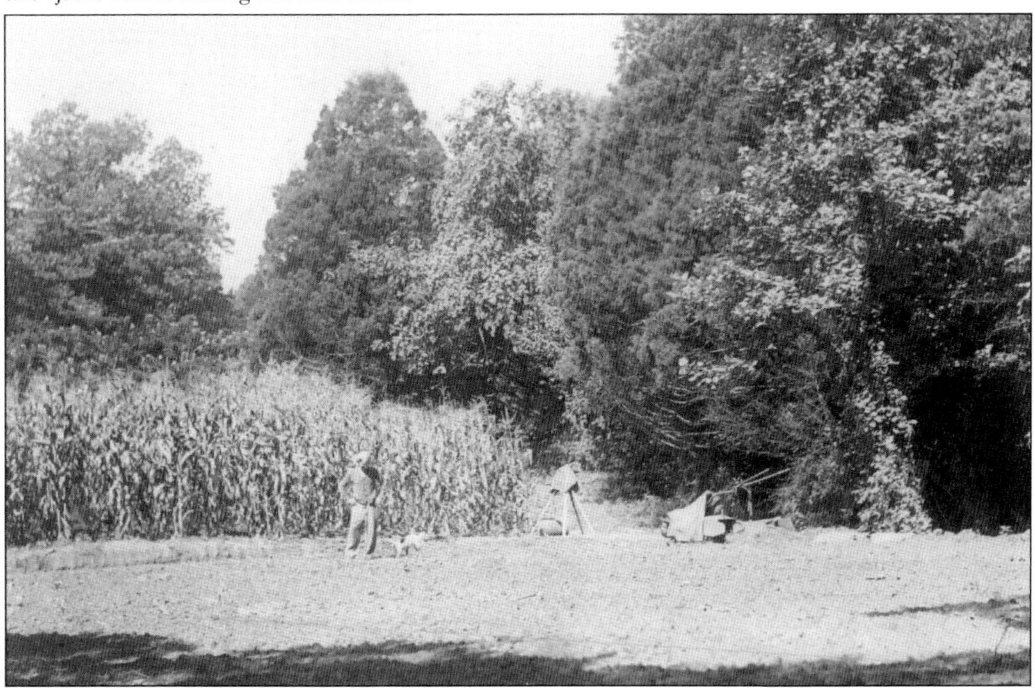

Although the term "farm" was loosely applied at the Ijams place, this long view of H. P. Ijams in front of a corn patch in the 1930s also shows a recently plowed field. Over the years, the property saw other uses, including, rather surprisingly, a tennis court that H. P. developed for his daughters in the mid-1920s.

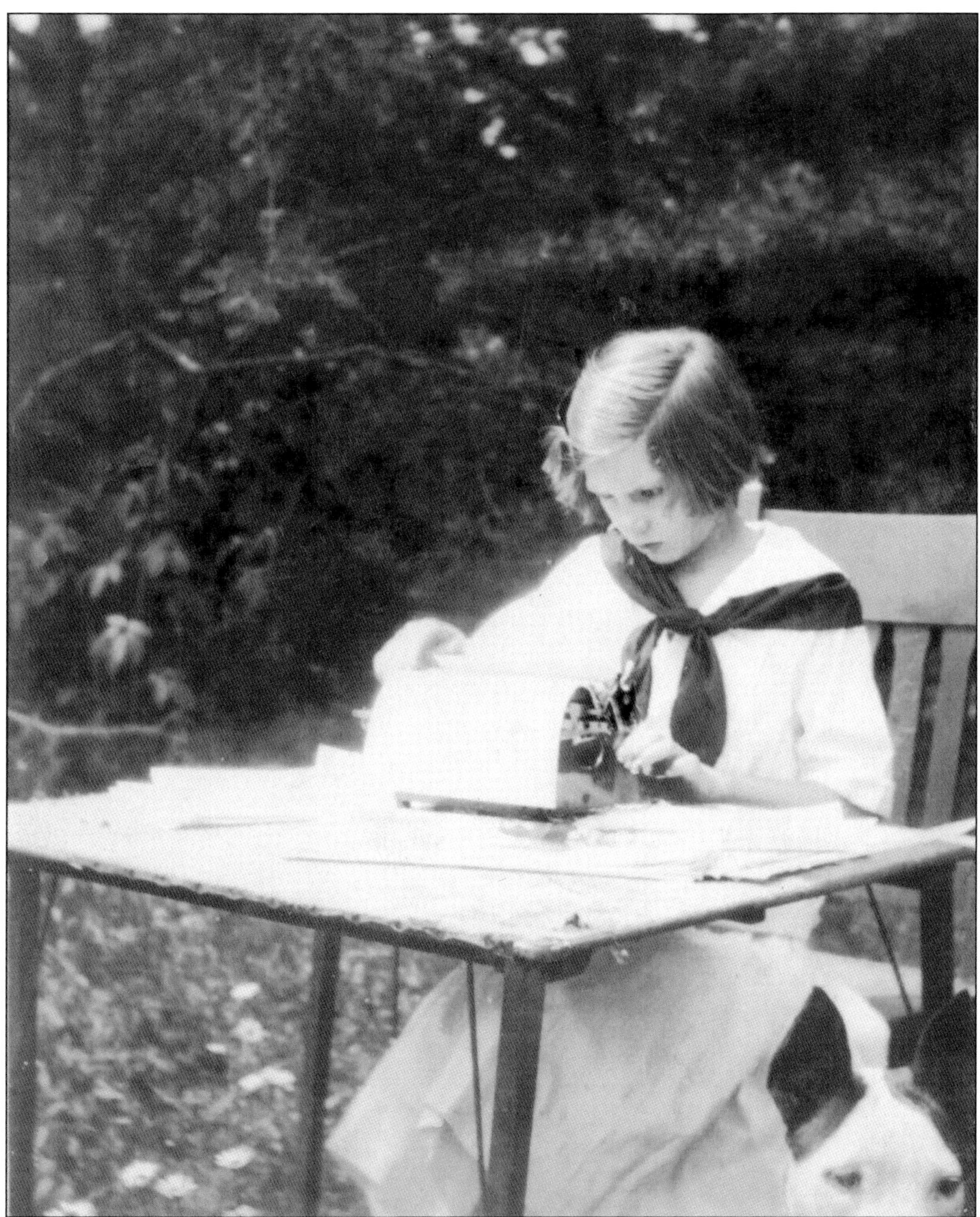

Jo Ijams began publishing the *Ijams Family Newsletter* in 1922 at age 10. The weekly edition reflected domestic activities, art, and poetry, and wildlife happenings. Jo initially produced multiple copies of the newsletter using a Corona typewriter and later employed a mimeograph called "The Duplicator" to render copies. Looking back, the newsletter now presents a fascinating glimpse of early-20th-century life at the Ijams place. Around the same time, an editorial appeared in the *New York Times* in response to a letter from Jo concerning the 1925 Scopes Monkey Trial in Dayton, Tennessee. As one might expect, the Ijams family's views on the teachings of Darwin's theory of evolution were progressive. In fact, H. P. placed a picture of Darwin above the front door and proclaimed, "Let 'em know where I stand!"

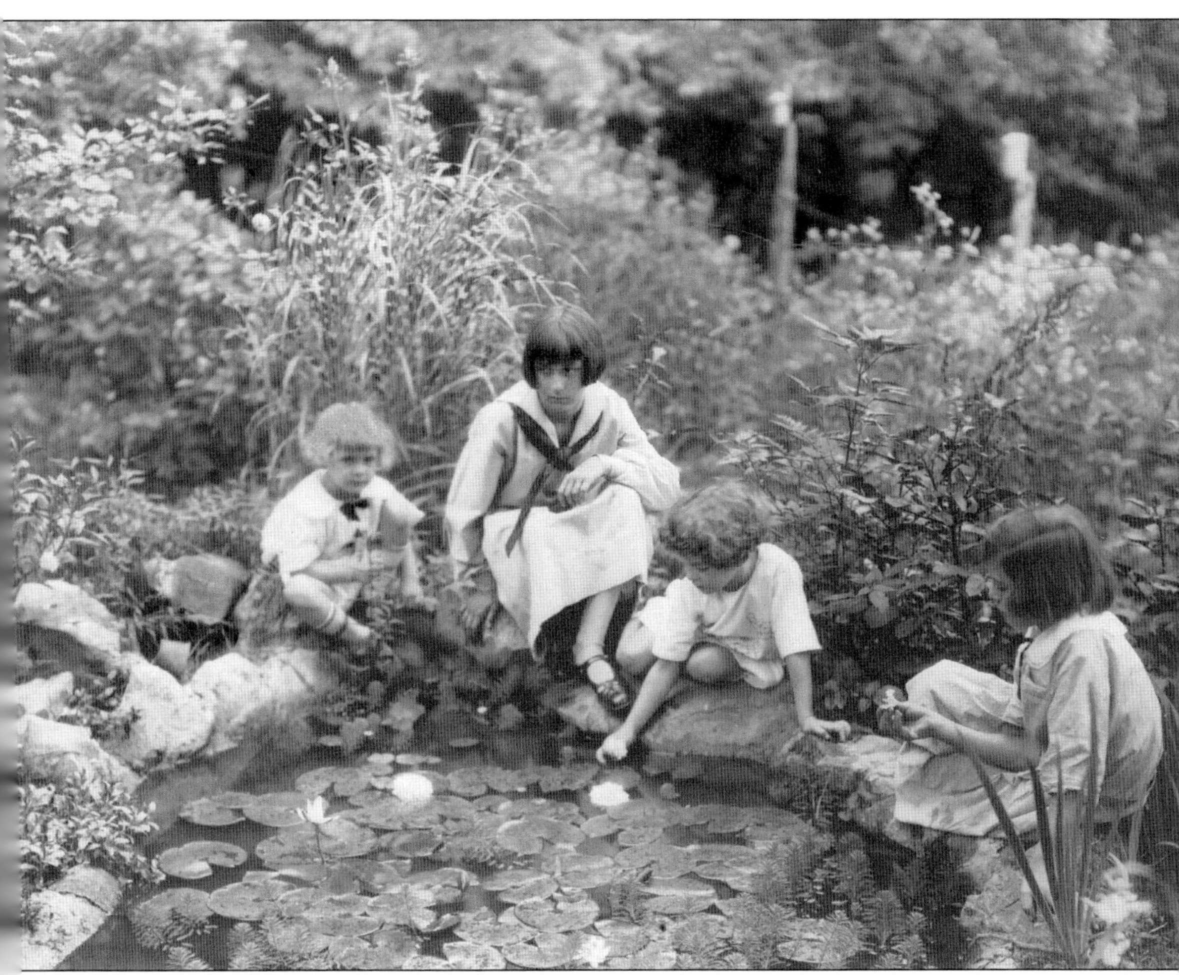

This is the full image of the cover photograph taken by Ben Curtis in July 1923. Like many of the Ijams family photographs, the background details are as important as the main subjects. The lush natural scenery indicates well-established grounds, leading one to think that H. P. Ijams concentrated first on the grounds of his property before renovating the house. As illustrator for a daily newspaper, H. P. was well placed to arrange memorable images, often bird-related, for the local press. A photograph similar to this appeared in the *Knoxville News Sentinel* on July 13, 1923. The headline accompanying the image read "Beautiful Girls in Beautiful Setting." From left to right are Martha, Elizabeth, Mary, and Jo Ijams.

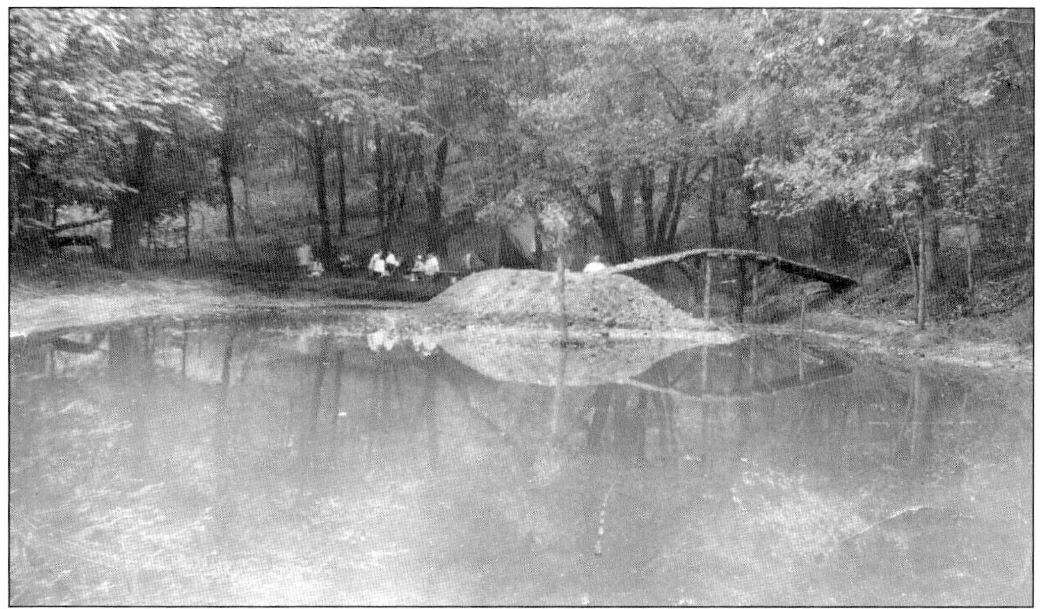

The Ijams family enjoyed frequent picnics next to Lake Avis, located down a short trail from the house. Taken in August 1922, this photograph shows a small bridge under construction and behind it, a tent often used by the young girls or visitors to the Ijams place.

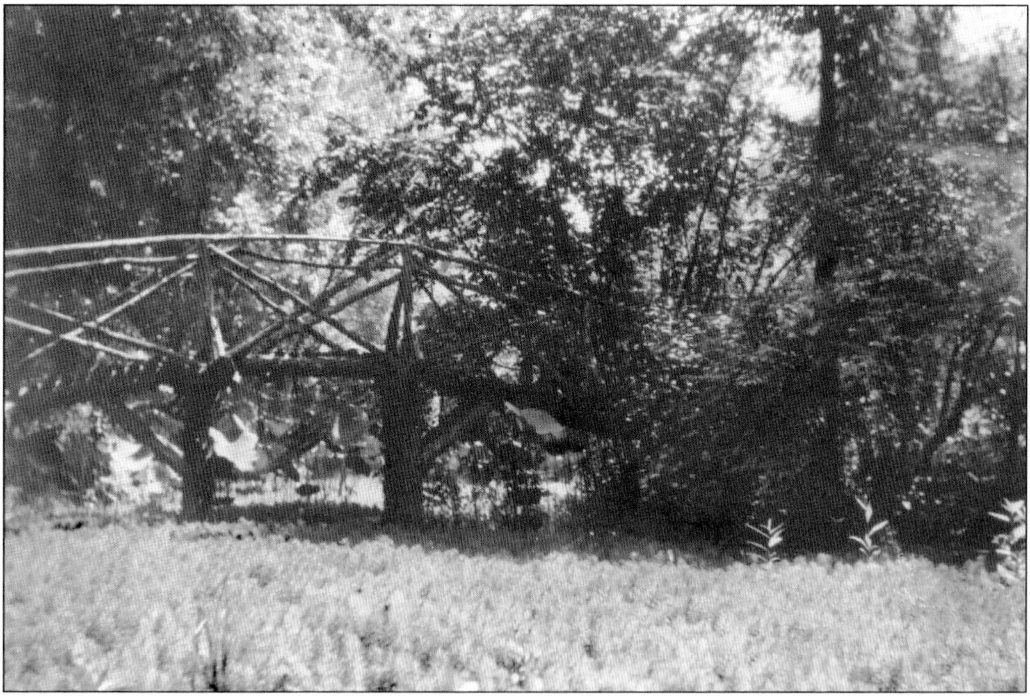

In the 1930s, Egyptian lotuses were planted in Lake Avis. Mrs. Oscar Lee Mitchell, a flower arranger and former State Garden Club president, visited from Chattanooga and commented, "In Mrs. Harry Ijams' garden there is a lotus pool that is too beautiful to describe. You approach the pool through a path that wanders down a woodsy trail, and all of a sudden there is the pool with its overwhelming blossoms before your very eyes."

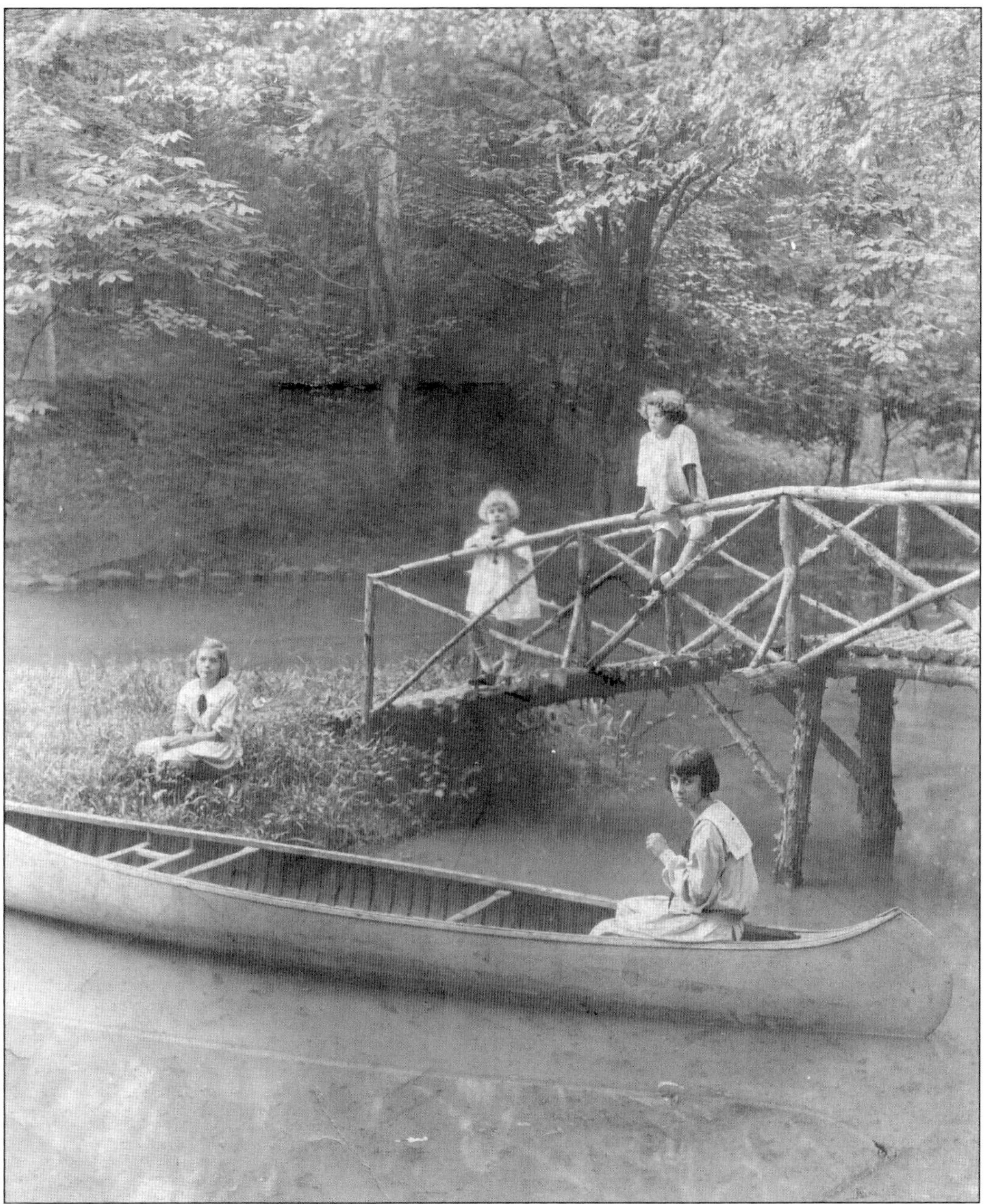

Many years later after this photograph was taken around 1923, H. P. Ijams told ornithologist Nancy Tanner that he built a spring-fed pool for his daughters to swim in more safely than in the sluice of the Tennessee River. To find a suitable name for the pond, which became known initially as Lake Avis, Jo Ijams ran a competition in the family newsletter. Later renamed Lotus Pond, the pool still exists today off the Discovery Trail and is a popular stopping point for visitors and school groups. A wide variety of wildlife may be seen at the pond, including snapping turtles, painted turtles, wood ducks, and even green herons. From left to right are Jo, Martha, and Mary, with Elizabeth in the canoe.

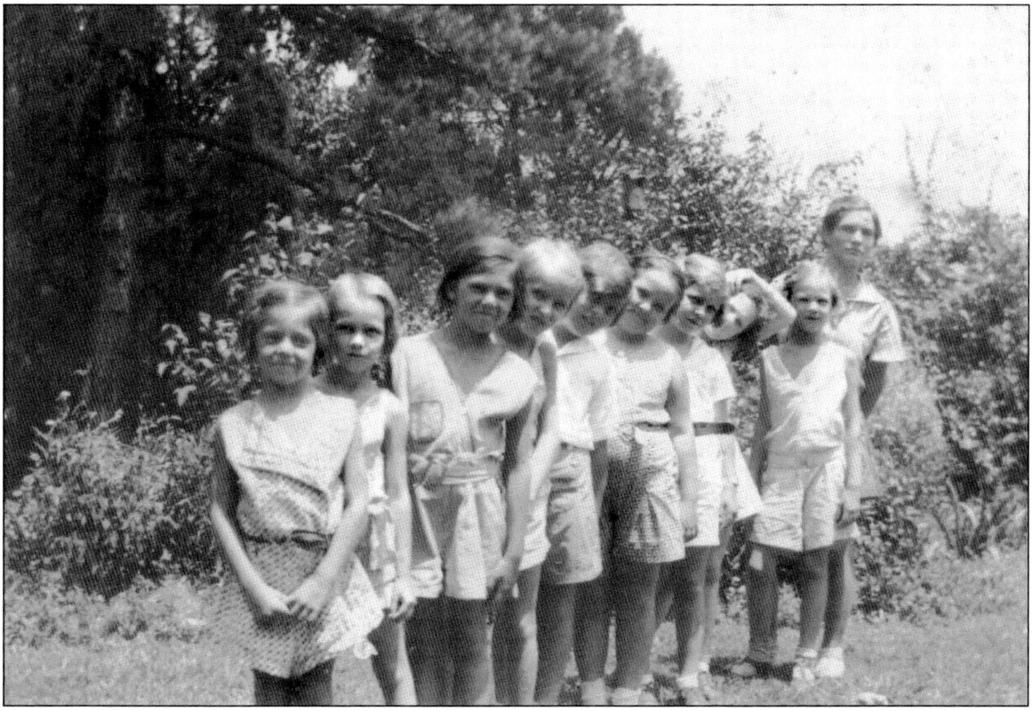

In the 1930s, Jo Ijams directed a "stay-at-home" summer camp for young girls at the home of Mr. and Mrs. Bruce Keener Jr. on Lyons View Pike. Camp activities included making splatter pictures, handicrafts, swimming, storytelling, and hikes. Day camps still play an important role in educational programming for young children at Ijams Nature Center today.

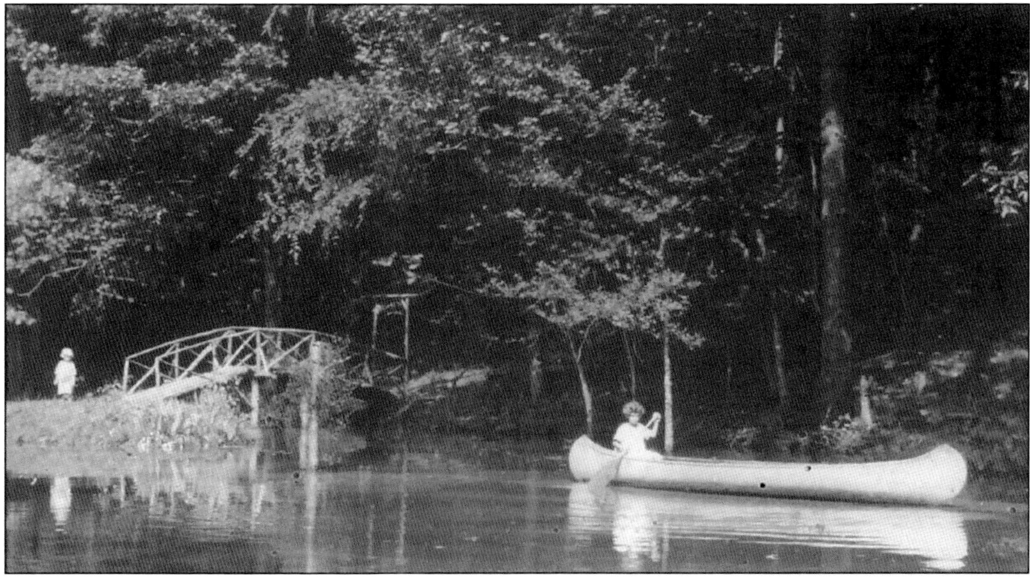

Here is another view of Lake Avis shortly after it was built, with Mary Ijams in the canoe and Martha watching from the island. For many years, the lake served as a training ground for the Ijams girls, who all became accomplished swimmers in the Girl Scouts or with the Knoxville Swim Team.

Martha Ijams poses for the *Knoxville Journal* with an Egyptian lotus from the Ijams Lotus Pond. The newspaper described the flowers as "shading from rose to pinkish white, measure from 10 to 12 inches around the blossom, and the flowers are 15 feet tall, 12 feet above the water and three feet below." The flowers followed the sun throughout the day, and many visitors from across town rode the Island Home streetcar just to see the natural spectacle.

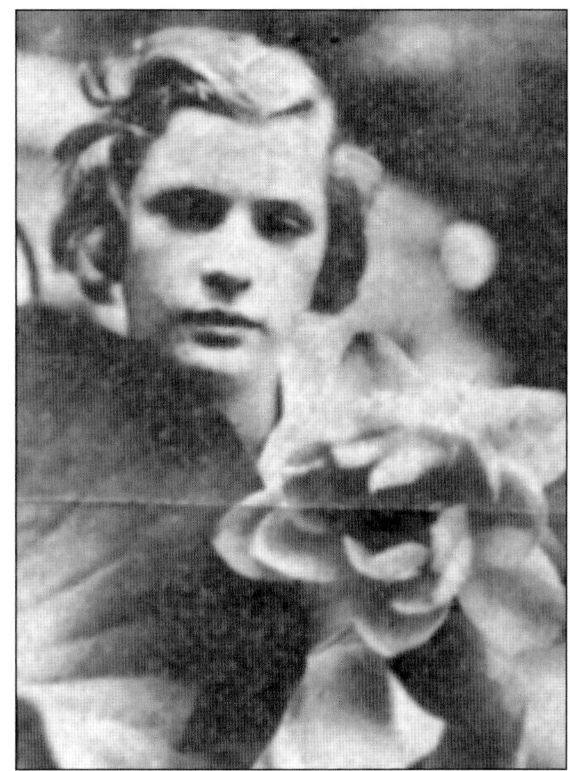

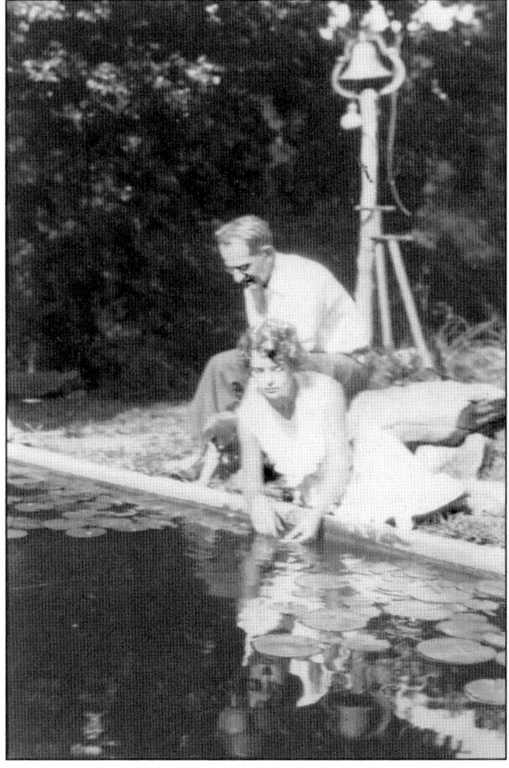

Here is a rare photograph of H. P. Ijams taking a break from ornithology with daughter Mary by the lily pond prior to her death in 1932. H. P. was elected president of the Tennessee Ornithological Society in 1932 and served for many years as the East Tennessee regional editor of the *Migrant*, the state organization's quarterly journal.

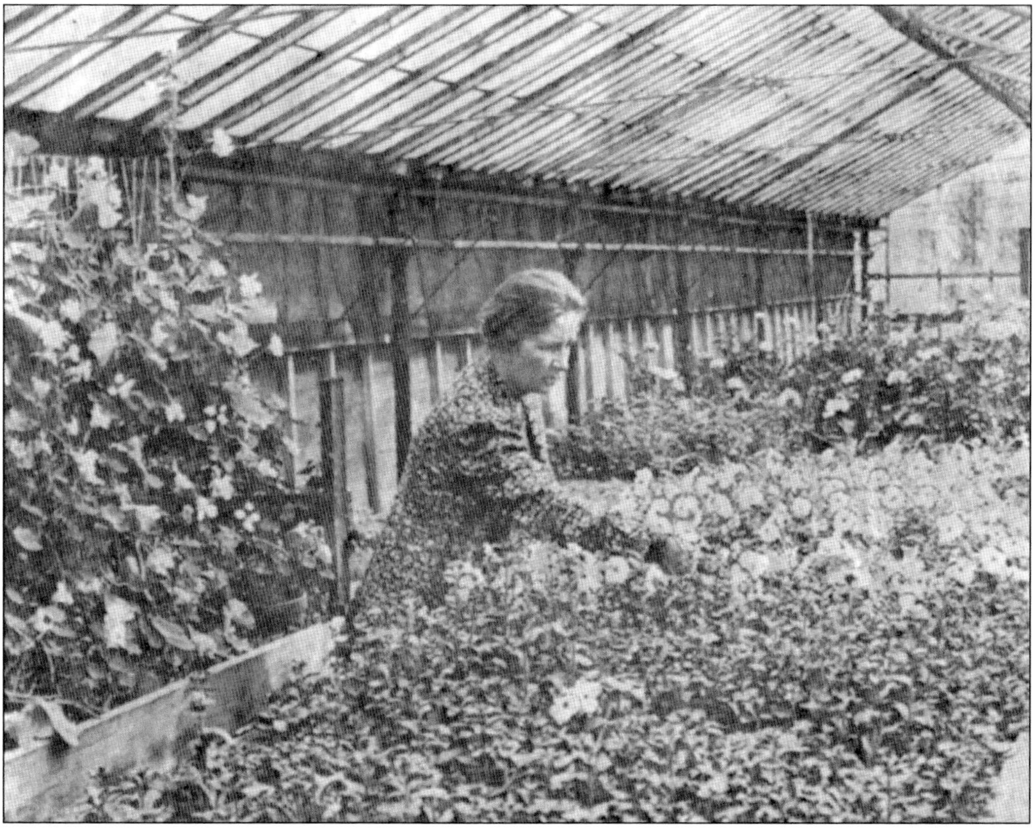

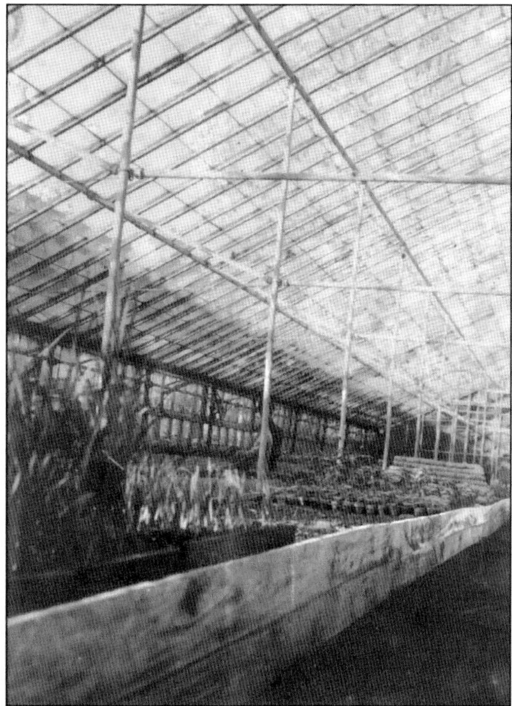

In the 1920s, Alice Ijams began Southside Greenhouses, a commercial venture that propagated and supplied flowers to Knoxville florist Brockway Crouch. The business included three huge greenhouses; the one that received the least sun was reserved for growing ferns. Alice also grew perennial plants outdoors.

Here is another glimpse into one of the greenhouses, which is stocked with varieties of native plants. Compared to today's green movement, Alice Ijams was clearly ahead of her time. Alice was an expert horticulturalist, and the Ijamses' phone was one of the busiest on the city exchange, with amateur and professional gardeners alike calling to "Ask Alice—she'll know." Indeed, she inspired the creation of several local garden clubs through her passion and philosophy of conservation and preservation.

Three

An Ijams Christmas

The Christmas season was a festive one at the Ijams place, and H. P. Ijams employed his artistic talents to full effect. Beginning in 1914, H. P. began a unique and long-standing family tradition: designing the Ijams Christmas postcard, which was mailed to family and friends. Early designs featured silhouettes of the family members cut out from black card stock, while others showcased H. P.'s inimitable pen-and-ink illustrations. Central to the creative process during those early years was keen participation from the Ijams girls, who would sit around the kitchen table eager to help. Each was given a different colored pencil, and they embellished the drawing as they went along the line.

Over the years, the Christmas postcards showcased a wide range of styles, including photographs of the Ijams household, a detailed map of the bird sanctuary, and charming birdlife, such as the noble cardinal or a goldfinch. Later, after the girls had flown the nest, the postcards depicted a more mature style, including a serene sandhill crane, a migrant species rarely seen in the region at the time. The postcards also allowed H. P. to employ his wit in at least two memorable scenes of Santa Claus during the Depression era and in happier times.

Another Ijams tradition that was relatively new to Knoxville during the early 20th century was to bring living trees into the house for Christmas. In 1952, Alice Ijams reminisced, "Our living Christmas tree group was one of the first in the city. Our scheme was simple. A desirable tree, one congenial to our soil, was purchased and came from the nursery with roots wrapped in burlap. This tree was placed in the living room, decorated, and gifts placed at its base. When the holidays were over, the tree was planted. All have thrived and developed except the ones that H. P. accidentally killed with a blow-torch in one of our periodic onslaughts against poison ivy and honeysuckle."

Today different festive activities persist at the Nature Center: an annual holiday craft party and recycling holiday greenery for the benefit of the Ijams grounds.

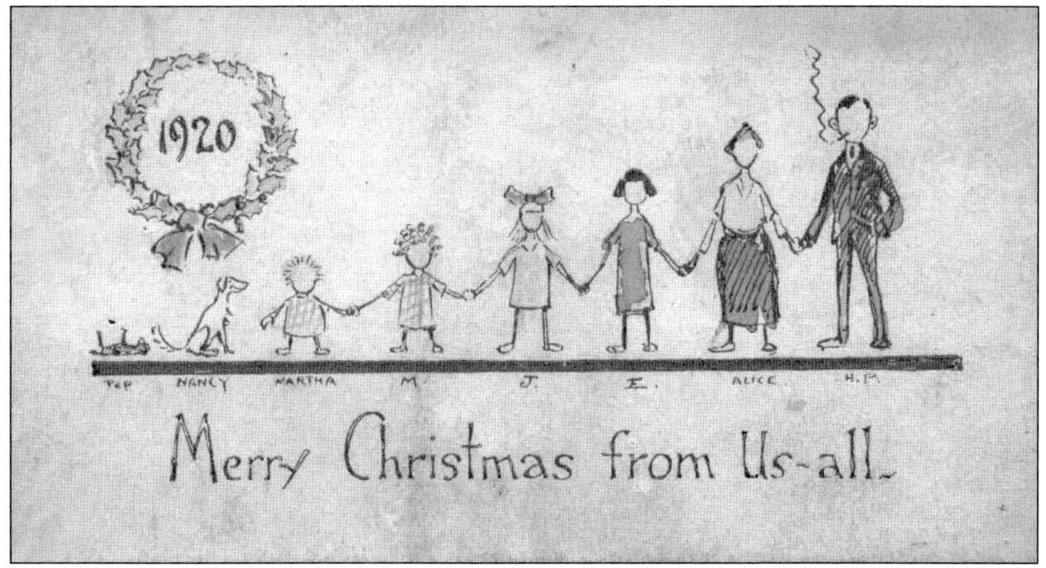

The entire Ijams family and pets appear on the 1920 Christmas postcard. The first dog on the left was a fox terrier named Pep, and the name was used for a series of pet terriers. A lifelong eccentric, H.P was later renowned for smoking a rather pungent brand of cigarettes, which would cause everyone to stand back after he lit one.

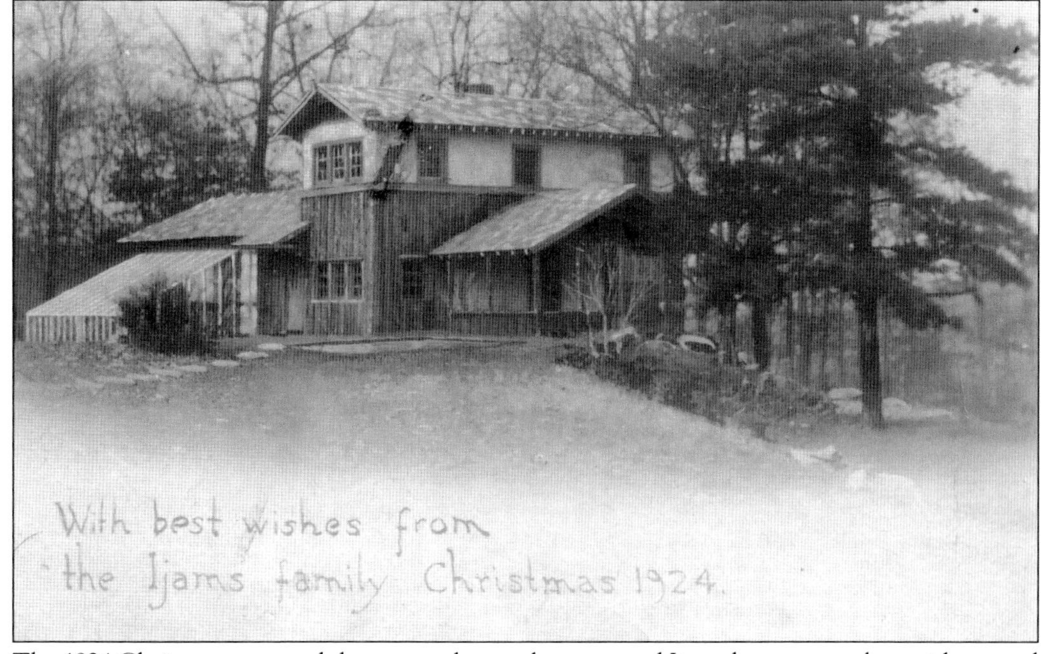

The 1924 Christmas postcard showcases the newly renovated Ijams home, complete with second story and greenhouse off the front porch.

The entire family is depicted in H. P. Ijams's remarkable silhouettes, which he made by drawing and then cutting the silhouettes out of black card stock.

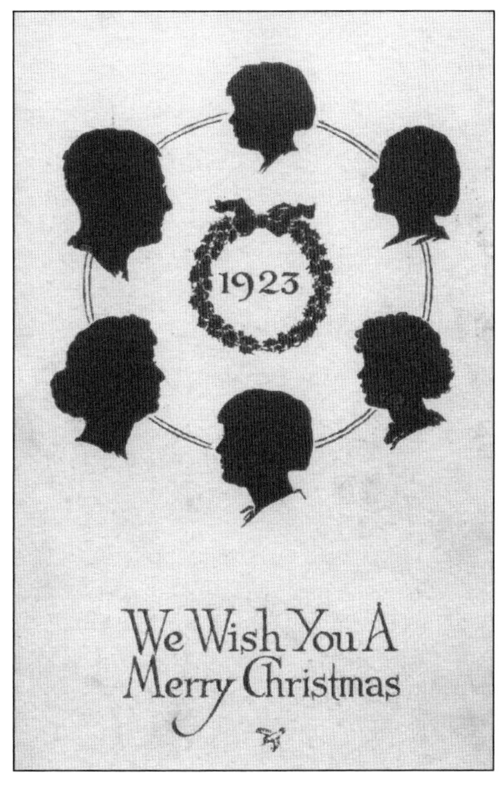

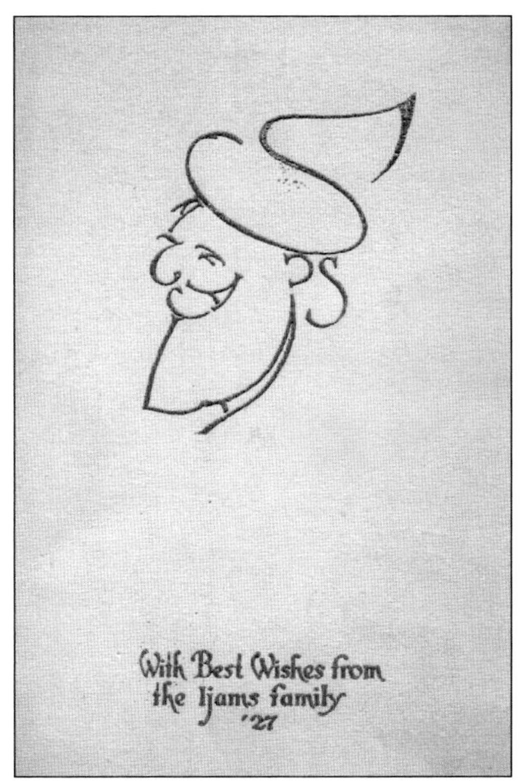

A creative genius, H. P. Ijams reduces Santa to his barest form in this simple yet elegant line drawing from 1927. On close inspection, the drawing reveals the letters from "Santa Claus" in sequence to form the jolly man in the red suit.

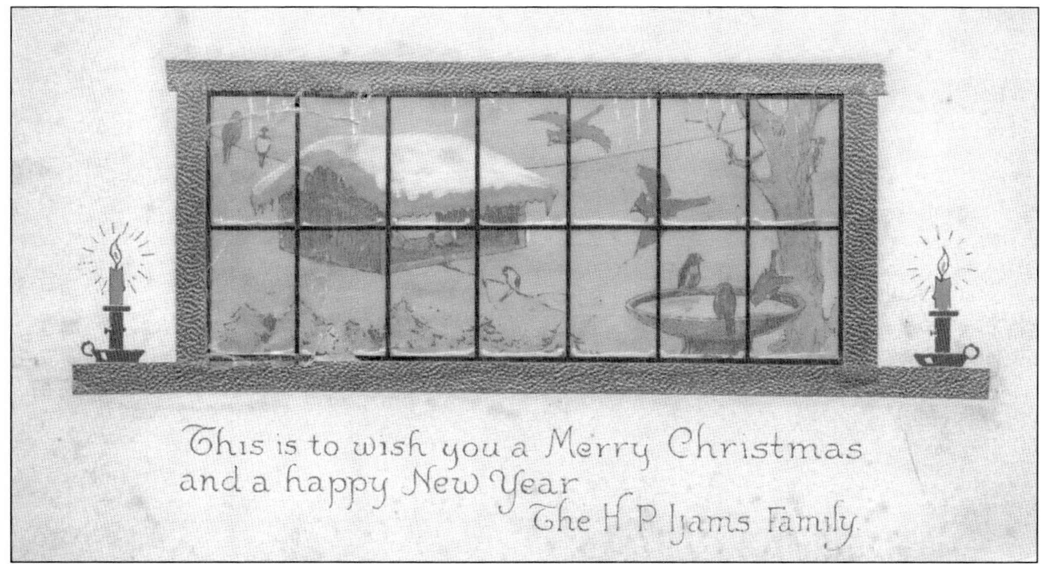

No doubt H. P. Ijams recreated this image from the view through his study window in this undated Christmas postcard.

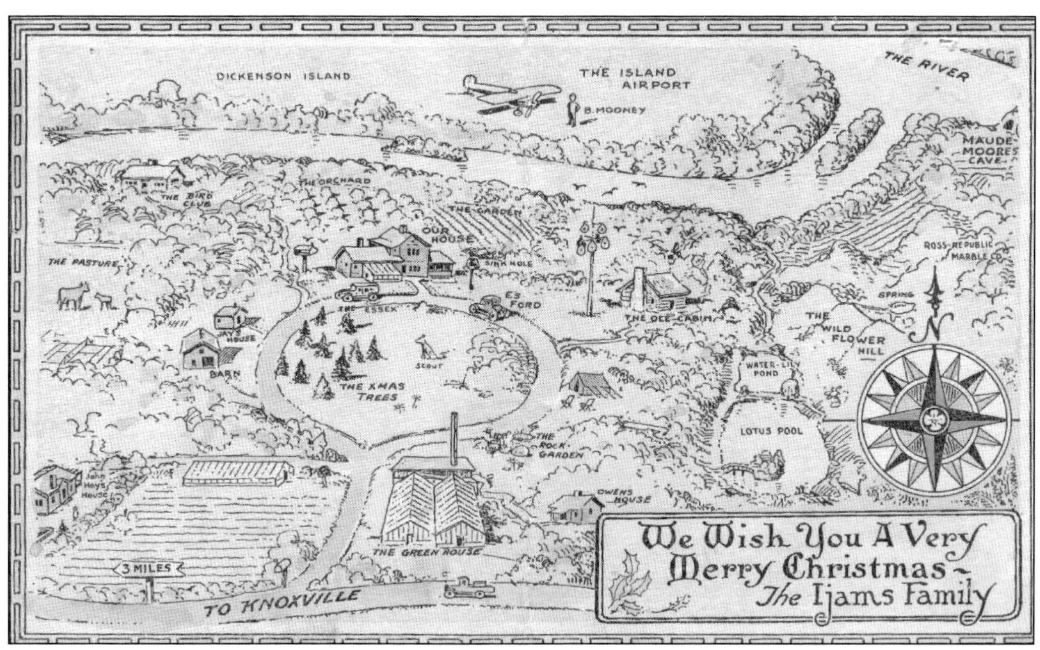

In 1930, H. P. Ijams captured the landscape at the Ijams farm, showing the location of the house, Lotus Pond (formerly Lake Avis), the Christmas tree patch, and Alice's greenhouses. Note that the Ijams property borders the Ross and Republic Quarry, later to become better known as Mead's Quarry. The bird club lodge is located at the upper left, overlooking the Tennessee River. The Ijams Visitor Center, built in 1997, now lies just above Wild Flower Hill.

A skinny Santa paradoxically lightened the mood during the Great Depression in this 1931 postcard. Note Santa's shabby outfit, toes poking through his boots, and the emaciated toy reindeer.

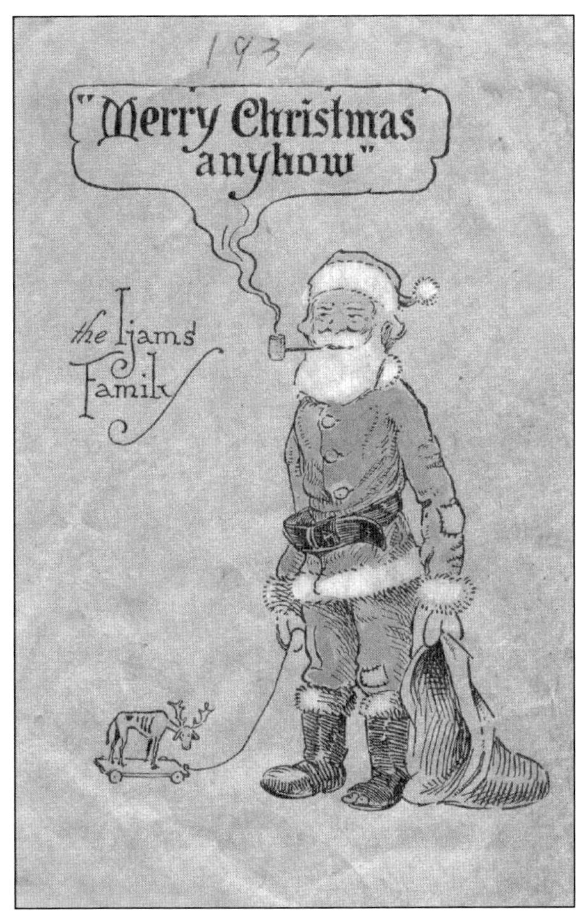

Emerging from depressed times, the 1933 Christmas postcard shows Santa Claus heralding a new hope by depicting the best that Knoxville and the region had to offer: the Great Smoky Mountains National Park, the National Forest, the Tennessee Valley Authority, and the East Tennessee Ornithological Society, as well the newly formed National Recovery Act, Civilian Conservation Corps, and others.

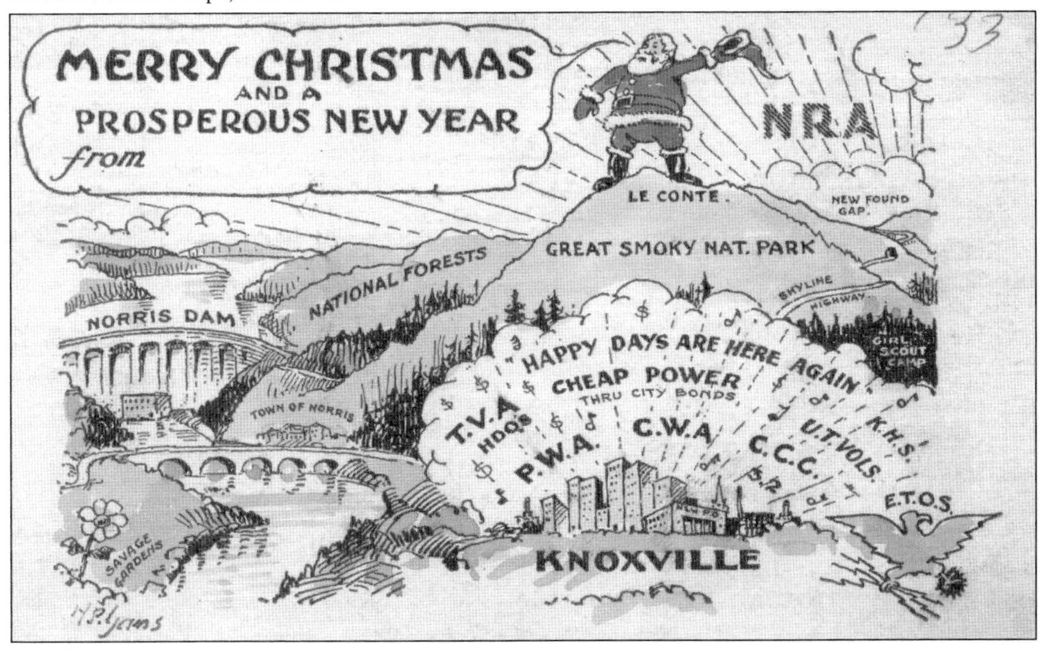

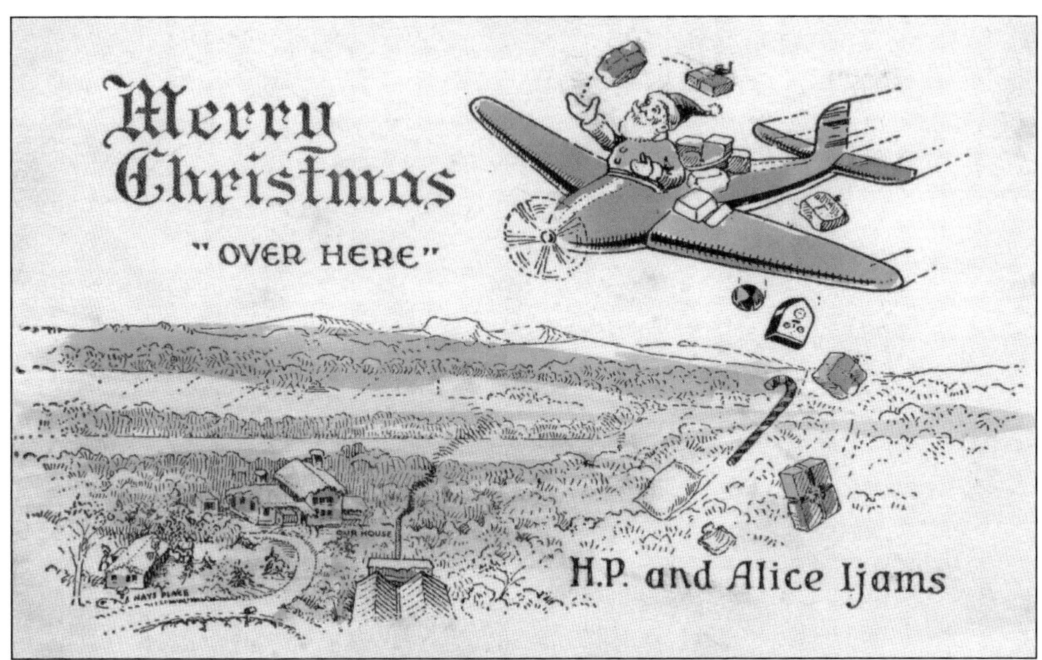

With its "over here" statement, it is possible that this undated postcard was made during World War II.

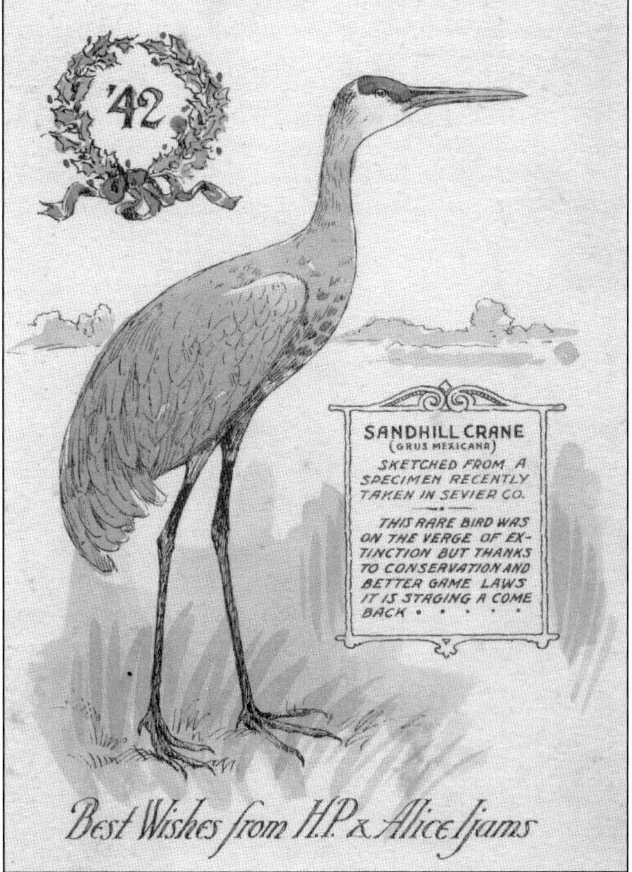

In 1942, a rare sandhill crane adorned the festive postcard. Although the species was making a good comeback, its larger cousin, the whooping crane, was virtually extinct at this time, with only 15 birds comprising the North American population. Conservation and improved game laws would serve both species well, and by the end of the 20th century, crane populations were significantly greater.

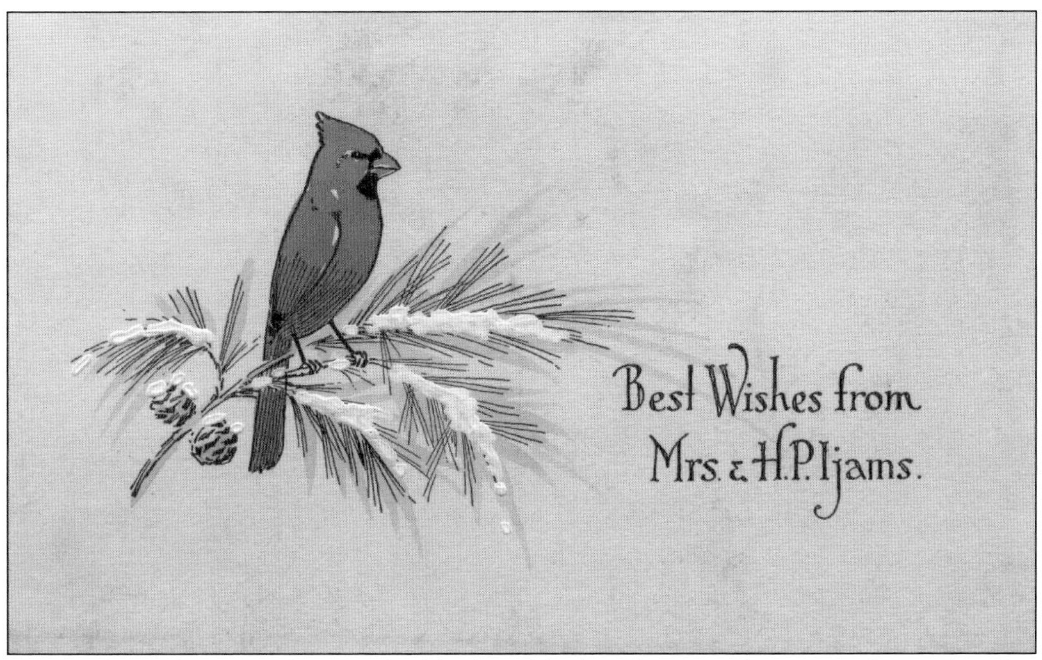

The cardinal, the most photographed backyard bird in the United States, is featured in this simple but charming postcard.

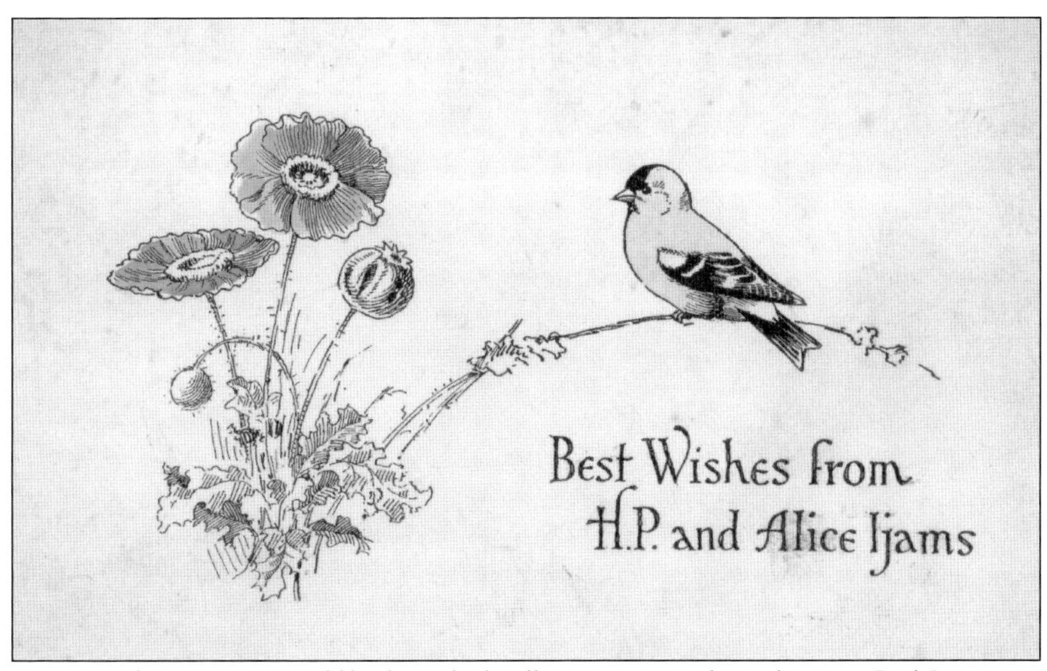

Poppies and an American goldfinch, undoubtedly a common sight at the Ijams Bird Sanctuary, adorn this undated Christmas card.

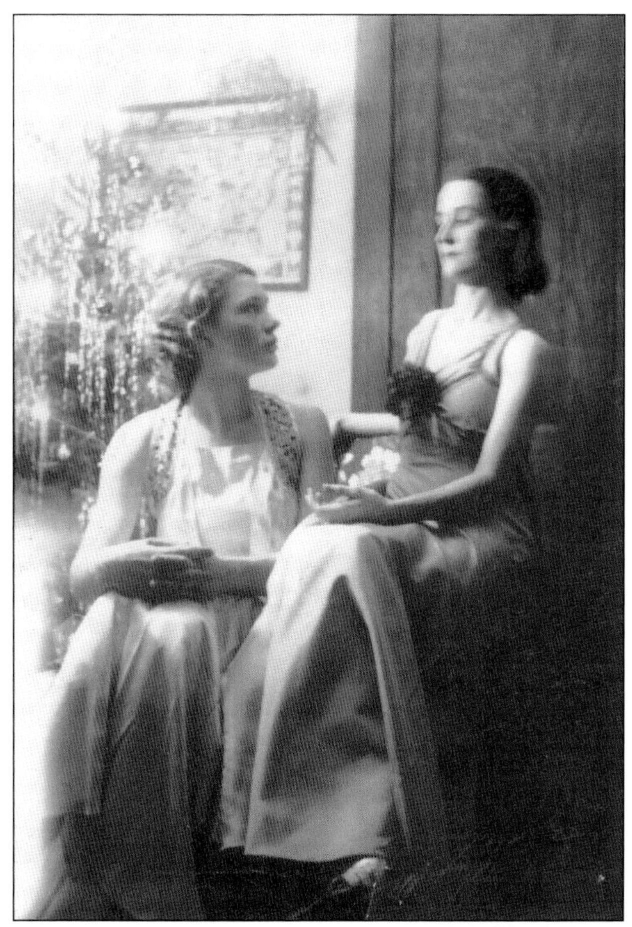

Jo (left) and Elizabeth Ijams take a break from being young naturalists to dress up for Christmas. A late 1920s *Knoxville News Sentinel* column entitled "What Comes Down Our Creek" extolled the virtues of live Christmas trees. "So pretty and sensible is Harry Ijams' scheme of a living Christmas tree! Each Christmas he obtains from a nurseryman an evergreen of some kind—hemlock, fir, balsam, or any variety he may choose. Mr. Ijams now has a little grove of 15 evergreens, growing more beautiful and valuable each year, and each and every one recalling a happy Christmas gone by."

A glimpse into a Christmas past shows a multitude of toys awaiting the Ijams girls under a live tree on Christmas day. The selection of toys included a pull-along horse, drum, car, turtle, teddy bear, and a Native American doll. The Ijams family radio sits to the right of the tree.

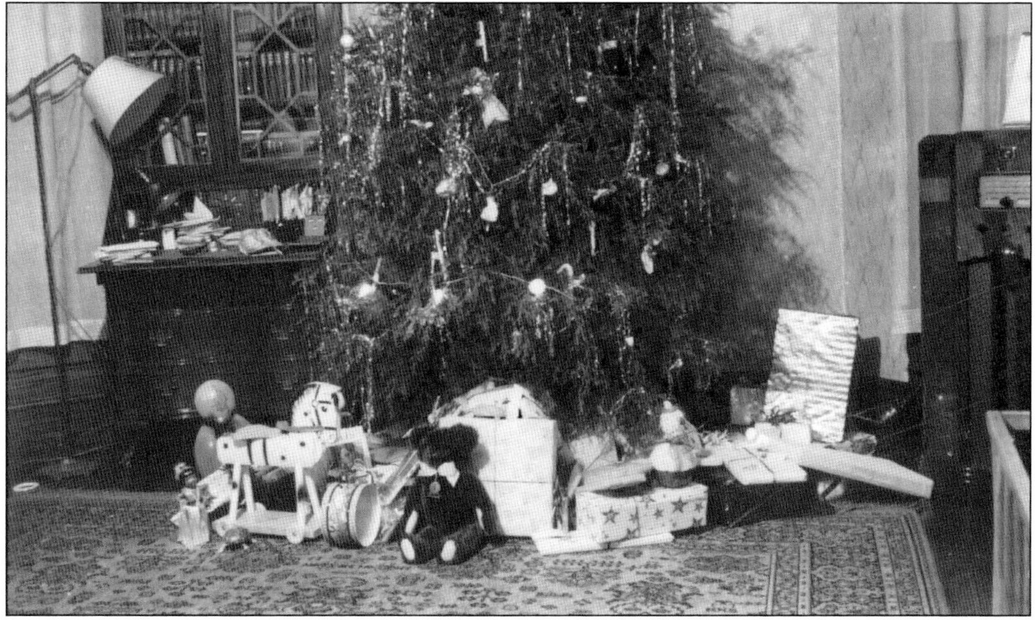

Four

MOUNT LECONTE

In his day, H. P. Ijams was an avid hiker in the Smoky Mountains, and being an expert ornithologist, he was well acquainted with the many different species, behaviors, and habitats of birds throughout East Tennessee. One fateful trip to the Smokies led to the establishment of the first official campsite on Mount LeConte.

In May 1925, H. P. Ijams accompanied fellow ornithologists Paul J. Adams and Albert Ganier on a birding trip to Mount LeConte. Adams had been an early treasurer with the East Tennessee Ornithological Society, while Ganier was a founding member of Tennessee Ornithological Society. After collecting eggs, a few specimens, and watching golden eagles soar off the peak, the trio discussed around the evening campfire the need for a permanent campsite on Mount LeConte. The idea for a national park in the southeast was already gathering momentum, and Knoxvillians such as Col. David S. Chapman (vice president of the Great Smoky Mountains Conservation Association) were already working tirelessly to ensure the Smokies was chosen. Ijams, Adams, and Ganier spent several days on the mountain, with Adams keen to discover the location of a natural spring on the peak which he had found years before and H. P. returning early to Knoxville to resume his duties at the *News Sentinel*. On his return, Adams discovered that H. P. had already contacted Col. Chapman to recommend him for the job of building the camp. However, there was one condition: Adams had to prove the existence of the spring, which Chapman felt was paramount to the success of the camp. Adams returned to LeConte shortly afterwards and finally located the spring, and he established the camp in July the same year.

H. P. Ijams also used his artistic talents in the Smoky Mountains as well as his birding expertise. As an illustrator for the *News Sentinel*, he produced at least two maps of the Smokies to promote the creation of the new national park in 1934. Showcasing H. P.'s inimitable pen-and-ink style, the maps charmingly captured the diverse characteristics of the region. Shortly afterwards, H. P. designed a set of poster stamps to be used in the promotion of the Smokies for the Smoky Mountains Conservation Association.

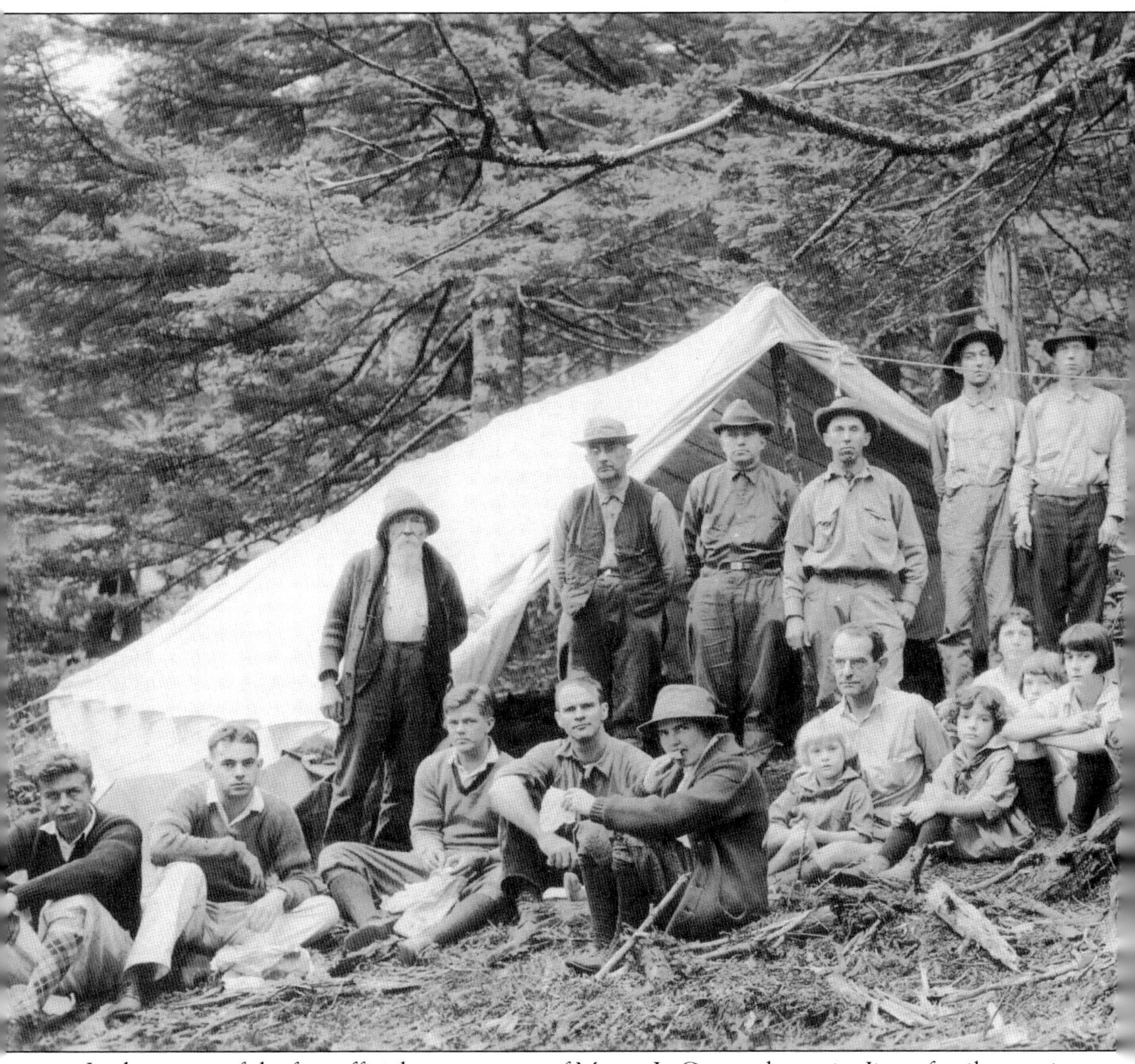

In the center of the first official camp on top of Mount LeConte, the entire Ijams family rests in front of the tent with members of the Smoky Mountain Hiking Club and other mountain folk. The photograph was taken on Saturday, July 19, 1925, just six days after Paul J. Adams had built the camp, and a few weeks after the birding trip with H. P. Ijams and Albert Ganier. Knoxville photographer Jim Thompson, in front of the tree, took great pains to compose this shot, which

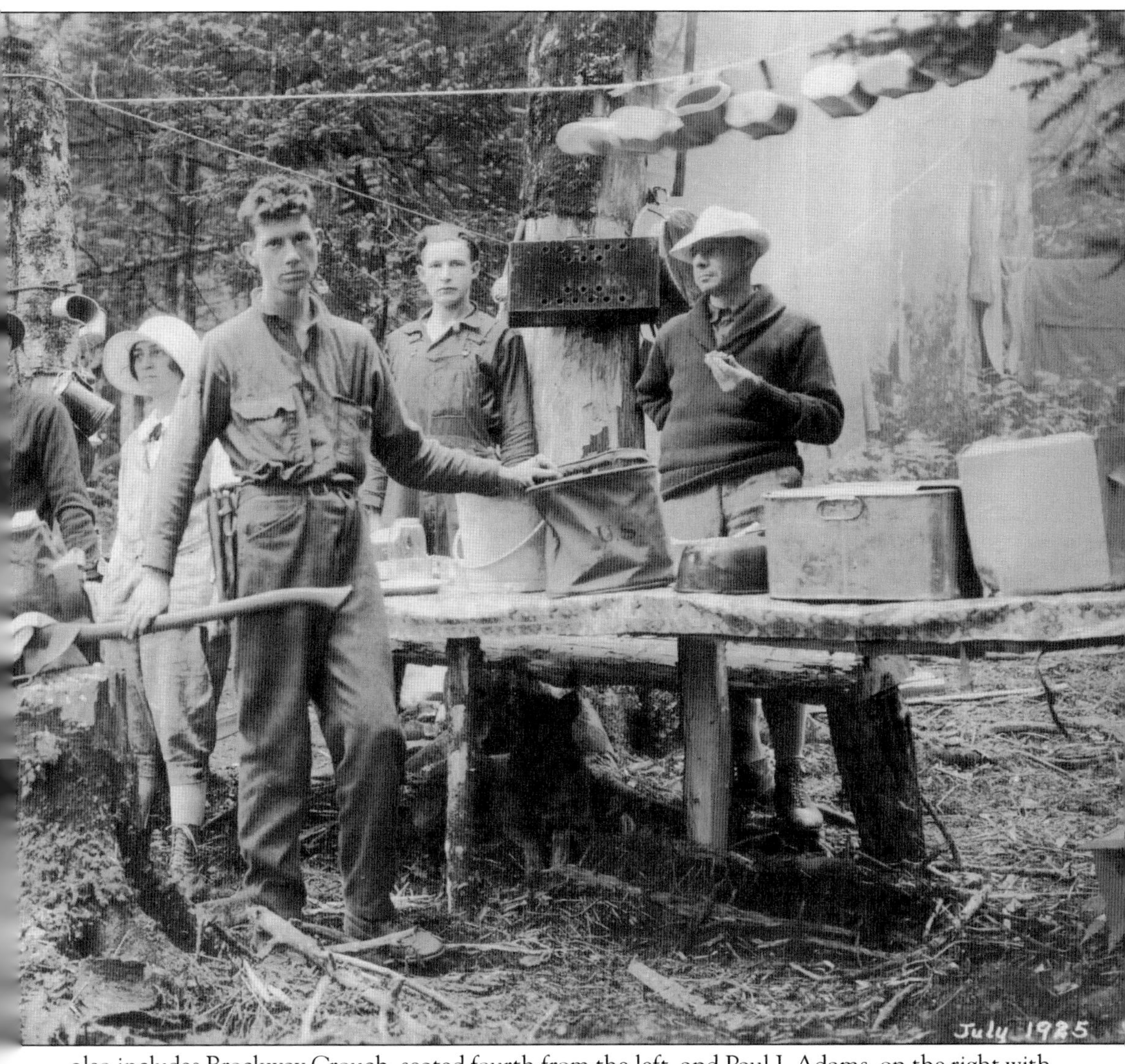

also includes Brockway Crouch, seated fourth from the left, and Paul J. Adams, on the right with the axe. Thompson was disappointed that Adams's legendary dog, Cumberland Jack, would not come out from under the table to join the adventurers. The photograph was taken by Robin Thompson. (Thompson Collection, Great Smoky Mountains National Park Archive.)

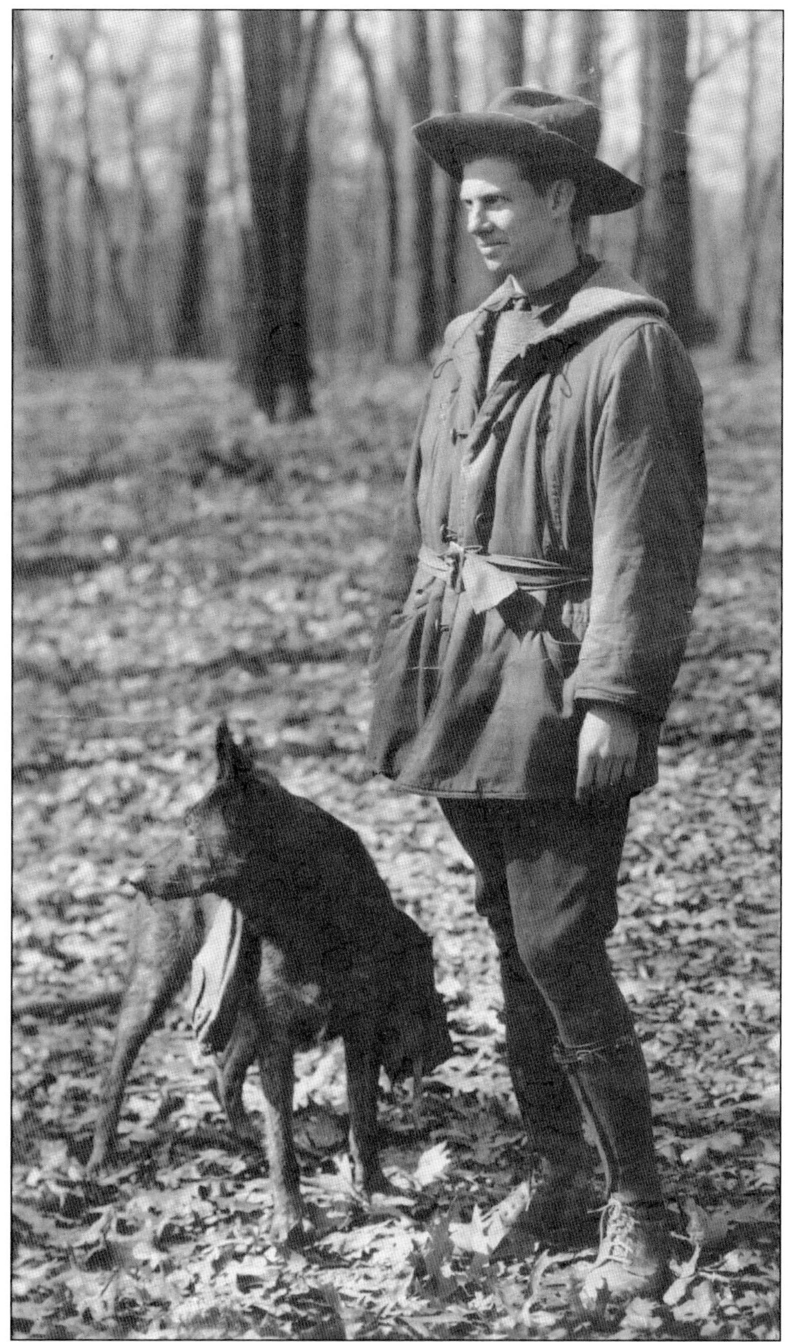

Paul J. Adams, employed at Brockway Crouch's florist shop on Gay Street, had been a frequent hiker on Mount LeConte. H. P. Ijams thought he was the right man for the job of creating the first official campsite on the peak. Adams's German shepherd, Cumberland Jack, is perhaps more famous than his owner. Kitted out with leather saddlebags, Cumberland Jack was frequently sent down the mountain to Charley Ogle's store in Gatlinburg, where he would be loaded up with supplies and return on his own back to the mountaintop. (Great Smoky Mountains National Park Archive.)

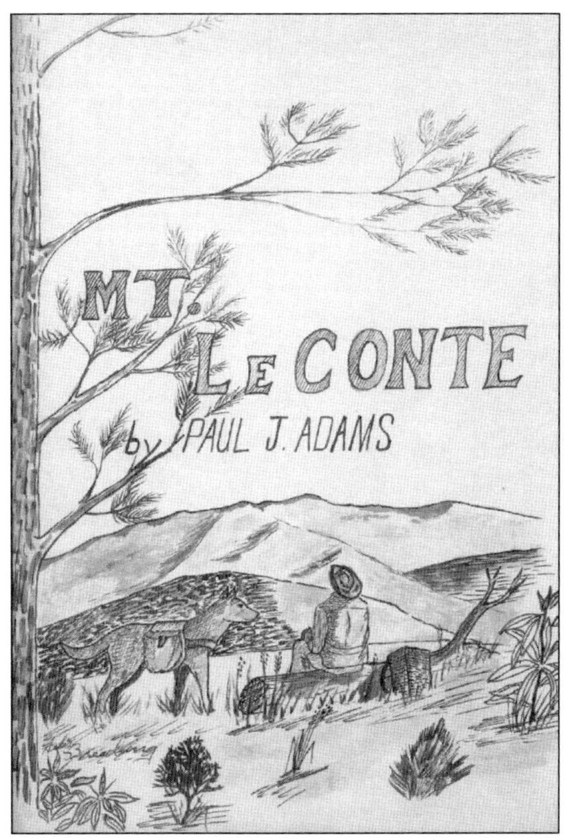

In 1966, Paul J. Adams reflected on his experiences as a mountain guide and a pioneer hiker of the Smokies in his book, *Mount LeConte.* Adams described in great detail the birding trip with Ijams and Ganier, as well as the often torturous efforts blazing previously uncharted trails up and down Mount LeConte to help establish what has since become the most visited of all national parks in the United States.

Col. David S. Chapman, pictured here with a caged bobcat, was one of the staunchest supporters of the Smokies becoming a national park. He probably worked harder than anyone in Knoxville to realize this goal and frequently organized trips for visiting dignitaries to experience the virtues of the mountains. Paul J. Adams often acted as a mountain guide on those trips. It is fitting that the main road from Knoxville to the Smoky Mountains, Chapman Highway, would be subsequently named after him. (Russell Harrison, Great Smoky Mountains Conservation Association.)

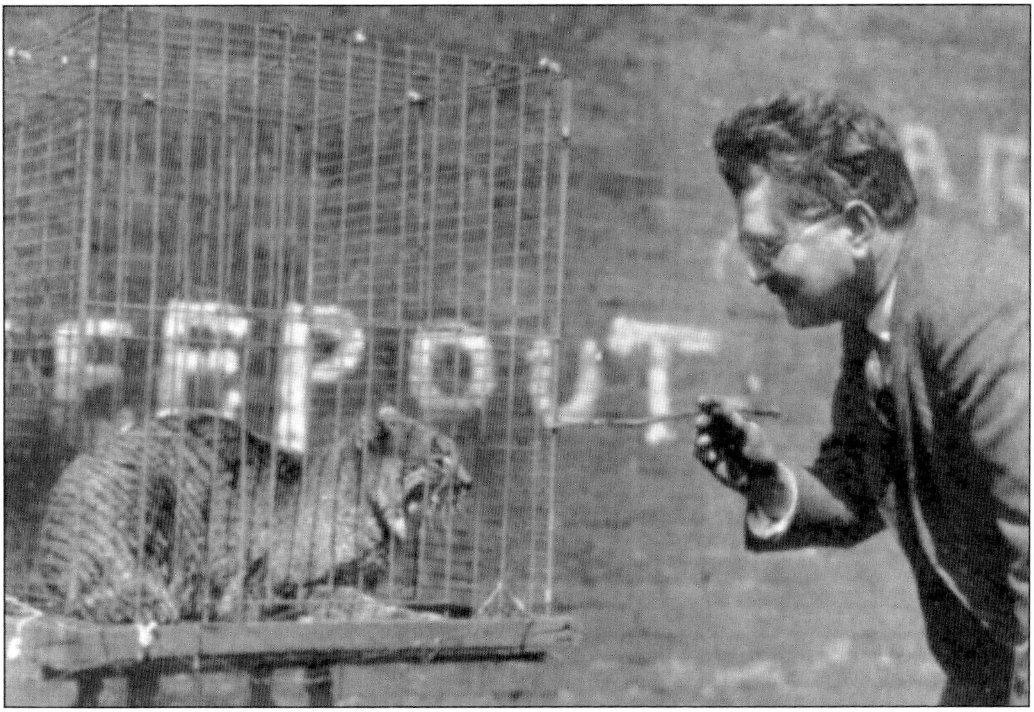

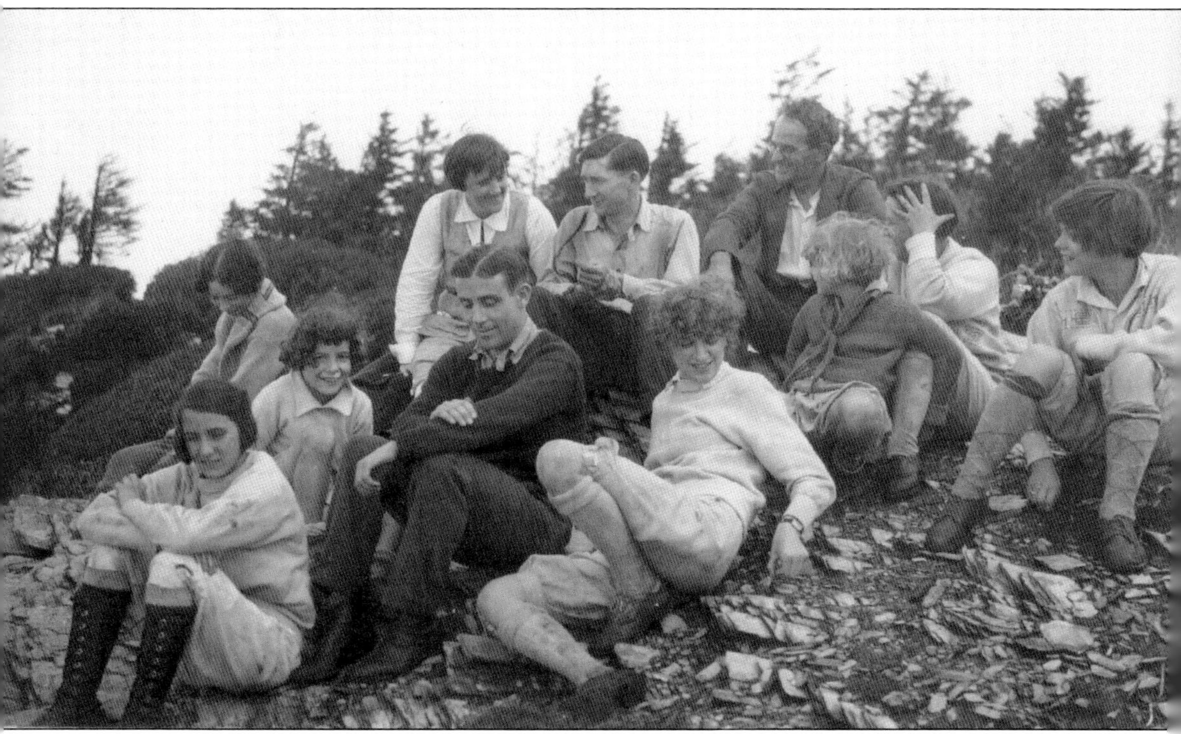

The Ijams family, seen here on top of Mount LeConte in June 1927, made frequent family trips to the Smokies. From left to right are Elizabeth Ijams, Willa Love Galyon, Mary Ijams, Ida Campbell, Lucien C. Greene, Harvey B. Broome, Frances Stout, H. P. Ijams, Martha Ijams, Alice Ijams, and Jo Ijams. Broome, an active member of the Smoky Mountain Hiking Club, became a founding member of the Wilderness Society in 1935. Carlos C. Campbell, who wrote *Birth of a National Park* in 1960, took the photograph. During the early 1940s, Campbell regularly brought his son, Jim, to see H. P. Ijams, who gave the young lad a pair of flying squirrels to look after. (Carlos C. Campbell, Great Smoky Mountains National Park Archive.)

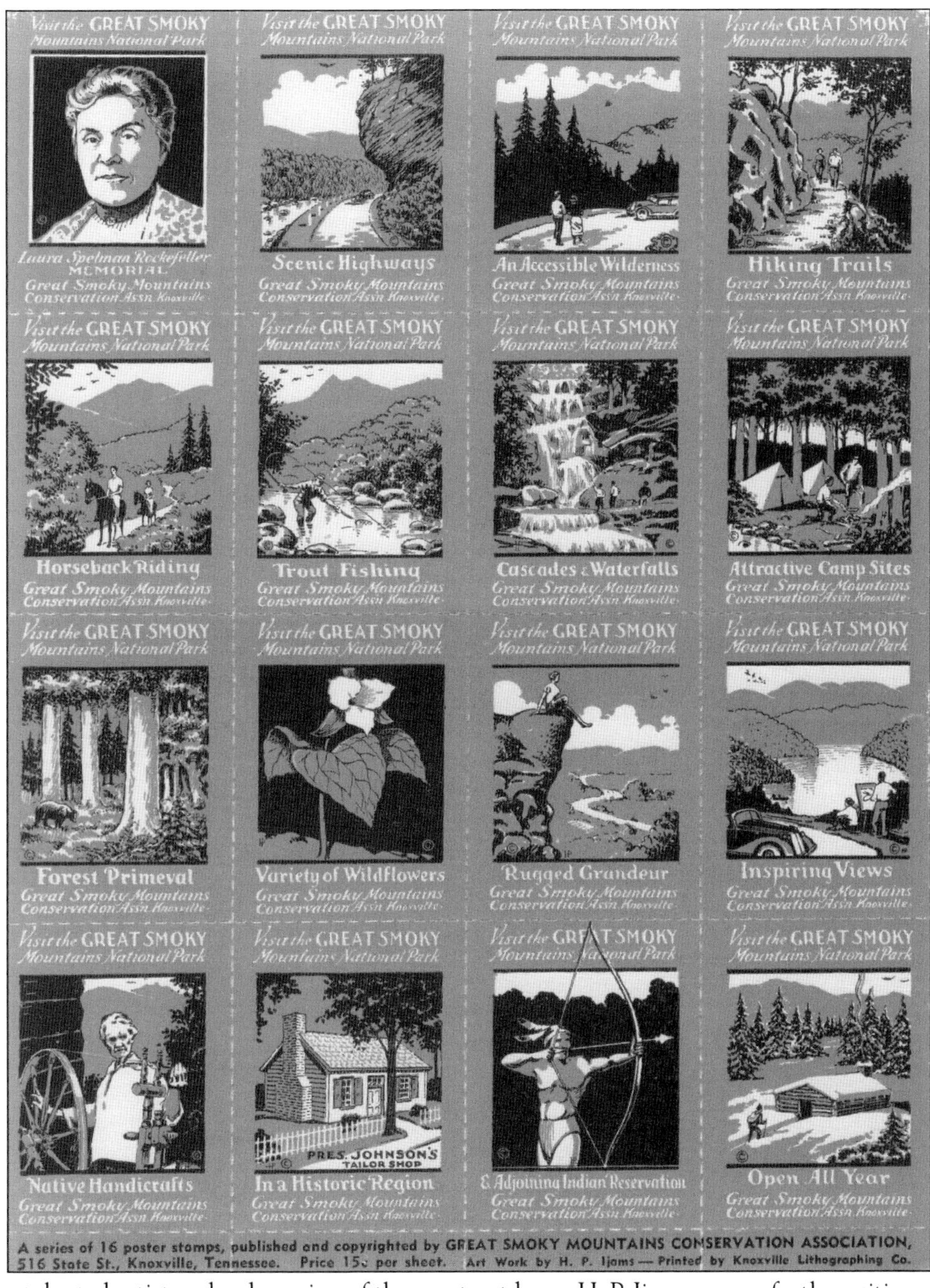

As a talented artist and a champion of the great outdoors, H. P. Ijams was perfectly positioned to lend a hand to help establish a national park in the Smokies. In the mid-1930s, H. P. created a set of 16 poster stamps for the Great Smoky Mountains Conservation Association. The Knoxville Lithographic Company, located near the Ijams home on Island Home Avenue, printed the stamps by the thousands. During the same era, H. P. also took on numerous commercial assignments outside of his daily post with the *Knoxville News Sentinel.* His logo of the day touted, "Designs, Blueprints, Patent drawings, electros, half-tones, and zinc etchings." (Great Smoky Mountains Conservation Association, Great Smoky Mountains National Park Archive.)

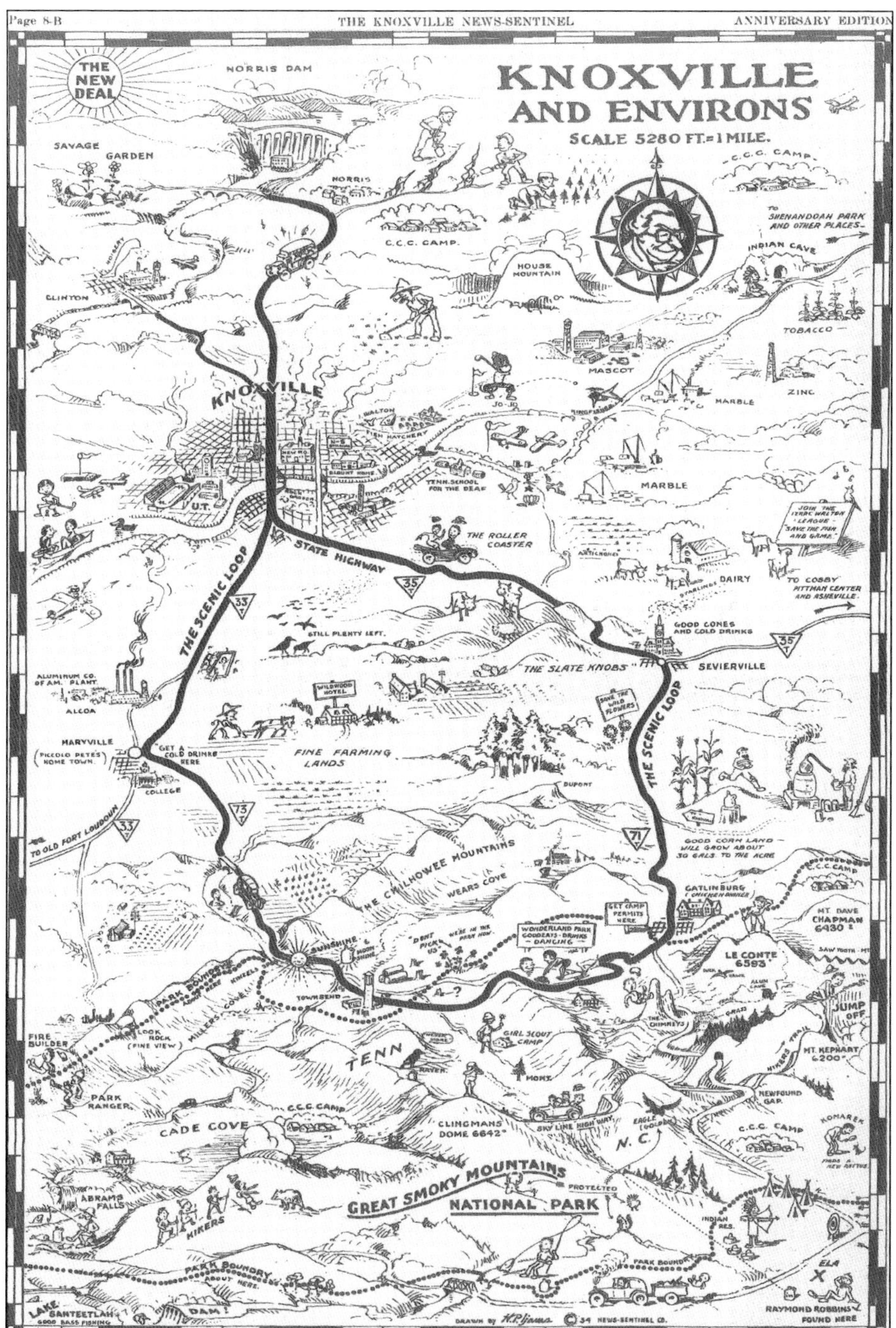

H. P. Ijams produced at least two pen-and-ink maps of Knoxville and the Great Smoky Mountains. The maps were undoubtedly used during the 1930s to promote the new national park, which was fast becoming a highly popular destination for an increasingly mobile population of nature seekers. H. P.'s talents are evident throughout the renderings, balancing a fine artistic style, a detailed knowledge of the region, and a keen sense of humor. (Great Smoky Mountains National Park Archive.)

Five

The Girl Scout Connection

A little-known fact is the connection between the Ijams and Townsend families. Col. W. B. Townsend, owner of the Little River Lumber Company and Railroad, brought logging to the Great Smoky Mountains in 1900. The local village, then called Tang in Tuckaleechee Cove, was subsequently named after him. Colonel Townsend's daughter, Mabel, married Ed Ijams, H. P. Ijams's elder brother, who was a superintendent at the Townsend Lumber Mill.

By the early 1920s, both Mabel and Alice Ijams had become active in the emerging Girl Scout movement, which had been established in the United States by Juliette Low in 1912. Both Mabel and Alice would become Girl Scout Council members, and later commissioners, for the region. Although the first informal Girl Scout camp in the region had been held in Calderwood, Tennessee, in 1923, the Knoxville Girl Scout Council was keen to locate a new permanent site. Mabel Ijams encouraged her father, Colonel Townsend, who owned thousands of acres, to help by donating land in the Smoky Mountains for a new camp. However, before it was built, Alice Ijams invited Girl Scouts to begin attending day camps at the Ijams place in 1923. The tradition of Girl Scout activities still persists at Ijams Nature Center today.

Established in 1925, the new Smokies camp, Camp Margaret Townsend, was named in memory of Mabel Ijams's mother, well known as a warm and generous lady, who died suddenly at the end of 1923. Both Mabel and Alice Ijams worked on the camp committee during those early years, and both Elizabeth and Jo Ijams enrolled the first summer. After being hired as the director of Knoxville Girl Scouts in 1929, Elizabeth Ijams also acted as camp director at Camp Margaret Townsend in 1932 and 1933.

Following the tragic death of their daughter Mary in 1932, H. P. and Alice Ijams found a fitting way to memorialize her. They donated two and a half acres of their property, including the former Audubon Society Woodward Lodge, to the Knoxville Girl Scouts. A competition to name the camp resulted in Camp Mary Ijams, which ran from 1939 until the late 1970s.

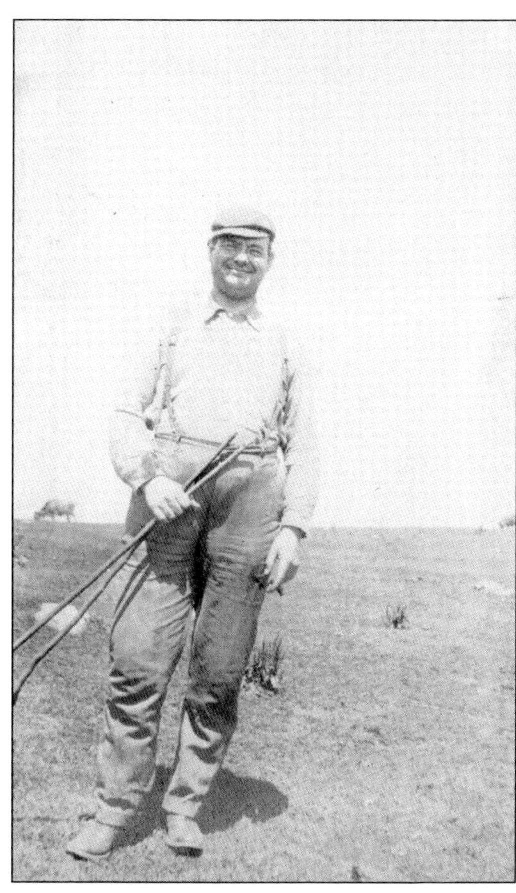

William Edwin (Ed) Ijams, H. P.'s elder brother, was born in 1869. After working in Knoxville as a commercial railroad agent, he became superintendent at the Little River Lumber Mill in Townsend. Ed married Col. W. B. Townsend's daughter Mabel in 1904. Their daughter Marnie, born in 1914, was an active Girl Scout with Mohican Troop 8, along with Elizabeth and Jo Ijams in Knoxville. (Franklin family, Ijams-Townsend family collection.)

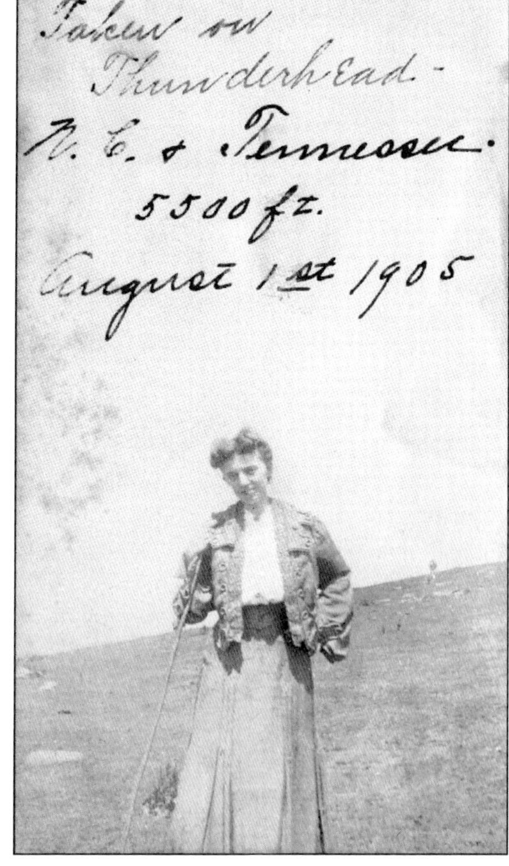

Mabel Townsend Ijams, born in Pennsylvania in 1882, moved to Tennessee with her father, Col. W. B. Townsend, in 1900. Along with her new sister-in-law, Alice Ijams, Mabel became deeply involved with the Knoxville Girl Scouts, first as a council member and later a commissioner. In 1929, Mabel hosted the Dixie Regional Conference at Whittle Springs Hotel, which was accompanied by a 1,000-word article written by Alice Ijams in the regional Girl Scout bulletin, the *Dixie Dynamo*. (Franklin family, Ijams-Townsend family collection.)

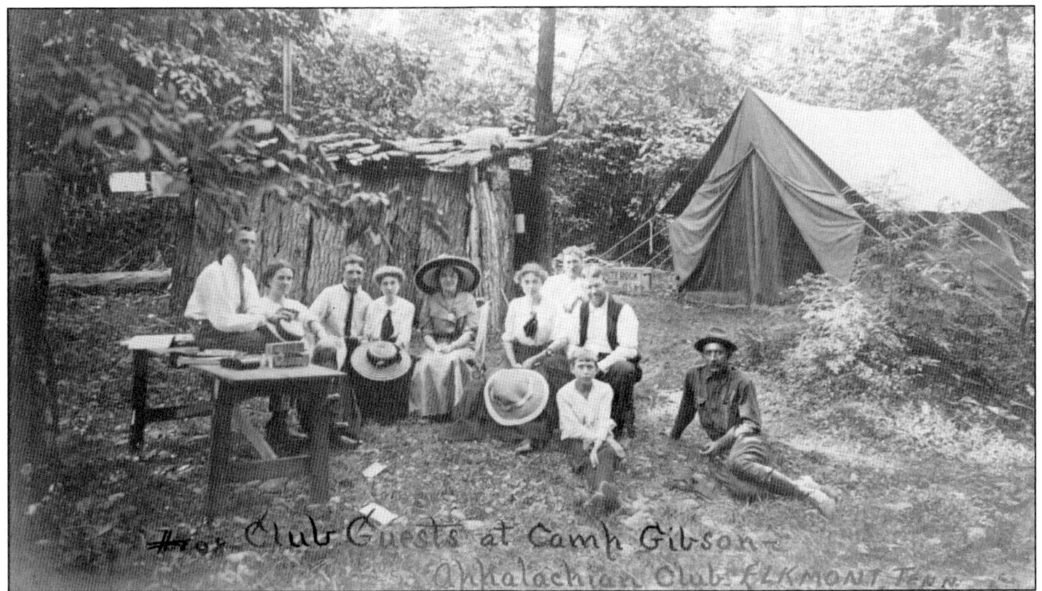

Before the Little River Lumber Company and Railroad excavated and laid tracks along the Little River through the Smokies, the enclave of Elkmont was a remote spot. This photograph featuring Ed and Mabel Ijams (seated second and third from right) was perhaps how H. P. and Alice Ijams found it on their honeymoon, shortly afterwards. (Franklin family, Ijams-Townsend family collection.)

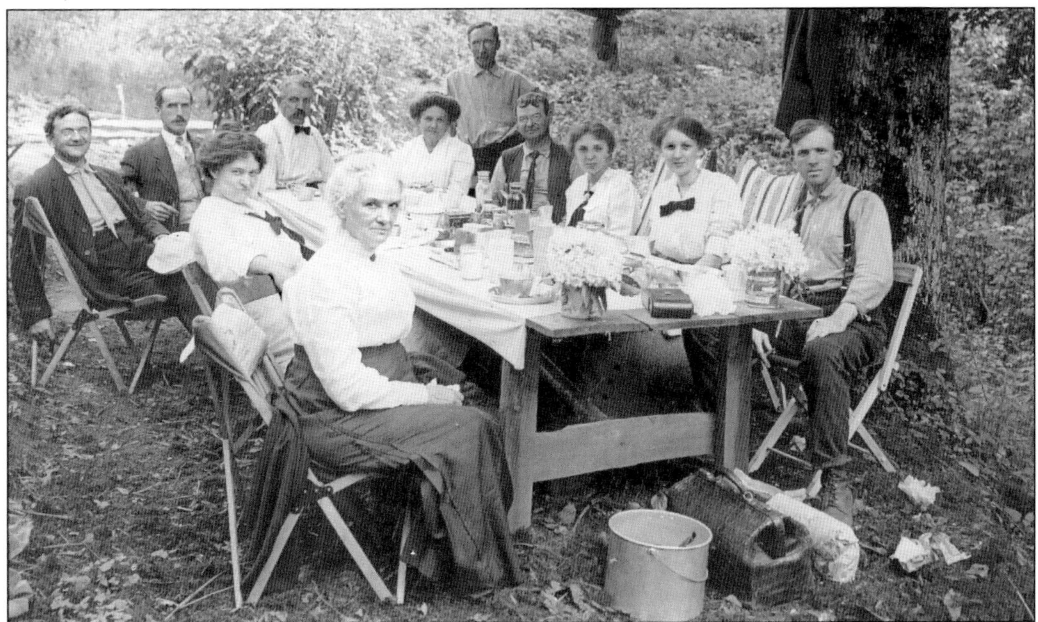

Seen here is a rare photograph of a Townsend family picnic with Col. W. B. Townsend at the head of the table. To the right of him are Margaret Townsend, Mabel Ijams, and Ed Ijams. In the foreground to the left of the table is Mary Aiken Ijams, the mother of Ed and H. P. Ijams. The Townsends also resided in Knoxville, and Colonel Townsend was active in community life, notably as a board member for the National Conservation Exposition in Knoxville in 1913. (Franklin family, Ijams-Townsend family collection.)

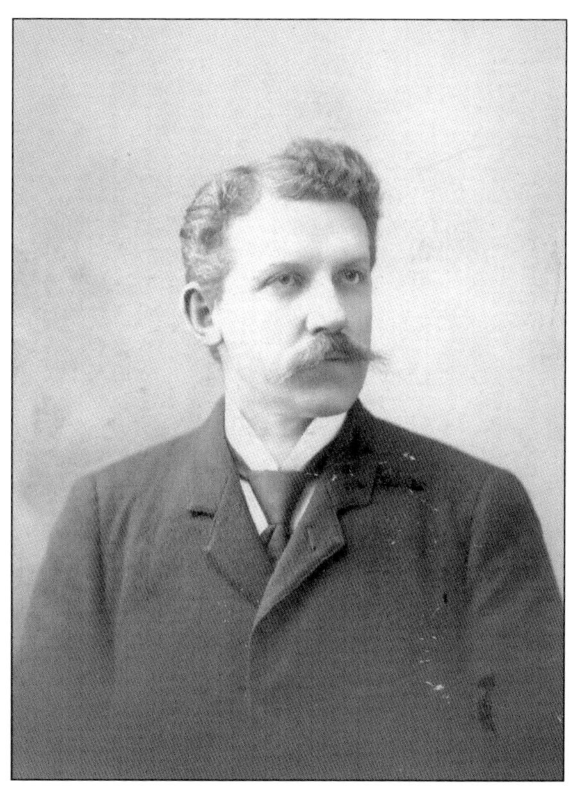

A successful Pennsylvania businessman in the lumber trade, Col. Wilson Bailey Townsend brought the Little River Lumber Company and Railroad to the Smokies in 1900. Extensive logging by his and other companies changed the shape of the land forever. Colonel Townsend later contributed to the creation of the Great Smoky Mountains National Park by selling 75,000 acres of his land at a greatly reduced price of only $3.59 per acre. (Franklin family, Ijams-Townsend family collection.)

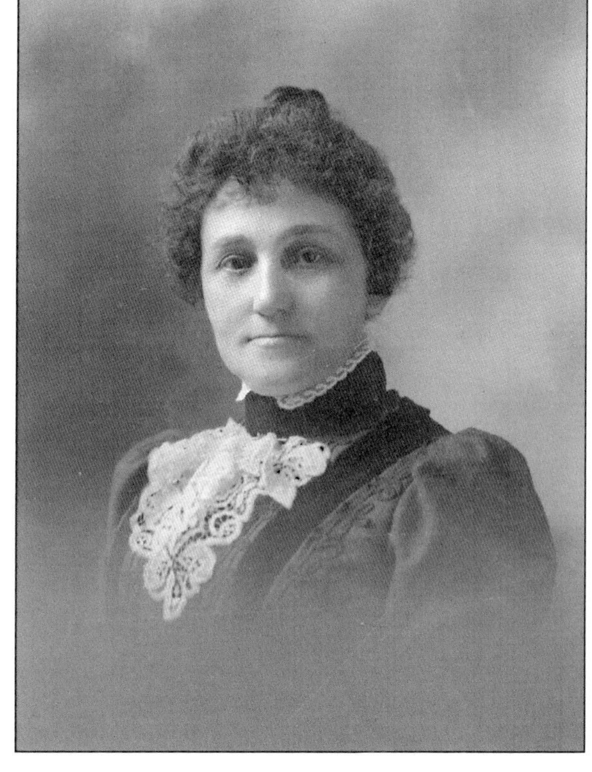

In 1903, Margaret Townsend introduced Christmas trees to the mountain community. A warm and generous woman, Margaret personally selected and purchased thoughtful Christmas gifts for hundreds of locals, especially children. Although thought to possess psychic abilities, Margaret stunned the family on New Year's Eve, 1923, when she announced during dinner that she must retire because "they are ready for me." Margaret Townsend died during the night, and her body was carried into Knoxville by a locomotive draped in black. She was buried in Old Gray Cemetery. (Franklin family, Ijams-Townsend family collection.)

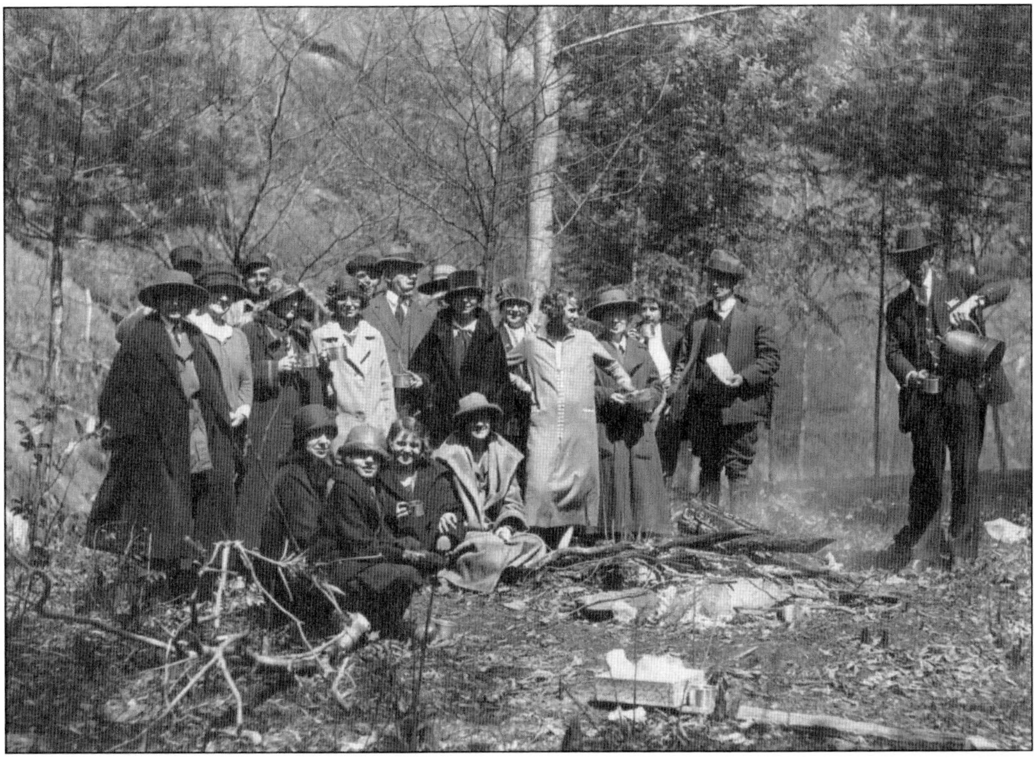

A group of well-dressed men and women are set to depart to look for a site for the new regional Girl Scout camp near Townsend some time in 1923. The group took a logging train up the east and west prongs of the Little River and found a lovely spot near Tremont in Walker Valley. Seated at left in the first row is Mabel Townsend, and next to her is her daughter, Marnie. On the second row, fifth from the left, is Col. W. B. Townsend. (Girl Scout Council of the Southern Appalachians.)

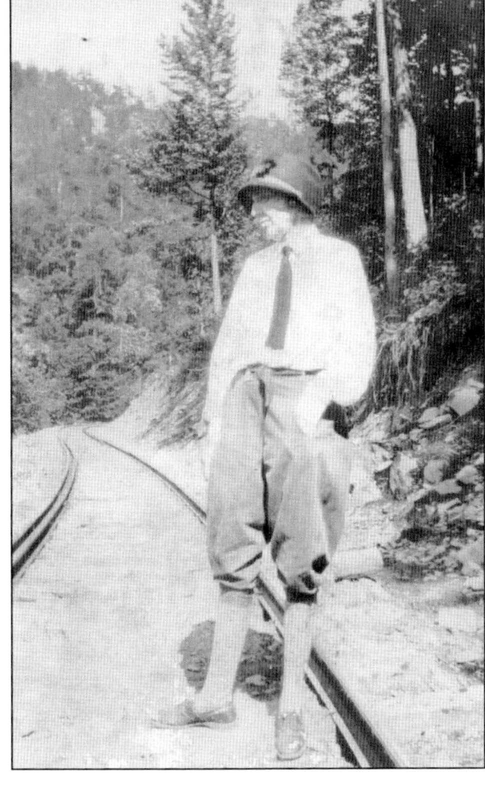

When the search party reached Walker Valley, Mabel Ijams described it as "little valley, sort of cleared out, with a little cabin on it, surrounded by yellow poplars." The cabin she had seen had belonged to "Black Bill" Walker, for whom Walker Valley is named. The site, which became Camp Margaret Townsend, opened in the summer of 1925 and operated until 1959. (Girl Scout Council of the Southern Appalachians.)

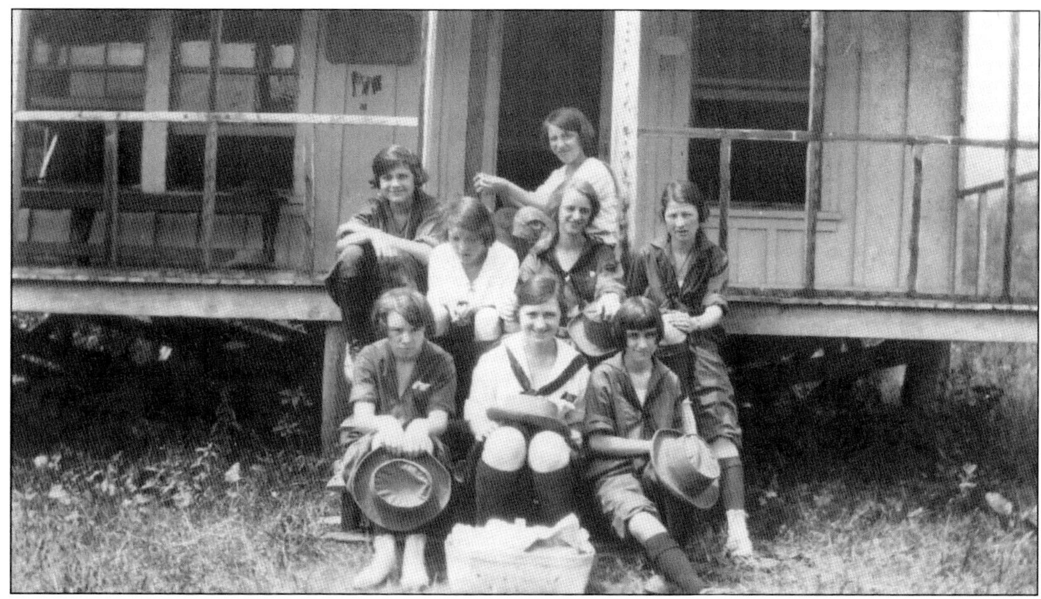

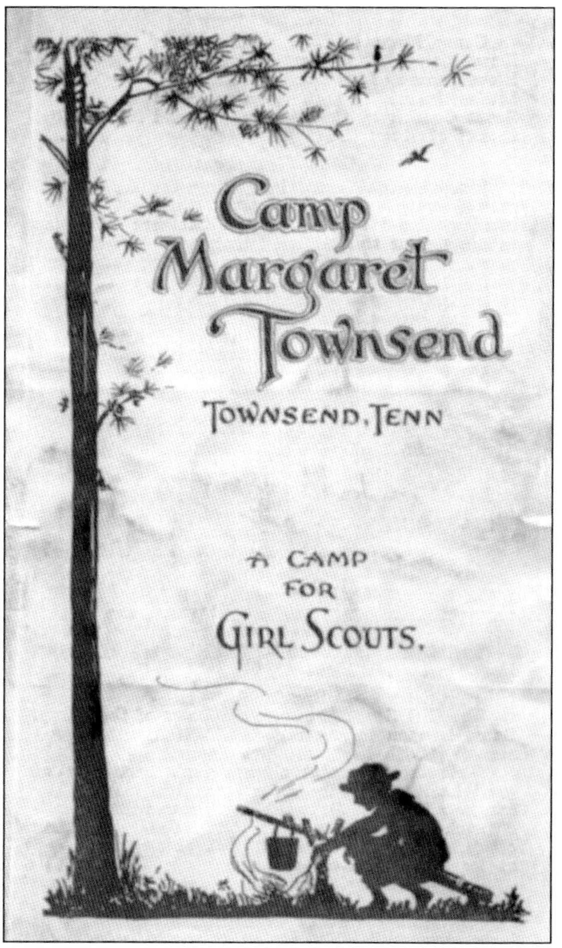

The first Girl Scout summer camp in East Tennessee was held at Calderwood in 1923 and was considered a marginal success, with cabins used instead of tents. Elizabeth Ijams, pictured at bottom right, was a member of the Opeeche Patrol Tribe, which won the overall camp prize for camp spirit, originality, and inspection. However, the inaugural camp raised expectations for a more suitable, permanent camp in the Smokies. (Girl Scout Council of the Southern Appalachians.)

Shown here is an early brochure for Camp Margaret Townsend, run by Knoxville Girl Scouts when it first opened in 1925. Among the staff conducting the camp were Alice Ijams and Mabel Ijams. That first year, no proper roads existed near the camp, and Girl Scouts from Knoxville and elsewhere arrived by logging train. Camp capacity accommodated 68 girls. (Girl Scout Council of the Southern Appalachians.)

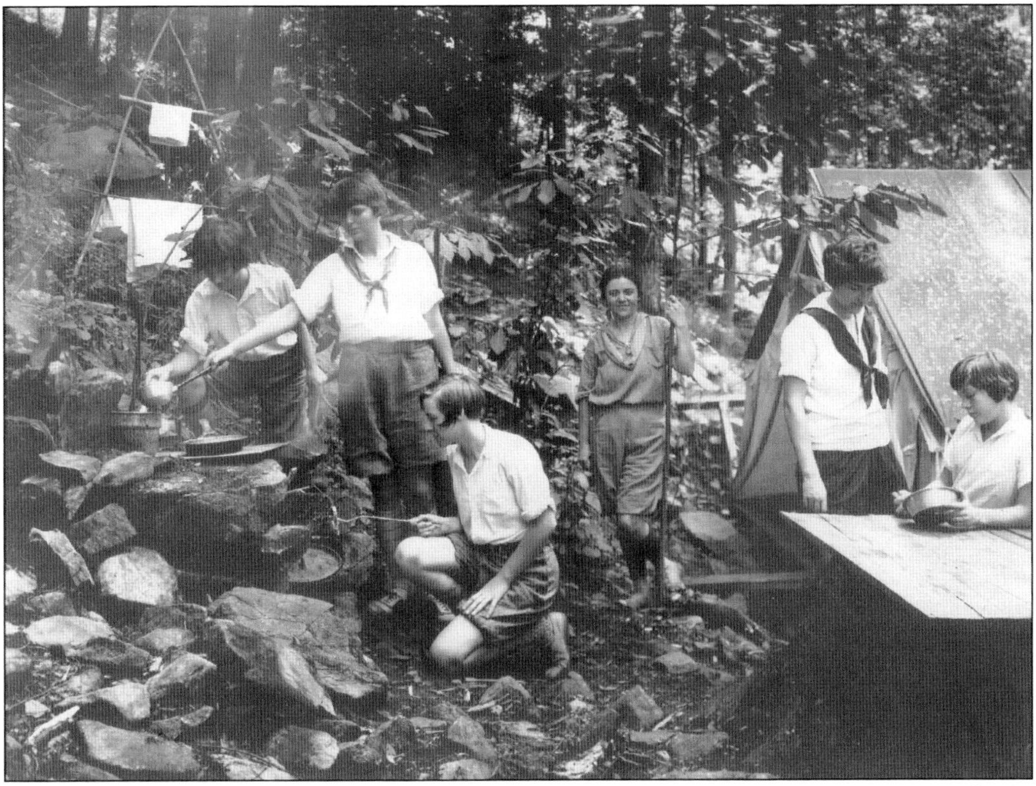

A group of Girl Scouts assumes cooking detail at Camp Margaret Townsend in 1927. On the far right is Jo Ijams, attending her third consecutive camp session. She would later serve as a camp swimming instructor. (Girl Scout Council of the Southern Appalachians.)

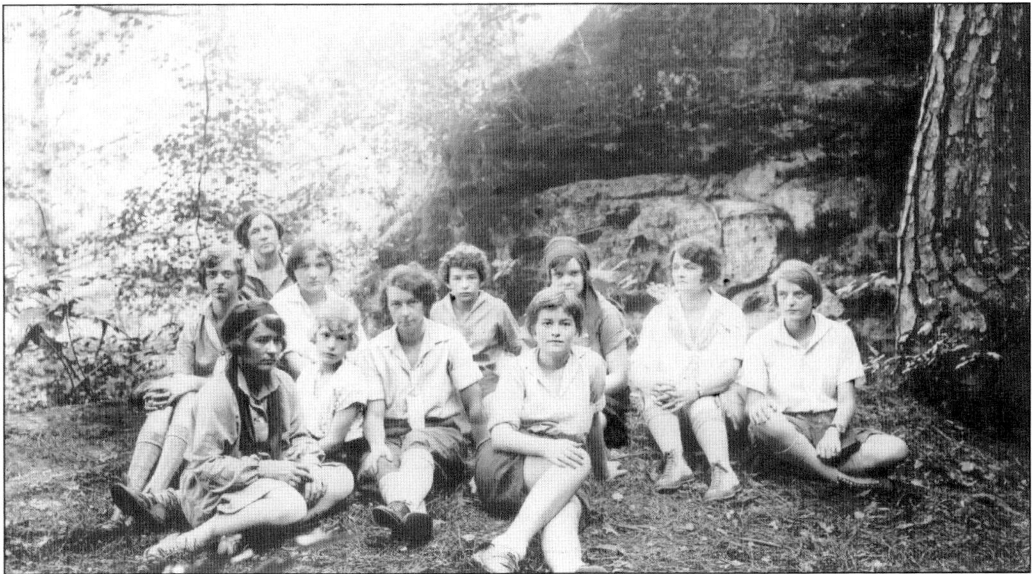

A group of Girl Scouts poses for the camera at Camp Margaret Townsend in the late 1920s. Martha Ijams is pictured second from left in the first row, while Mary Ijams is third from the left in the second row. Alice Ijams is seated in the rear.

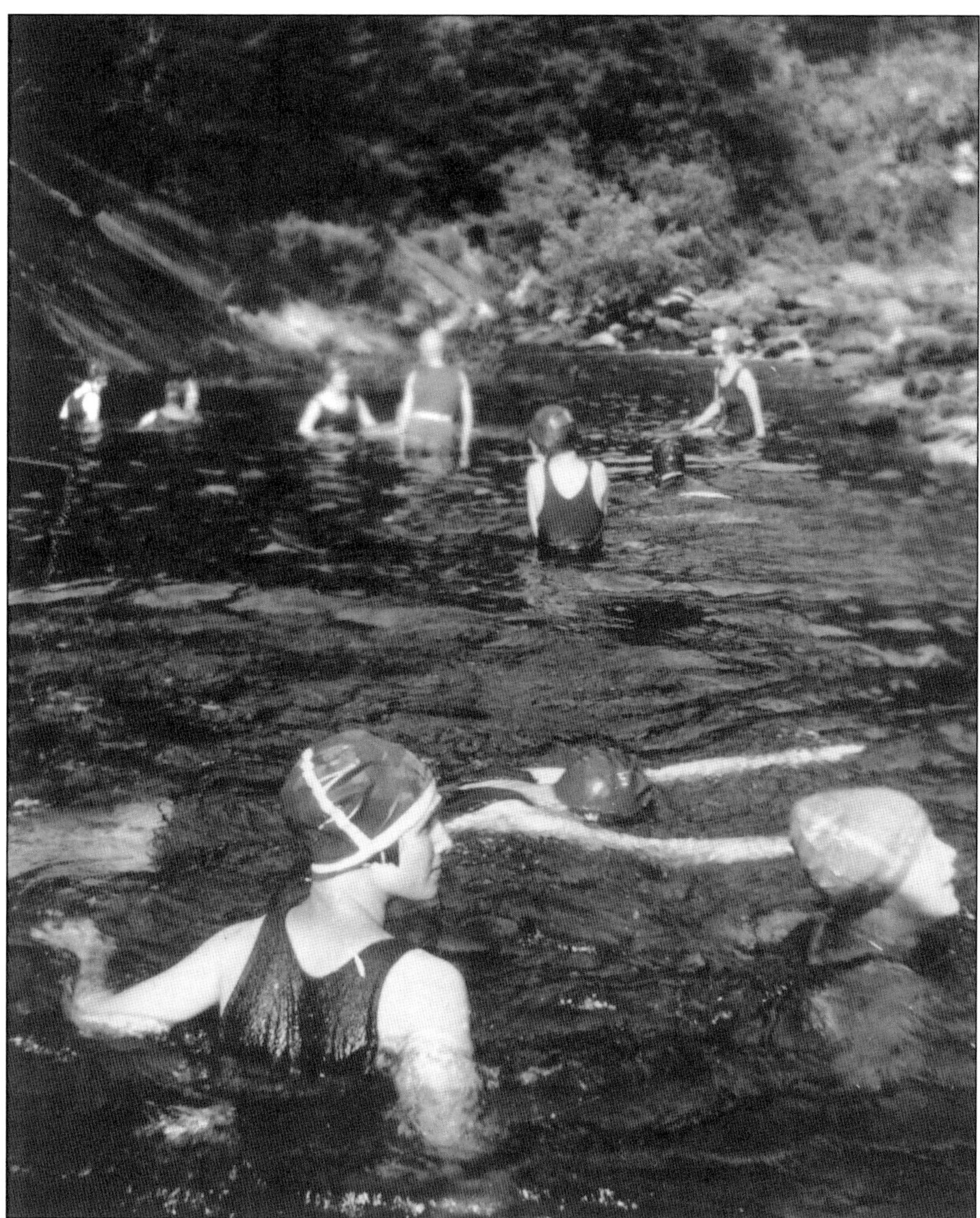

Girl Scout campers were awakened each day with the sound of a bugle, followed by a brisk dip into the swimming hole before breakfast. In the foreground, Elizabeth Ijams, camp director at Camp Margaret Townsend in 1932 and 1933, keeps a watchful eye on the swimmers at the camp's swimming hole. Each year, the annual water pageant and swimming competitions were key highlights of the summer. In *Memories of a Lifetime: A History of Tanasi Girl Scout Council* by Jerry Warwick, Mabel Hood Houk King shared her thoughts on her camp experiences around the time Elizabeth Ijams was in charge. She wrote, "Girl Scouting taught us to live in harmony with nature, to survive in nature with only a minimum of civilization's accoutrements, and to respect and protect Earth like the mother that she is." (Girl Scout Council of the Southern Appalachians.)

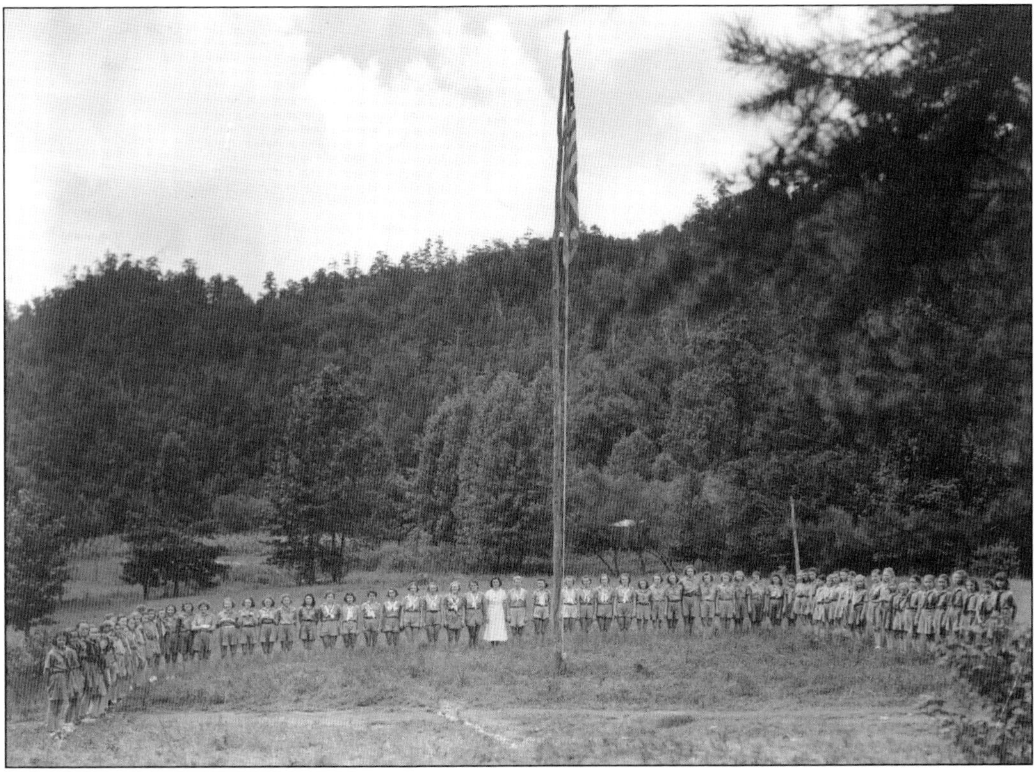

Girl Scouts stand at attention around the flag at Camp Margaret Townsend during the early 1930s. Daily activities included swimming, horseback riding, nature handicrafts, games, hikes, and evenings around the campfire. (Girl Scout Council of the Southern Appalachians.)

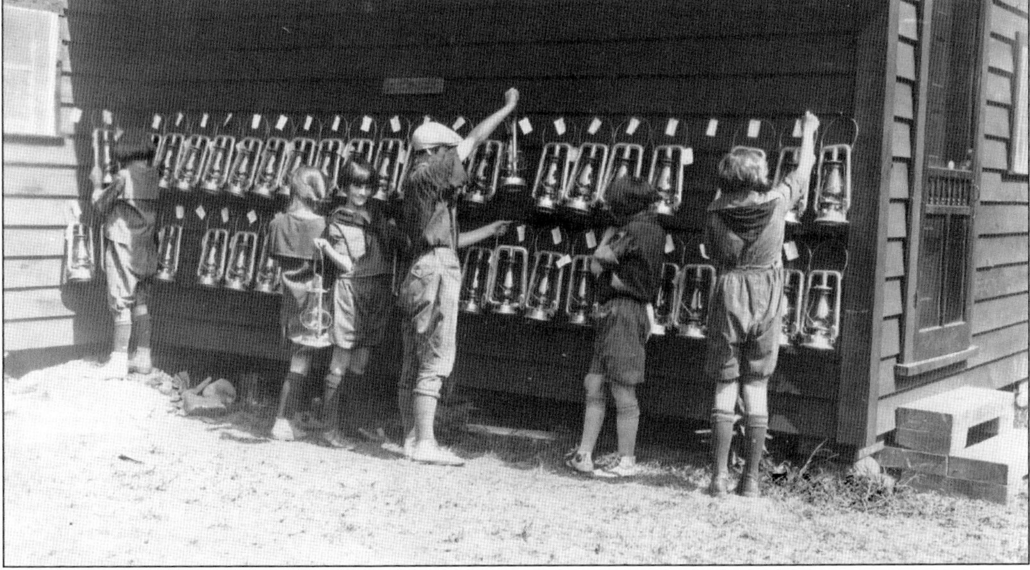

Young campers prepare for lantern duty at Camp Margaret Townsend during the late 1920s. During those days there was no electricity, with the campfire and oil lanterns being the only illuminations after dark. (Girl Scout Council of the Southern Appalachians.)

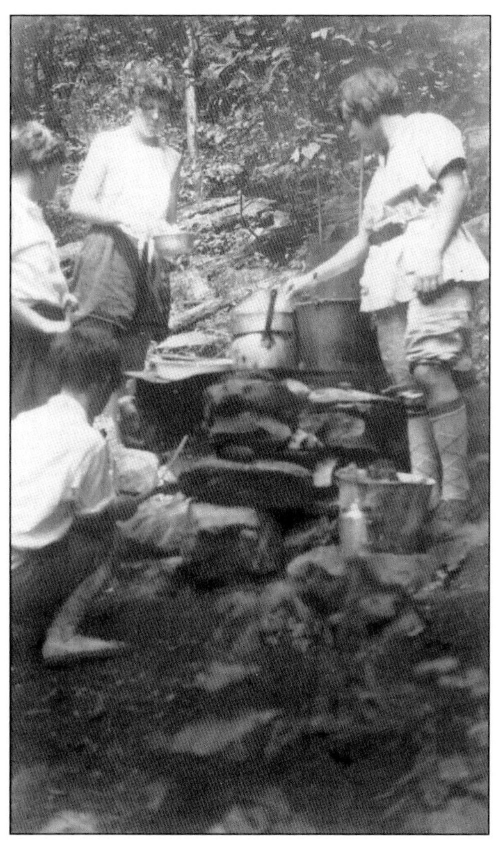

At 8:00 a.m. every day, campers performed daily chores known as "Kapers," which included chopping wood, stuffing mattresses, washing dishes, doing laundry, and carrying water from the local spring. For second-class Girl Scouts over the age of 14, Pioneer Camp was situated more than a mile away from the main camp, and activities there led to the Pioneer merit badge. Here Jo Ijams, far right, performs kitchen duties for her own merit badge. (Girl Scout Council of the Southern Appalachians.)

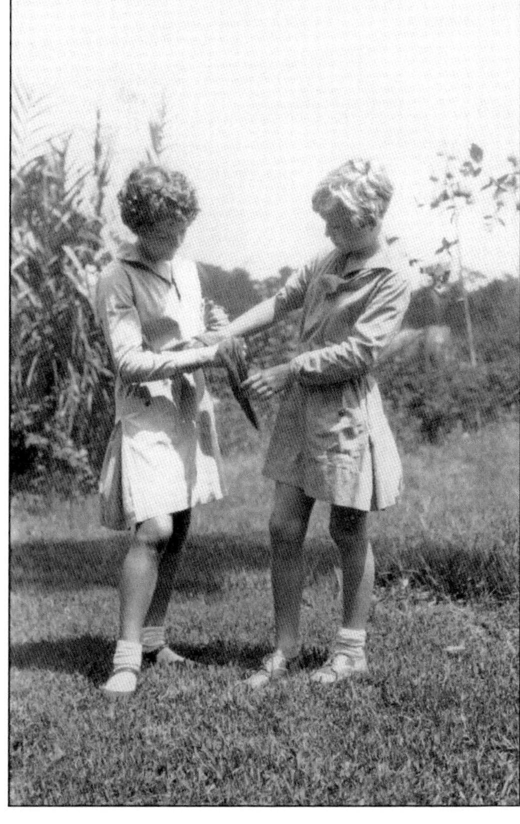

Mary (left) and Martha Ijams practice first aid on each other at a Girl Scout meet at the Ijams place during the summer of 1929. After Mary's death, Margaret Kent, field secretary for Knoxville Girl Scouts, paid the following tribute to the young Scout: "No one knew quite as much about birds, flowers, and trees as Mary. She was a perfect camper, a good woodsman, an expert swimmer, and a very, very unusual girl."

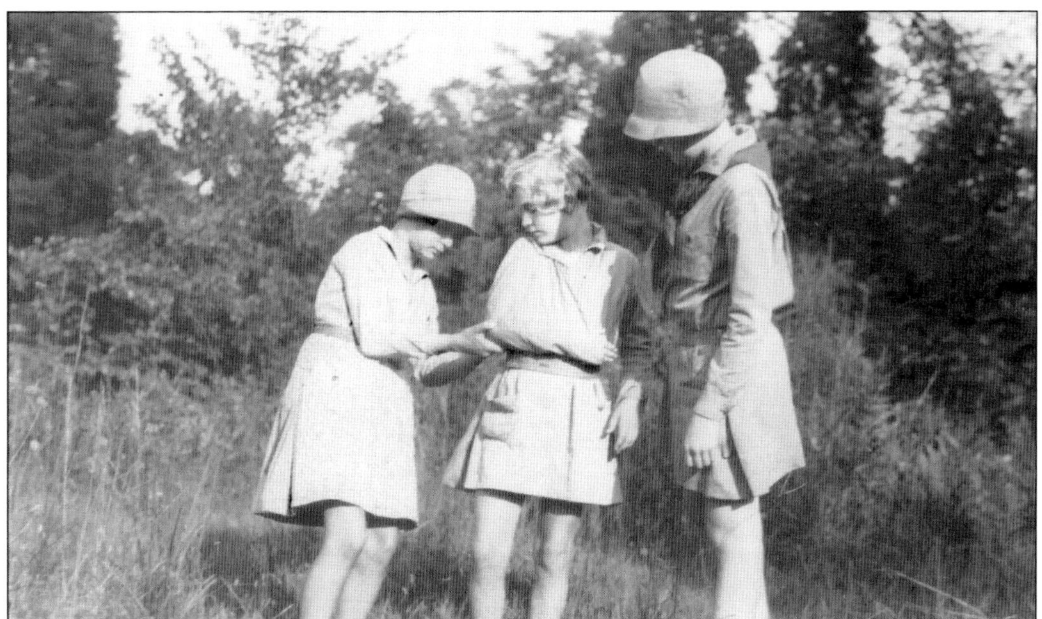

Girl Scouts Mary (left) and Martha Ijams prepare a sling, assisted by Edna Bentley (right) during the summer of 1929. Edna, who lived nearby on Peachtree Street off Island Home Pike, was a frequent visitor to the Ijamses' place, as well as a close friend and fellow student of Mary's at South Knoxville Elementary School.

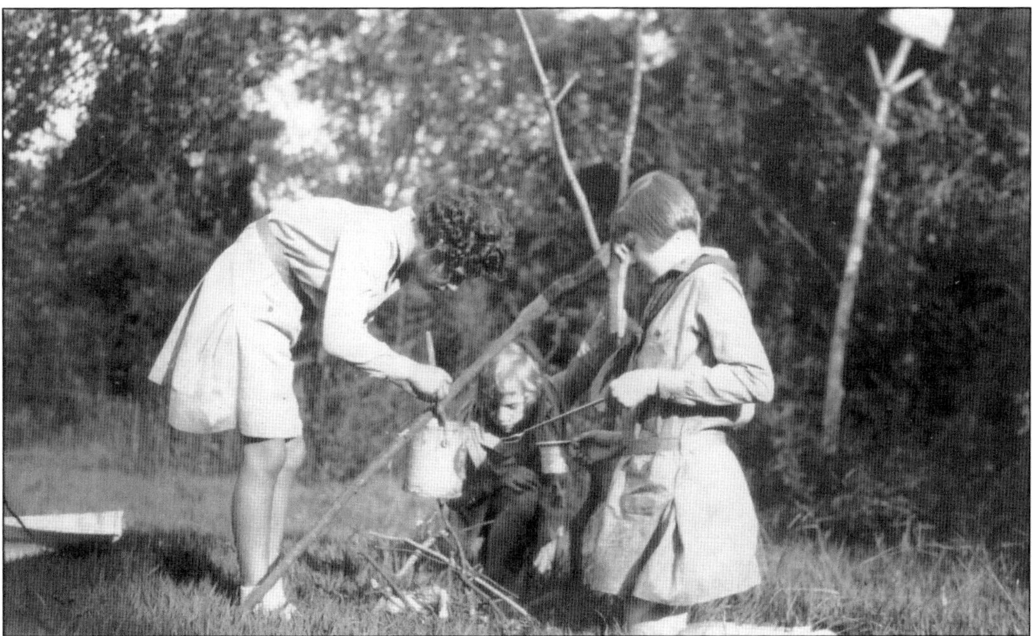

Mary (left) and Martha Ijams prepare a meal over an open fire with Edna Bentley (right) at a Girl Scout meet at the Ijams farm in 1929. Edna enjoyed many years with the Girl Scouts, including a career as buyer of supplies at Camp Margaret Townsend and later as director of Camp Mary Ijams in the late 1950s and early 1960s. Edna's father, Gordon M. Bentley, was a professor of entomology at the University of Tennessee during the early 20th century.

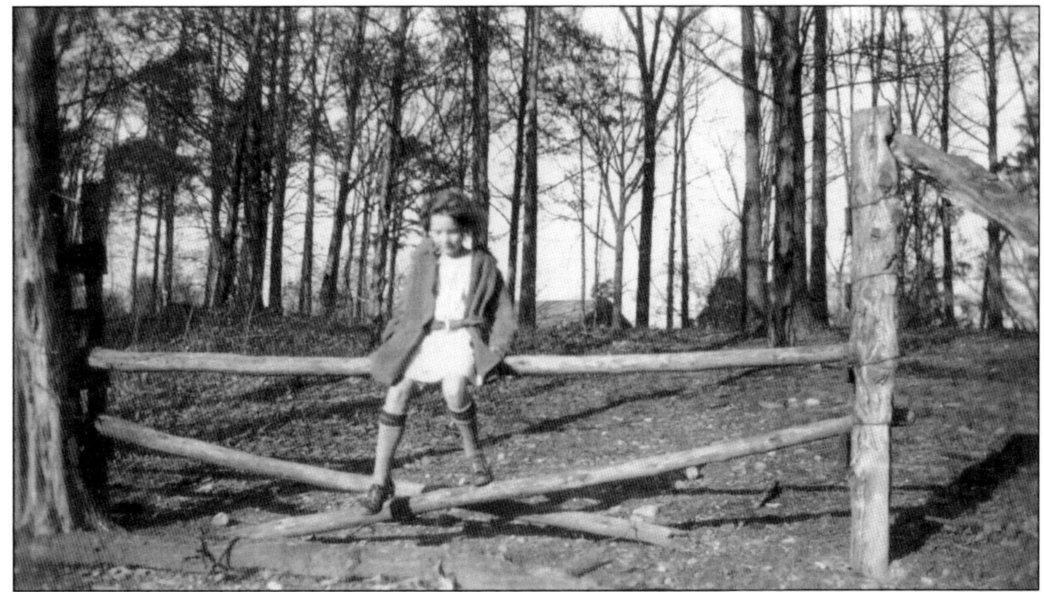

Mary Ijams rests on a fence with a trail behind her leading to Magnolia Woodward Lodge. A competition was held to name the new camp, and the winning entry, Camp Mary Ijams, was submitted by Ethelynn Allen of Troop 16 at Park Junior High School. From 1939, the site would serve as a camp location for Knoxville Girl Scouts in her memory.

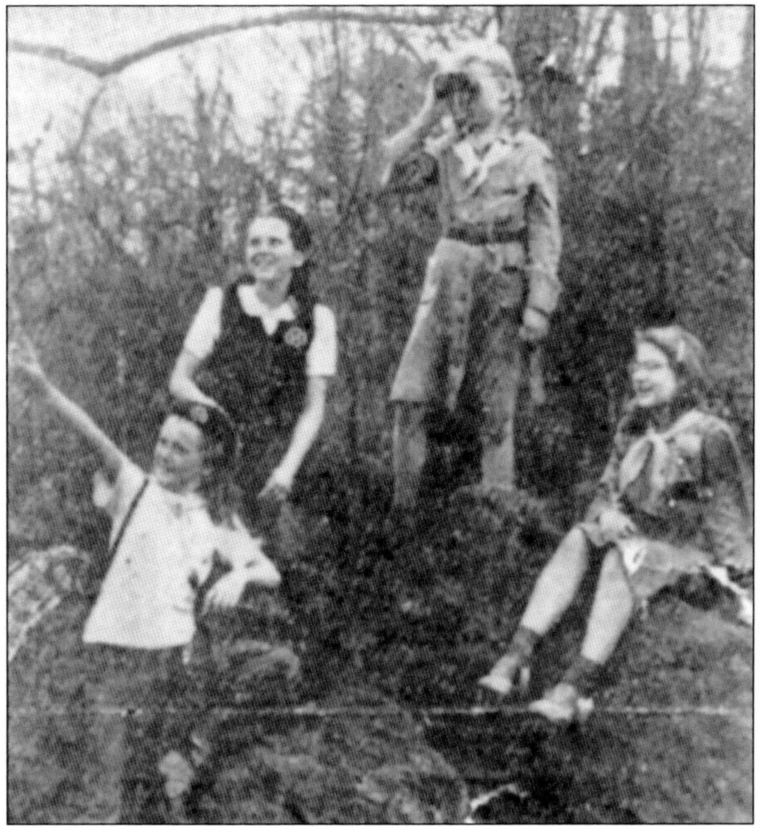

Four members of Troop 41, Graystone Presbyterian Church, look for birds at Camp Mary Ijams during the spring of 1948. To gain an ornithologist badge, Girl Scouts walked the Ijams Bird Sanctuary with H. P. Ijams, who even in old age became animated in helping them identify numerous species. From left to right are Emily Sue Trotter, Ija Jo Davis, Lynn Mitchell, and Floice Smith. (*Knoxville News Sentinel.*)

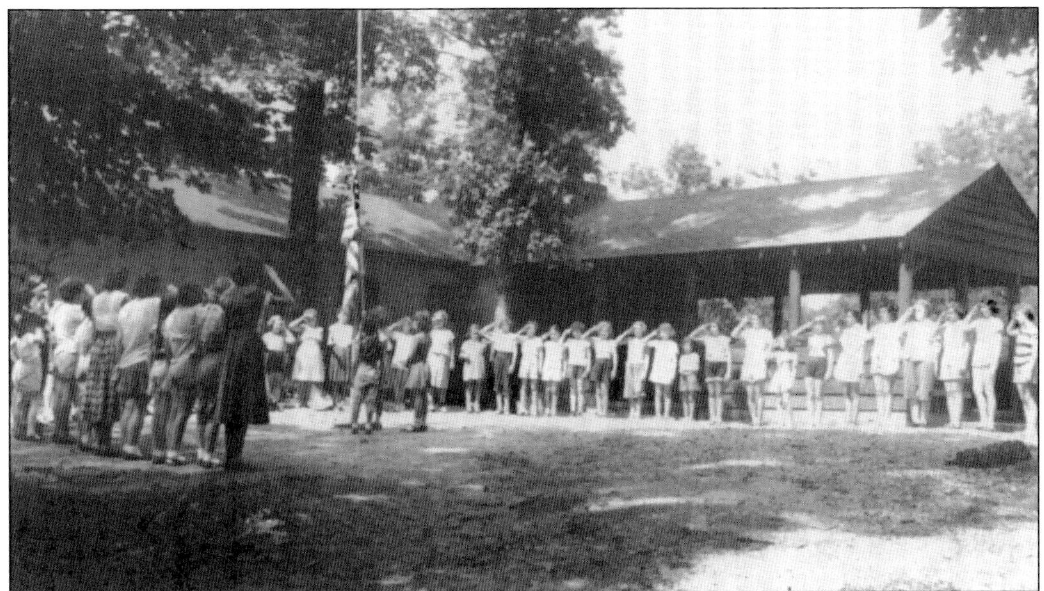
After Magnolia Woodward Lodge burned in the mid-1940s, a new structure was built. Camp Mary Ijams continued as both a day camp and summer camp until the late 1970s. In this photograph from the 1950s, Girl Scouts stand at attention around the flagpole. The year 1951 was particularly busy, with 218 campers attending under the directorship of Mrs. Darwin Stout. (Girl Scout Council of the Southern Appalachians.)

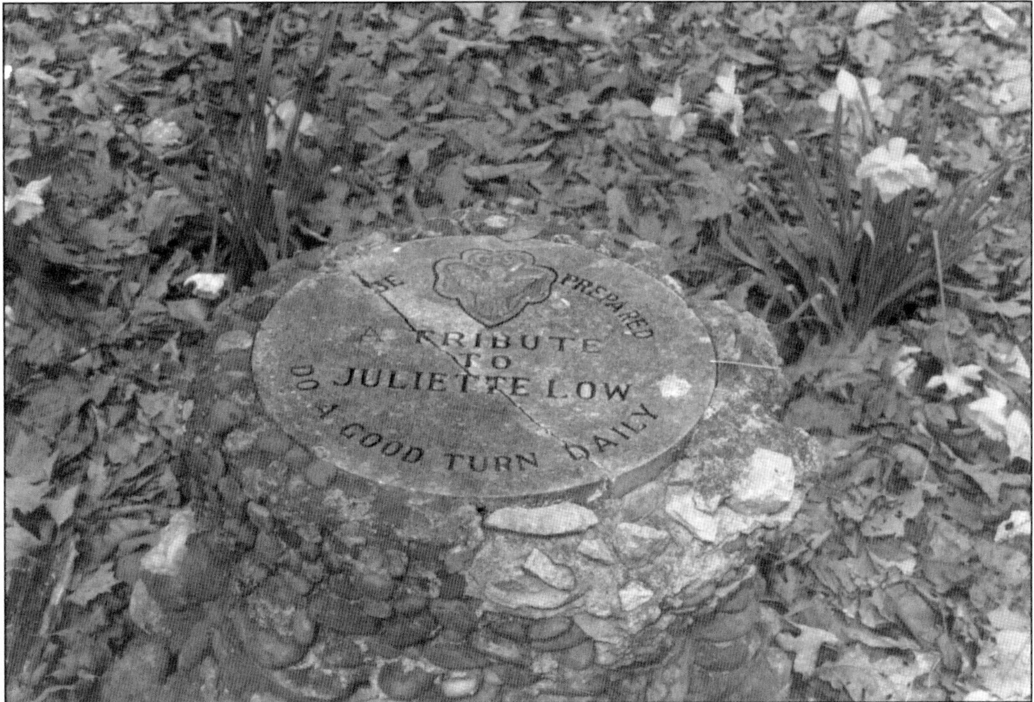

Pictured here is a memorial stone at Camp Mary Ijams in remembrance of Juliette Low, founder of the Girl Scout movement in the United States. (Girl Scout Council of the Southern Appalachians.)

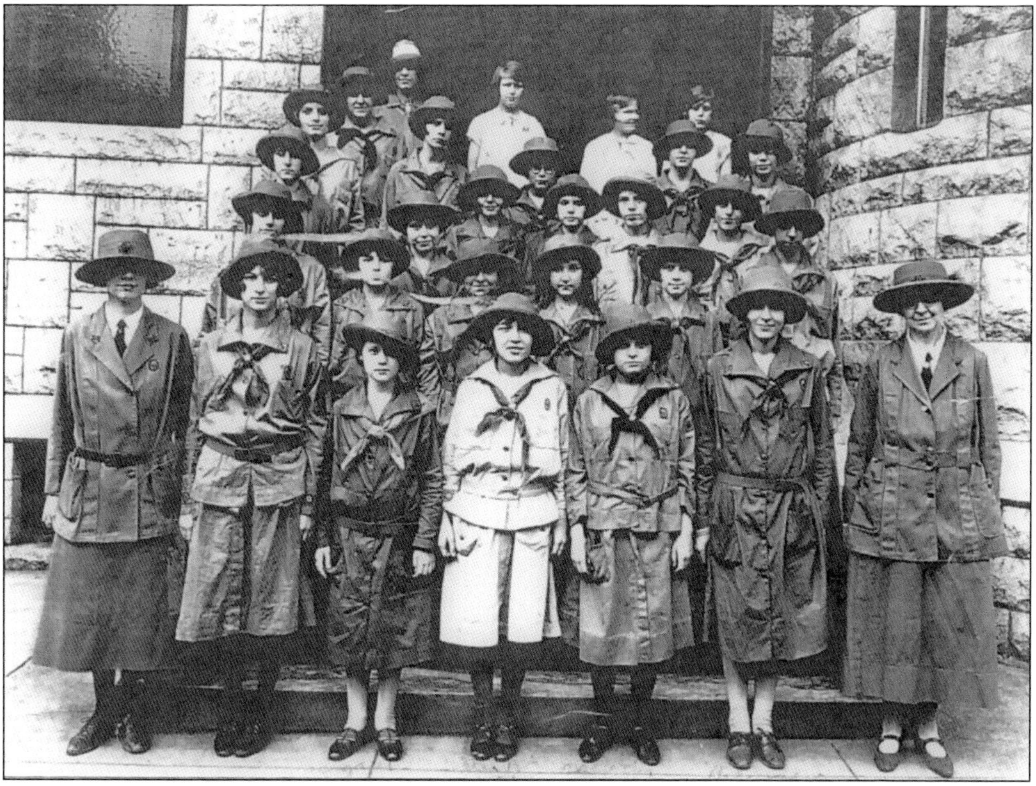

Girl Scouts from Mohican Troop 8 pose on the steps of St. John's Episcopal Church in the mid-1920s. Bea McClennaghan was troop leader on front row, far right. In the third row are Elizabeth Ijams (left), Marnie Ijams (second from left), and Jo Ijams (third from left). (Sherrie Carris.)

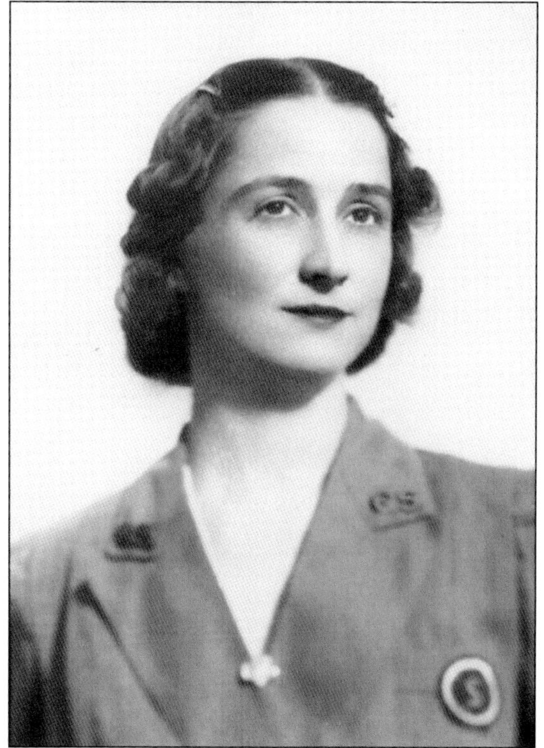

In 1933, Elizabeth Ijams moved to middle Tennessee, where she became director of Nashville Girl Scouts. Elizabeth also worked with the Girl Scouts in Winston-Salem, the national office in New York City, and finally in Trentwood, New Jersey, before she retired. Elizabeth passed away in 1988.

Six

The Bird Sanctuary

Birds have played a crucial role throughout the history of Ijams Nature Center. H. P. Ijams's fascination with his feathered friends and the knowledge and passion he extended to fellow birders truly earned him a reputation as the father of Knoxville ornithology. In addition, the native plants and intelligent landscaping introduced at the Ijams Bird Sanctuary have subsequently sustained many resident and migratory bird populations.

H. P. Ijams and fellow ornithologists were originally active with the East Tennessee Audubon Society at a time predating the formation of the Tennessee Ornithological Society by a group of Nashville birders in 1915. The National Conservation Exposition held in Knoxville in 1913 was a defining moment for many birders, especially those who appreciated the opportunity to increase the public knowledge and appreciation of birds. However, the local Audubon Society was firmly divided on the benefits of the exposition, and many members voted not to invest a single moment or a single dime on the event. The "progressive" members such as H. P. were forced to expend their own time and resources to participate, and the results were memorable: an impressive educational booth named the Bird Court held at the Land Building at Chilhowee Park far outstripped members' hopes and significantly raised genuine awareness about the value of birds.

During the early 1920s, members of East Tennessee Ornithological Society were far more united in their efforts, which led to the creation of a significant bird reserve to rival any in the state. Magnolia Woodward reported in 1922 that a 1,000-acre bird reserve in South Knoxville was being established. The heart of the reserve was the Ijams farm, and many members throughout the Island Home area had obtained permits to post their own grounds for the protection of birds and other wildlife. It was an unprecedented achievement and one that centered on H. P. Ijams's generosity in providing the location for a members lodge on his property. Further foreshadowing the educational mission of the future nature center, students from local schools and the University of Tennessee were also invited to the reserve to conduct bird studies. And so an enduring legacy of ornithology in East Tennessee was born.

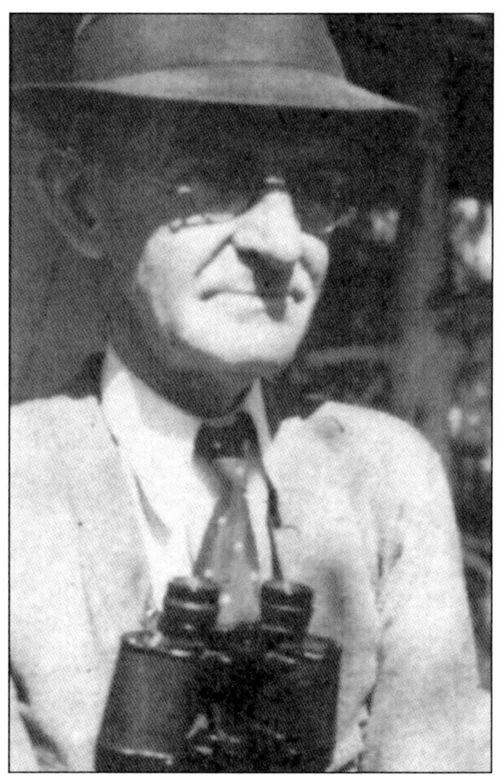

H. P. Ijams spearheaded the ornithologist movement throughout Knoxville and East Tennessee. The consummate bird expert, specializing in conservation and migration, H. P. was genuinely regarded as Knoxville's first ornithologist. In May 1949, the Knoxville bird club held "Harry Ijams Day" in his honor, resulting in a record-breaking total of 123 bird species observed within the Knoxville area. (The *Migrant*, Tennessee Ornithological Society.)

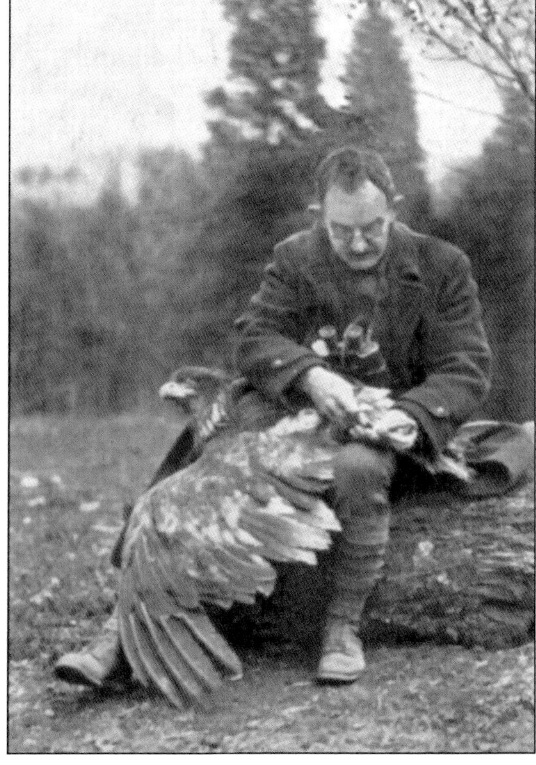

Birders across the region frequently brought injured or distressed birds to H. P. Ijams. Here, H. P. bands a juvenile bald eagle in 1925. Details of the bird are unknown, but the species would have been a rare sighting in Knoxville, despite the Ijams farm being located on the banks of the Tennessee River. (Russell Harrison, Great Smoky Mountains Conservation Association.)

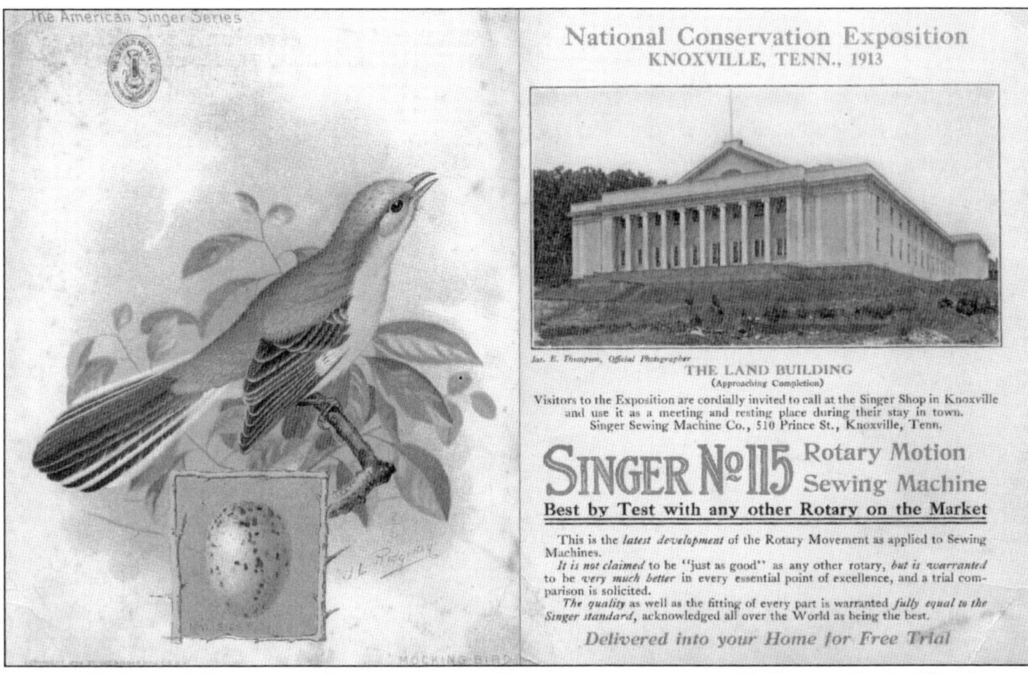

Knoxville hosted the National Conservation Exposition in 1913 at Chilhowee Park. The Singer Sewing Machine Company promoted bird conservation and the exposition on one of a series of bird cards. The card featured the mockingbird—Tennessee's state bird—on the front, and on the reverse was the Land Building, which housed a significant presence by the East Tennessee Audubon Society. H. P. Ijams was a known supporter of the expo and was likely involved in staging birding activities. (Stephen Lyn Bales.)

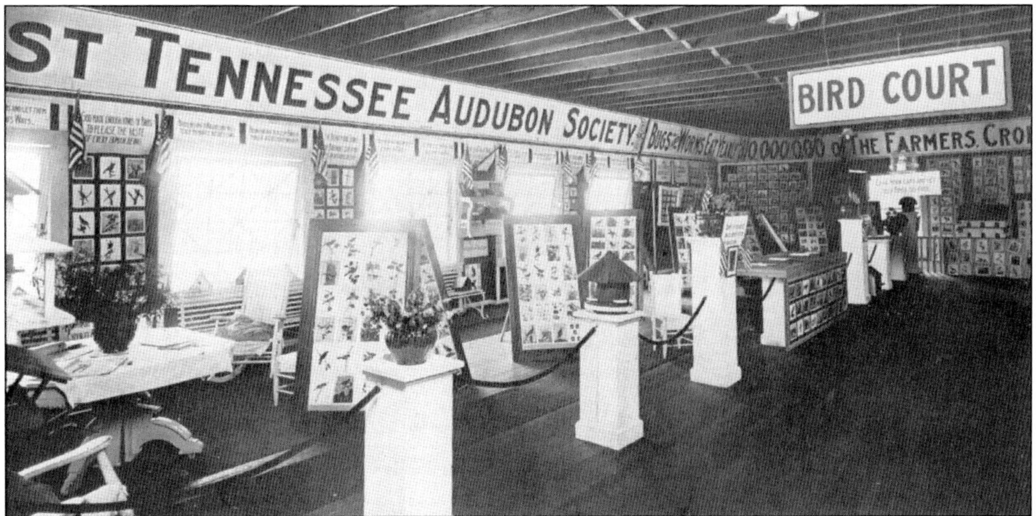

Members of the East Tennessee Audubon Society saw an opportunity to spread its mission of bird protection and education at the National Conservation Exposition. The resulting Bird Court boasted more than 1,000 bird illustrations, pamphlets, and books. The banner on the wall reads, "Bugs and worms eat yearly $80,000 of the farmers' crops." A smaller hanging sign addresses the ornithologist's arch nemesis, the household cat: "Cage your cats and let your birds go free." (Knox County Two Centuries Photograph Project, McClung Historical Collection.)

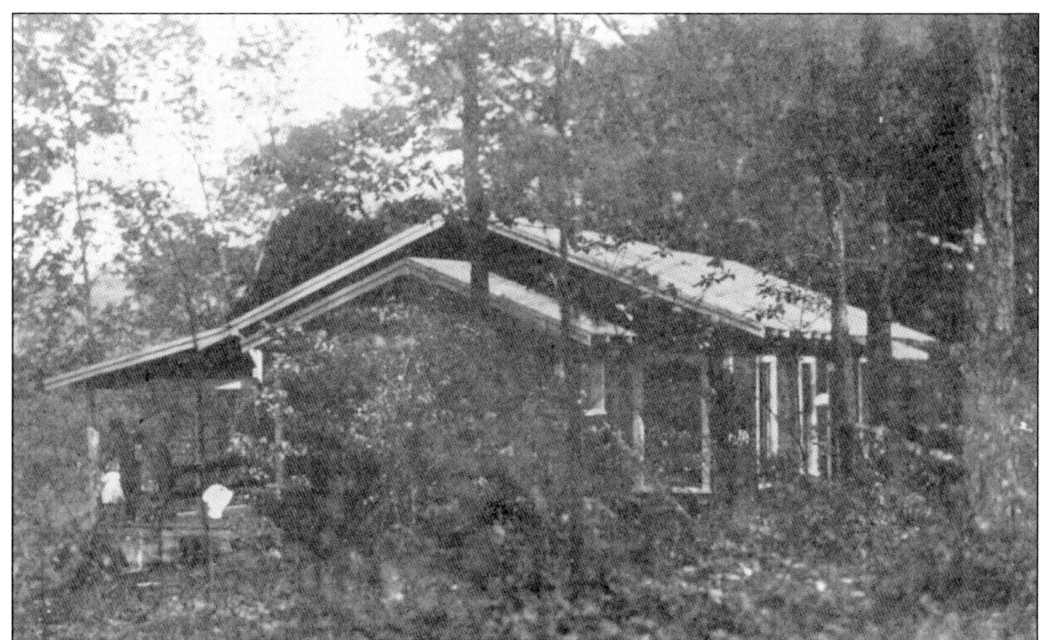

As an active member of the East Tennessee Audubon Society, H. P. Ijams presented a proposal that the society couldn't refuse: to build a members clubhouse on the Ijams farm for meetings and educational purposes if its members posted their own land as protected bird habitat. The members rallied, and more than 1,000 acres were protected. The clubhouse, named in honor of Magnolia Woodward, who conducted the first bird count in the state of Tennessee in 1902 and who helped establish Audubon activities in Knoxville, was duly built in 1922.

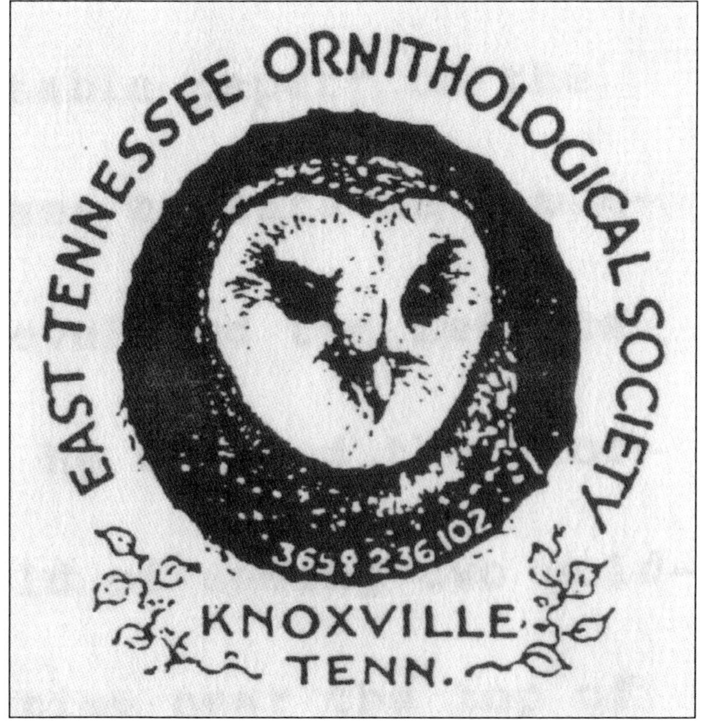

By the early 1920s, H. P. Ijams and fellow birders Brockway Crouch, Paul Adams, and Arthur Ogden, among others, formed a breakaway group from the Audubon Society to focus more on bird study. The group began annual spring bird counts, which continued when they formed the East Tennessee Ornithological Society in January 1924. Among the list of charter members was a junior member, Elizabeth Ijams. The club's logo, likely designed by H. P. Ijams, incorporated a barn owl banded on Dickinson Island during the summer of 1923.

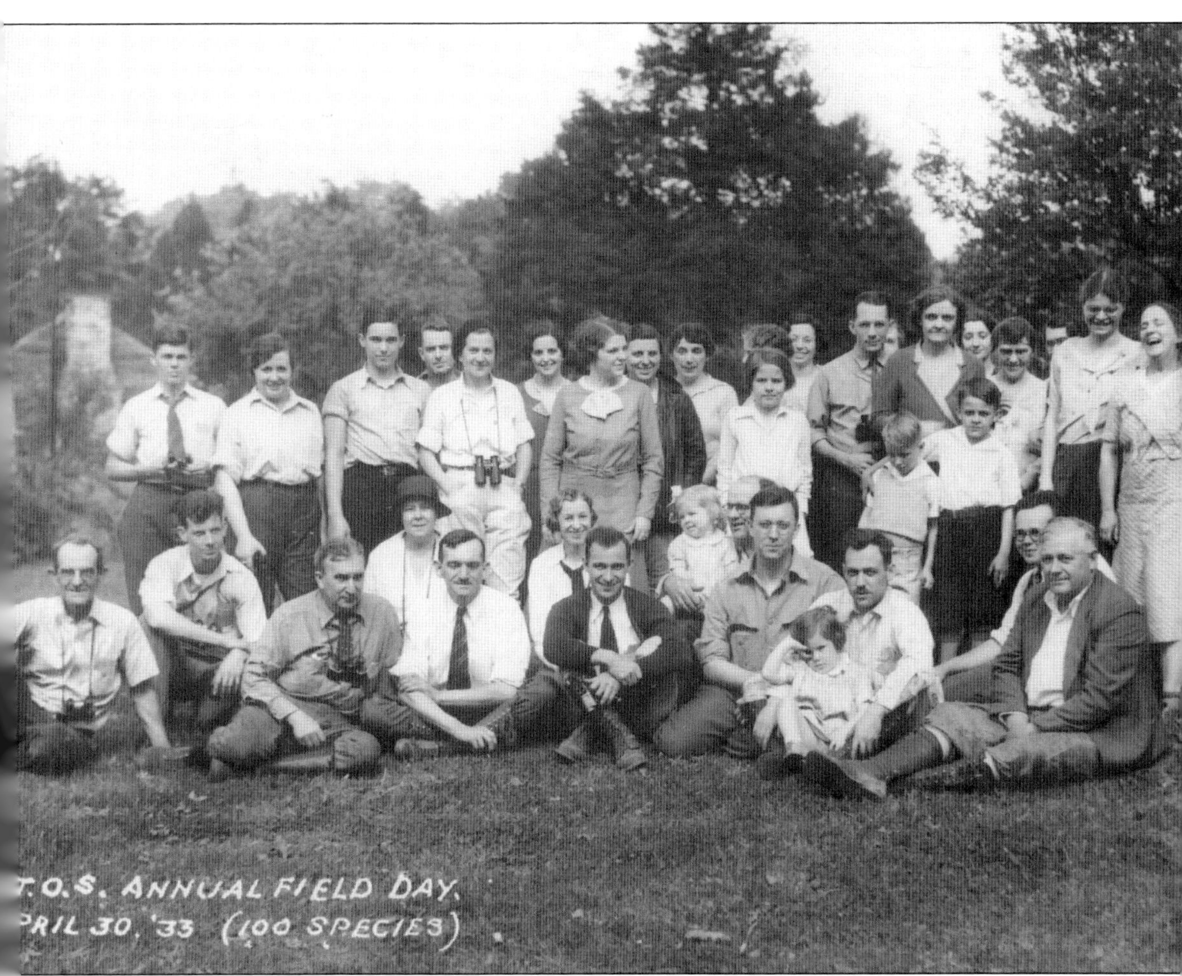

Alice Ijams, standing at far right, obviously enjoyed the company of fellow birders in this group shot of the East Tennessee Ornithological Society in 1933 where it held its annual bird census every May. From left to right are (first row) H. P. Ijams, Paul Adams, Samuel Ogden, Mary Beard, Albert Ganier, two unidentified, Jane Crouch, Brockway Crouch, William Johnson, unidentified, ? Ressler, unidentified, and Dr. Edwin Powers; (second row) unidentified, Barbara O'Brien, two unidentified men, Minnie Leonard, unidentified, Elise Crouch, Edith Lynn, Mrs. William Johnson, Edwine Powers, three unidentified people, Pauline Powers, four unidentified people, Mary Ruth Chiles, and Alice Ijams.

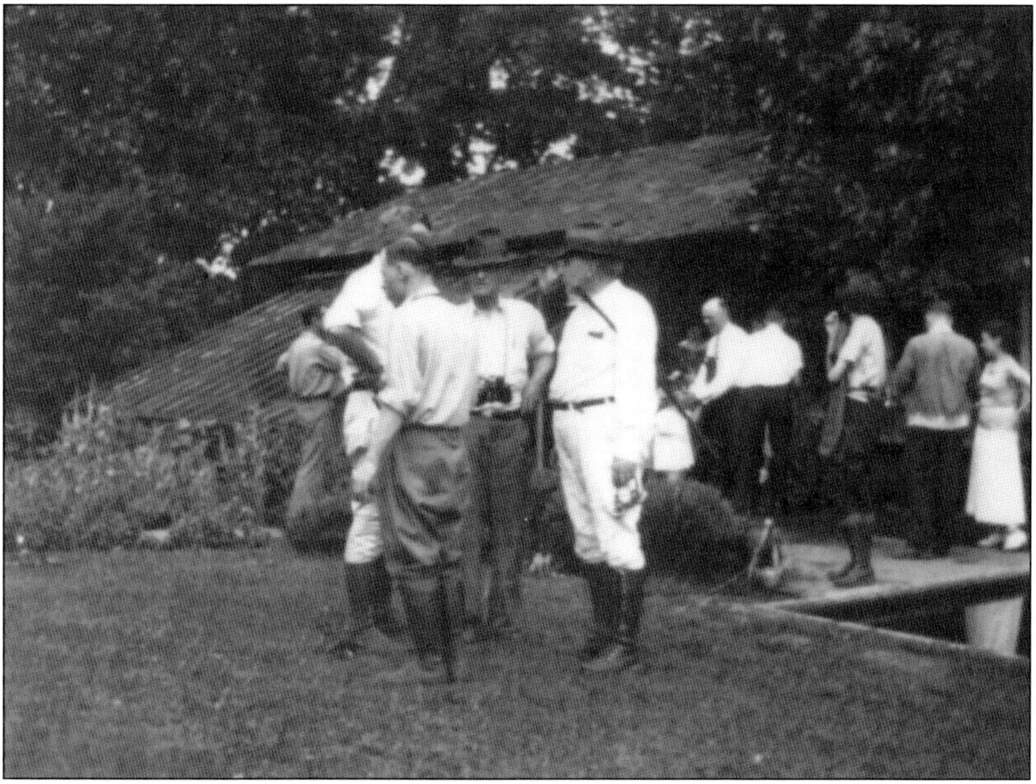

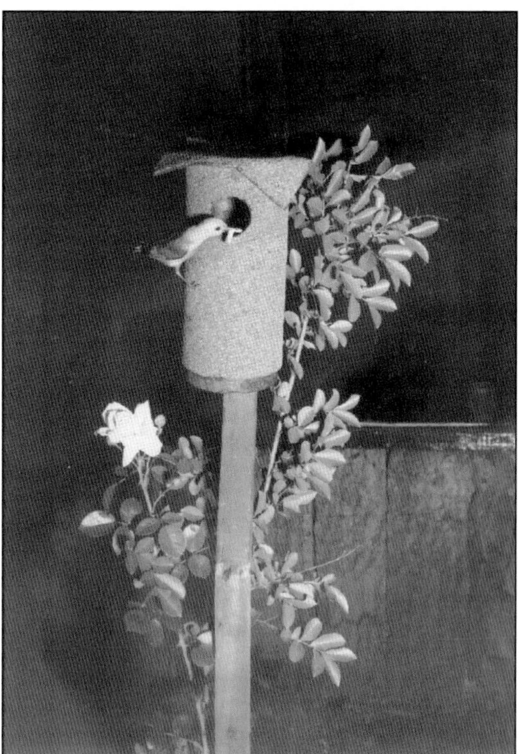

H. P. Ijams (center with binoculars) and fellow birders prepare to head out on the annual bird census in May 1935. Brockway Crouch is the only member identifiable in front of the house. H. P. was the President of the Tennessee Ornithological Society in 1932 and served as regional editor of the quarterly journal the *Migrant* for many years. (Knox County Two Centuries Photograph Project, McClung Historical Collection.)

One of H. P. Ijams's birding successes was attracting prothonotary warblers to nest frequently in a bird box by his screen porch overlooking a small lily pond behind the house. In 1952, Alice Ijams wrote, "We keep two feeding stations in operation the year 'round. Of course, the birds do not require feeding in the summer, but we like to have them around and do everything we know to attract them; and it is well for them to become accustomed to an all-season feeding station so that in time of sleet or snow they know where to find shelter and sustenance."

For many years H. P. Ijams kept scrupulous records of bird species, nesting periods, and eggs laid and hatched on his property. His own patented nesting boxes were numbered and spaced all over the grounds and tabulated on a map hung in his study. H. P. was also an inventor. In the October 1927 edition of *Popular Mechanics*, an article featured a horse and tackle hitch invention, one of a series of labor-saving devices that he employed.

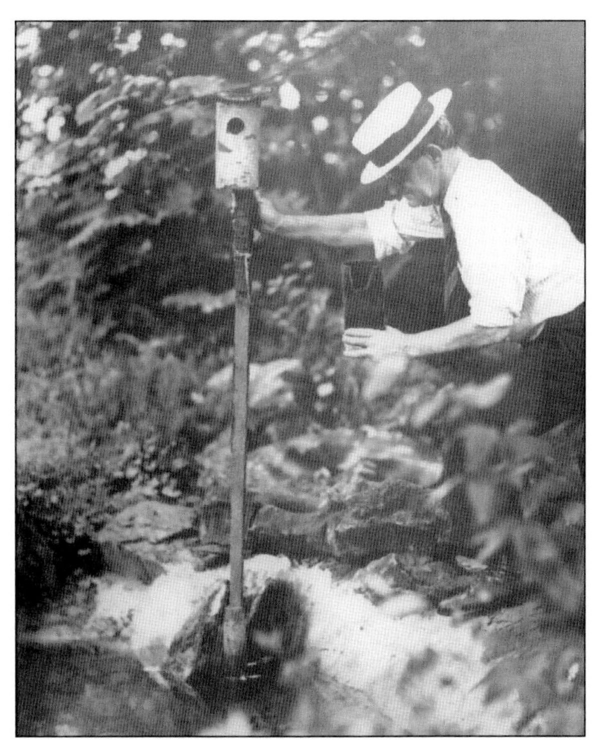

In the early 1930s, John Bamberg, ornithologist and teacher at Park Junior High School, published a booklet for Boy and Girls Scouts entitled *How to Know Our East Tennessee Birds.* The illustrations were by H. P. Ijams and included a kingfisher perched on a can of JFG Coffee, a Knoxville company that still exists today. (Kathleen Hancock.)

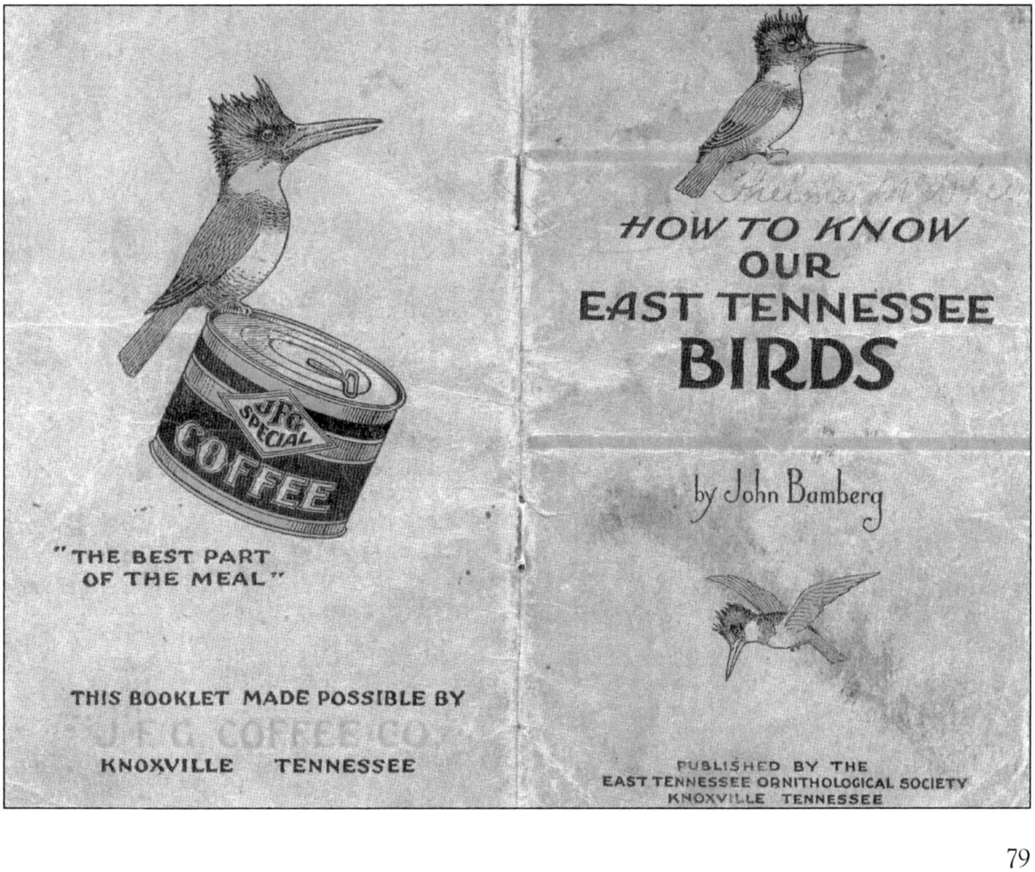

JFG SPECIAL
COFFEE

"THE BEST PART
OF THE MEAL"

THIS BOOKLET MADE POSSIBLE BY
J. F. G. COFFEE CO.
KNOXVILLE TENNESSEE

HOW TO KNOW
OUR
EAST TENNESSEE
BIRDS

by John Bamberg

PUBLISHED BY THE
EAST TENNESSEE ORNITHOLOGICAL SOCIETY
KNOXVILLE TENNESSEE

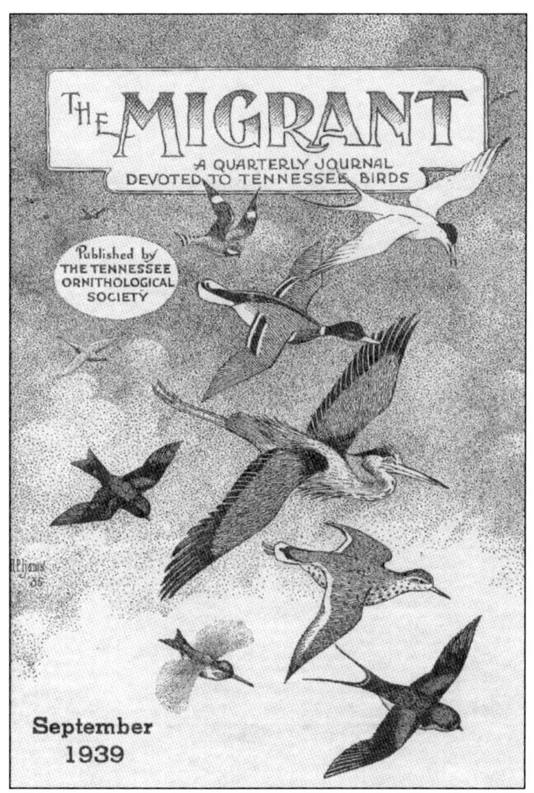

In 1935, H. P. Ijams produced a new cover design for the *Migrant*, the Tennessee Ornithological Society's quarterly journal. The previous illustration had featured a great horned owl, but Ijams's design captured the broad diversity of Tennessee bird life so well that despite a brief pause in 1940, it ran on the cover for a staggering 57 years, from 1935 to 1991. (The *Migrant*, Tennessee Ornithological Society.)

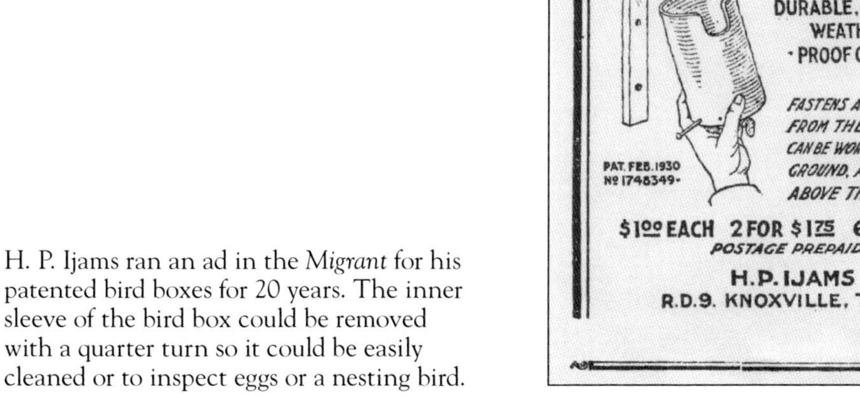

H. P. Ijams ran an ad in the *Migrant* for his patented bird boxes for 20 years. The inner sleeve of the bird box could be removed with a quarter turn so it could be easily cleaned or to inspect eggs or a nesting bird.

In 1928, H. P. Ijams filed a patent for his unique bird box design. At one time, more than 100 of these bird boxes were in place around the Ijams Bird Sanctuary.

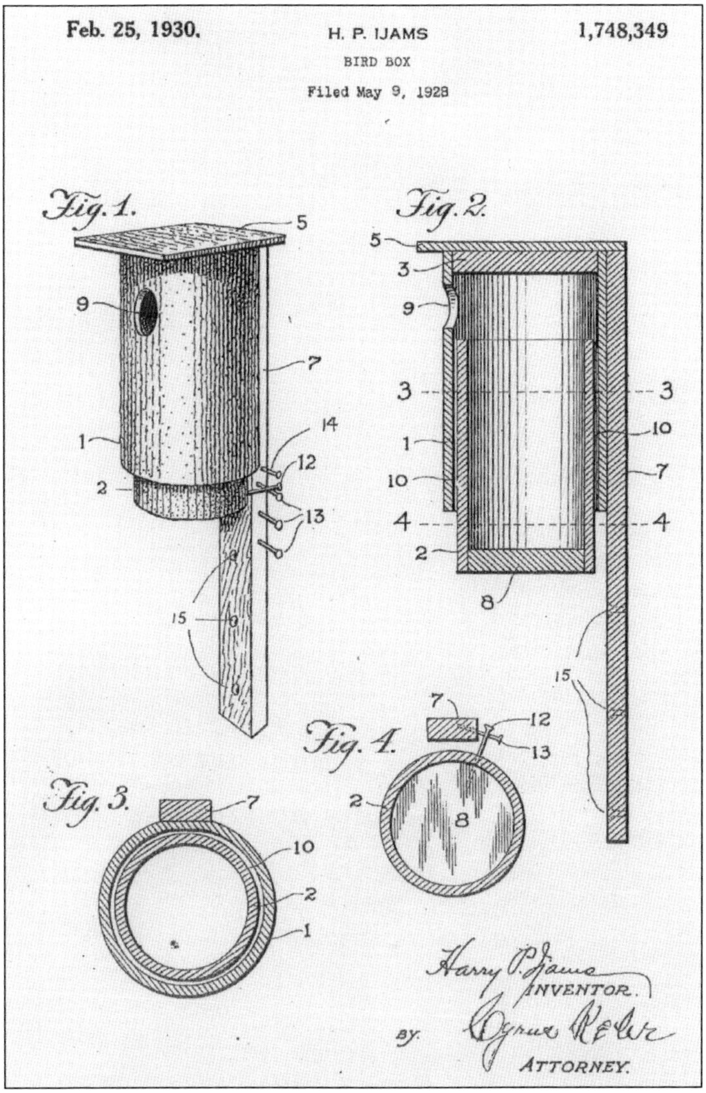

Feb. 25, 1930. H. P. IJAMS 1,748,349

BIRD BOX

Filed May 9, 1928

Fig. 1.

Fig. 2.

Fig. 3.

Fig. 4.

Harry P. Ijams INVENTOR.

BY Cyrus Kehr ATTORNEY.

This illustration of an eastern towhee, drawn by H. P. Ijams in 1945, was featured in the *Migrant*. The species would have been a year-round resident at the bird sanctuary.

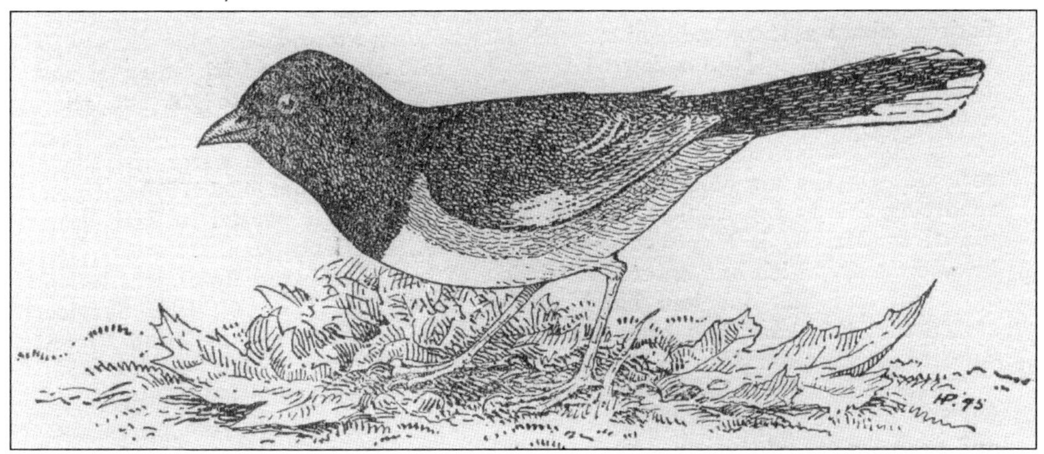

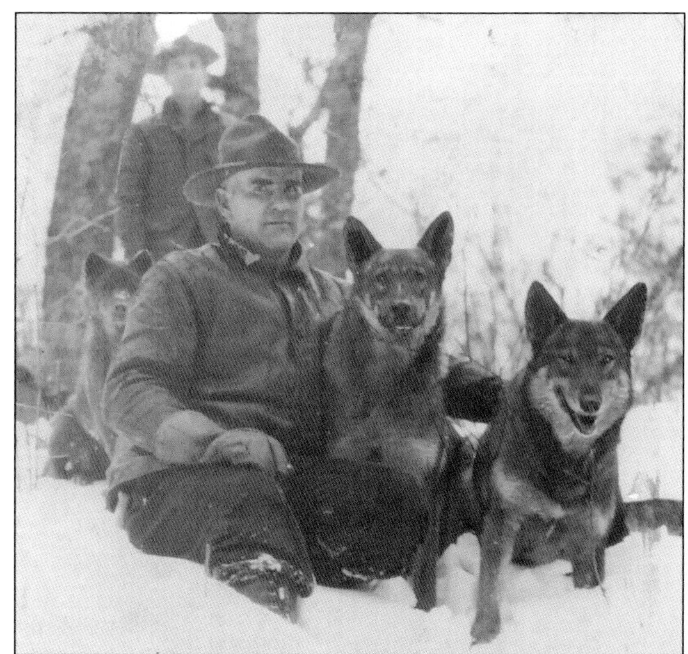

Along with H. P. Ijams, Brockway Crouch was one of Knoxville's leading ornithologists. Born in 1896, he married Elsie Wayland, a fellow member of the Smoky Mountain Hiking Club, in 1927. Both were frequent visitors to the Ijams Bird Sanctuary. Crouch was also widely known for his fondness for dog breeding and is seen here with a pair of German shepherds. He died in 1971 and at the time was the longest-serving member of the bird club.

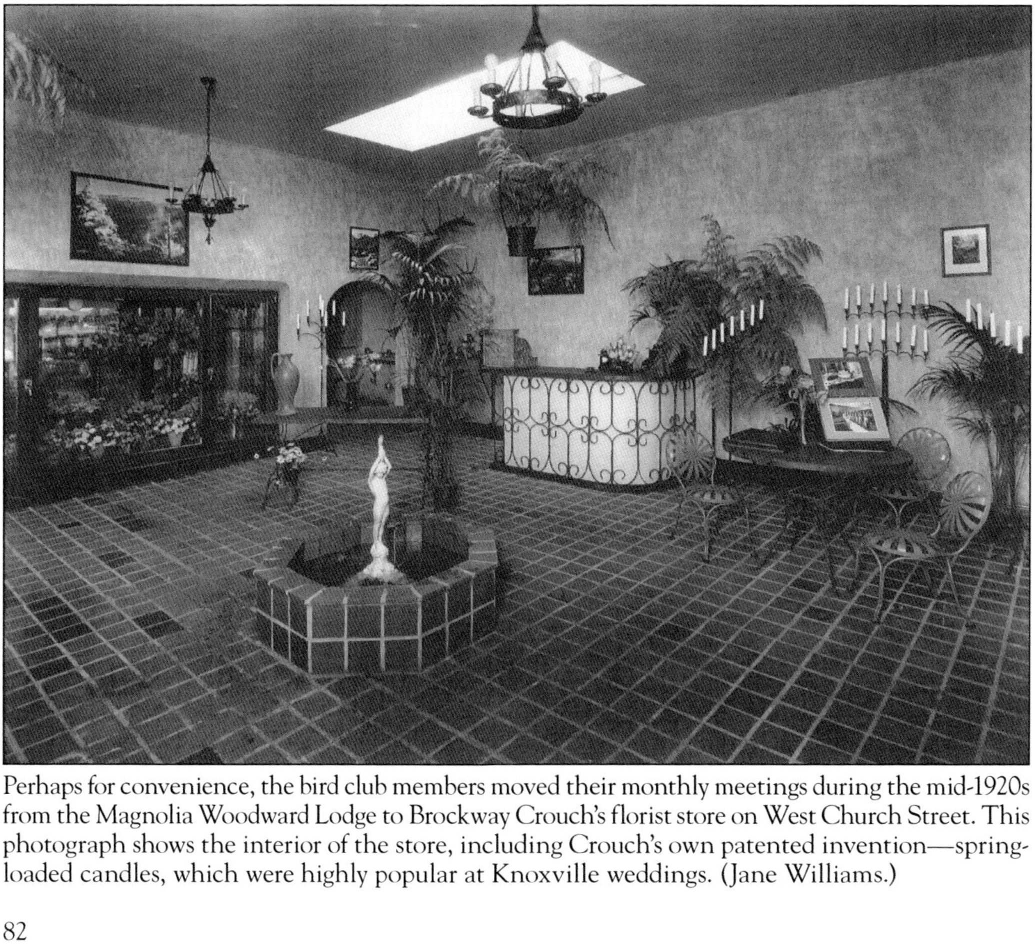

Perhaps for convenience, the bird club members moved their monthly meetings during the mid-1920s from the Magnolia Woodward Lodge to Brockway Crouch's florist store on West Church Street. This photograph shows the interior of the store, including Crouch's own patented invention—spring-loaded candles, which were highly popular at Knoxville weddings. (Jane Williams.)

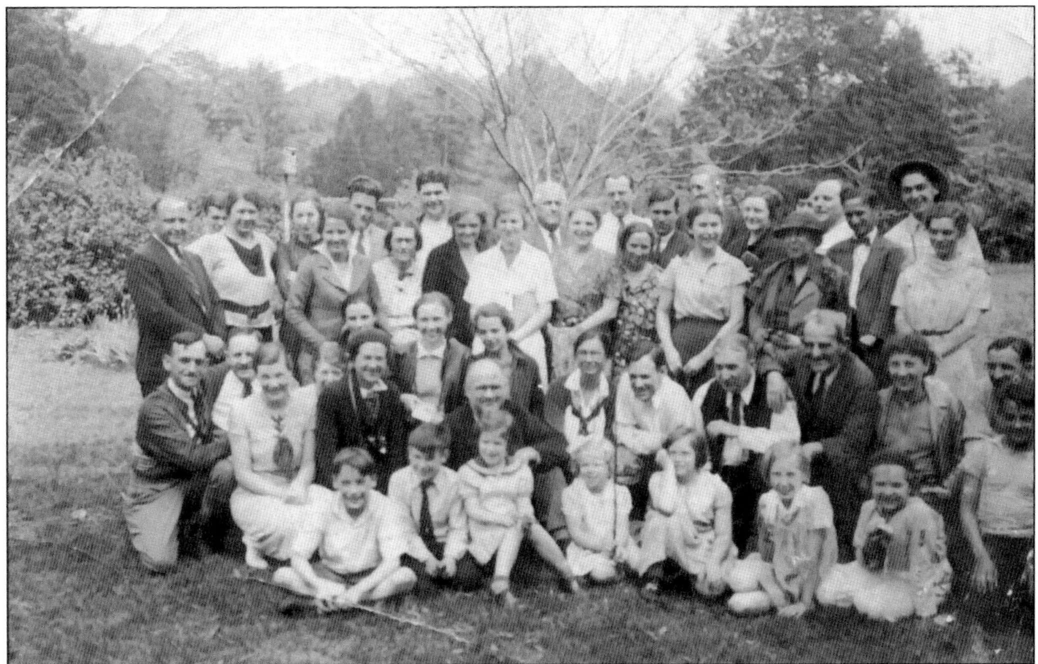

Members of the East Tennessee Ornithological Society pose for the camera in May 1936. Overnight campers enjoyed warm hospitality on the Ijams lawn, rising early in search of local and migrating birds. Often more than 100 species were recorded before noon. In the center of the front row is Jane Crouch, a frequent visitor with her parents, Brockway Crouch (sitting just behind the children), and Elsie Crouch (next to Alice Ijams, third row, fifth from right).

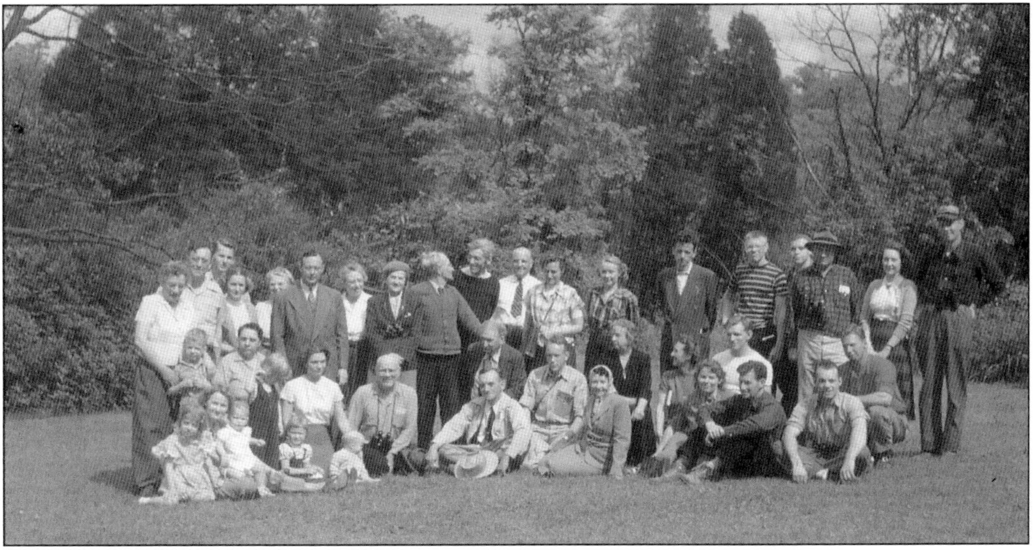

In 1952, the bird club meets on the Ijams lawn during the annual bird census. A fairly recent newcomer to Knoxville was one of Tennessee's most respected ornithologists, Dr. James Tanner, who is the fourth man from left on bottom row. As a graduate of Cornell University's Lab of Ornithology in 1935, Tanner filmed what may have been one of the last surviving populations of ivory-billed woodpeckers in Louisiana. Tanner was also the only known person ever to band an ivory-bill, which he achieved in 1938 during a three-year research and conservation study.

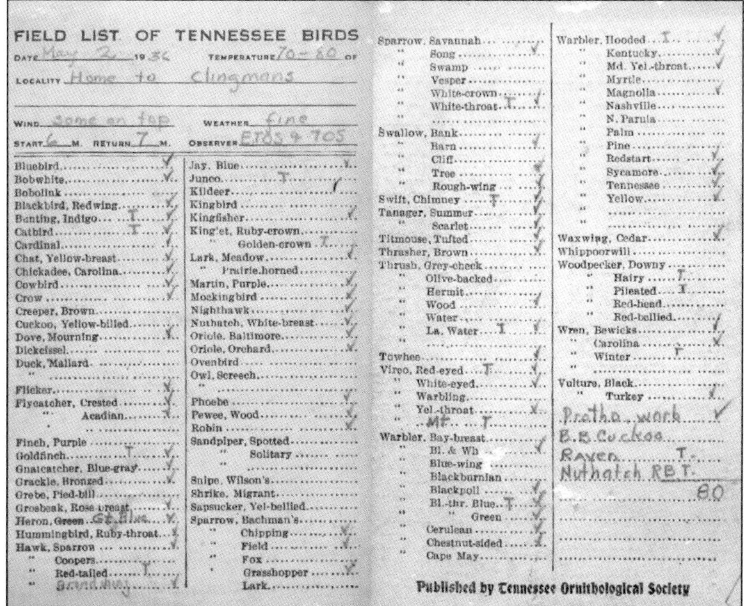

FIELD LIST OF TENNESSEE BIRDS

DATE May 2, 1936 TEMPERATURE 70–80 °F

LOCALITY Home to clingmans

WIND some on top WEATHER fine

START 6 M. RETURN 7 M. OBSERVER EIOS & 705

Bluebird
Bobwhite
Bobolink
Blackbird, Redwing
Bunting, Indigo
Catbird
Cardinal
Chat, Yellow-breast
Chickadee, Carolina
Cowbird
Crow
Creeper, Brown
Cuckoo, Yellow-billed
Dove, Mourning
Dickcissel
Duck, Mallard
"
Flicker
Flycatcher, Crested
" Acadian
"
Finch, Purple
Goldfinch
Gnatcatcher, Blue-gray
Grackle, Bronzed
Grebe, Pied-bill
Grosbeak, Rose-breast
Heron, Green
Hummingbird, Ruby-throat
Hawk, Sparrow
" Coopers
" Red-tailed
"

Jay, Blue
Junco
Kildeer
Kingbird
Kingfisher
Kinglet, Ruby-crown
" Golden-crown
Lark, Meadow
" Prairie.horned
Martin, Purple
Mockingbird
Nighthawk
Nuthatch, White-breast
Oriole, Baltimore
Oriole, Orchard
Ovenbird
Owl, Screech
"
Phoebe
Pewee, Wood
Robin
Sandpiper, Spotted
" Solitary
"
Snipe, Wilson's
Shrike, Migrant
Sapsucker, Yel-bellied
Sparrow, Bachman's
" Chipping
" Field
" Fox
" Grasshopper
Lark

Sparrow, Savannah
" Song
" Swamp
" Vesper
" White-crown
" White-throat
"
Swallow, Bank
" Barn
" Cliff
" Tree
" Rough-wing
Swift, Chimney
Tanager, Summer
" Scarlet
Titmouse, Tufted
Thrasher, Brown
Thrush, Grey-cheek
" Olive-backed
" Hermit
" Wood
" Water
" La. Water
"
Towhee
Vireo, Red-eyed
" White-eyed
" Warbling
" Yel.-throat
" Mt.
Warbler, Bay-breast
" Bl. & Wh
" Blue-wing
" Blackburnian
" Blackpoll
" Bl.-thr. Blue
" " Green
" Cerulean
" Chestnut-sided
" Cape May

Warbler, Hooded
" Kentucky
" Md. Yel.-throat
" Myrtle
" Magnolia
" Nashville
" N. Parula
" Palm
" Pine
" Redstart
" Sycamore
" Tennessee
" Yellow
"
"
Waxwing, Cedar
Whippoorwill
Woodpecker, Downy
" Hairy
" Pileated
" Red-head
" Red-bellied
Wren, Bewicks
" Carolina
" Winter
"
Vulture, Black
" Turkey
Protho. work
B.B. Cuckoo
Raven
Nuthatch RBT.
80

Published by Tennessee Ornithological Society

An official Tennessee Ornithological Society bird observation field list, completed by H. P. and Alice Ijams in May 1936, detailed 80 species of birds observed between the Ijams home and Clingman's Dome in the Great Smoky Mountains National Park.

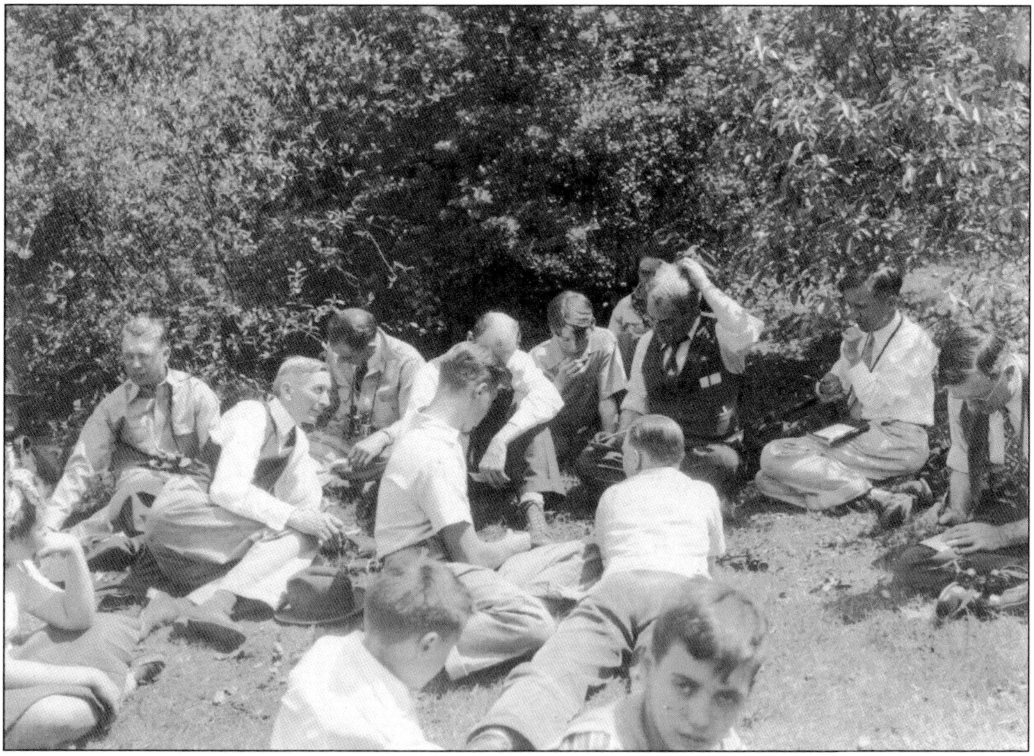

Members of the East Tennessee Ornithological Society put their heads together while reviewing observations during the spring bird census around 1940. George Mayfield (fourth from left, with hat and waistcoat) was a founding member of the Tennessee Ornithological Society in 1915. Next to Mayfield is Dr. Earl O. Henry (fifth from left), who joined the bird club as a junior member in 1929.

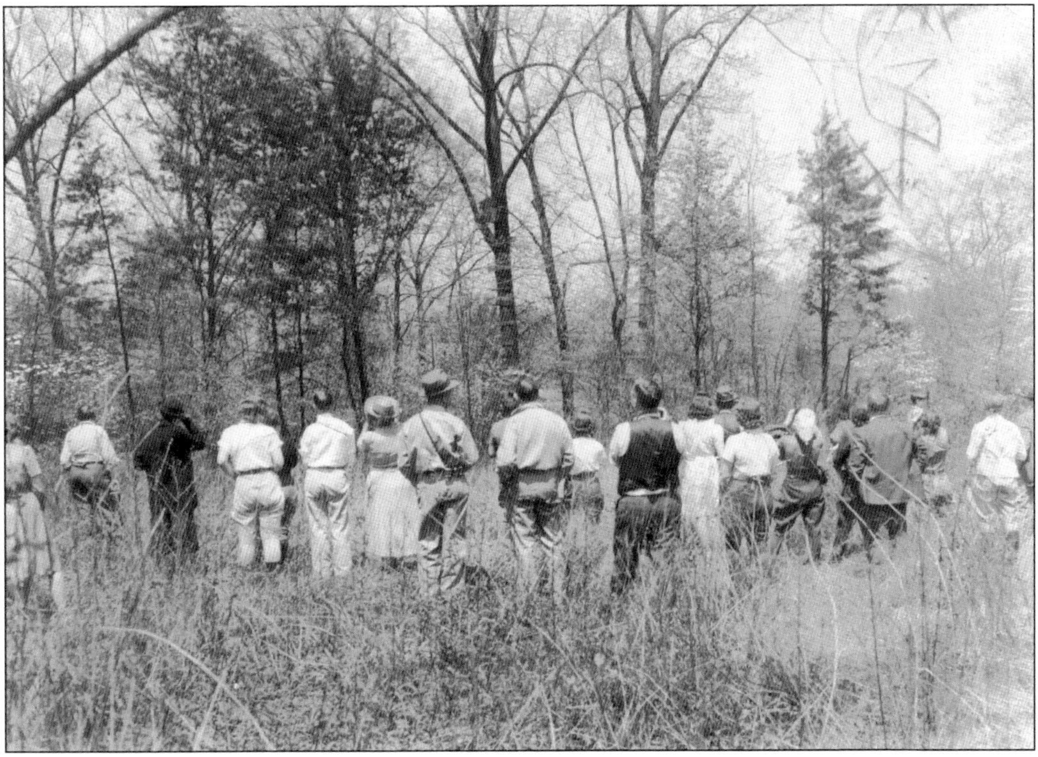

A group of ornithologists at the Spring bird census at the Ijams Bird Sanctuary study an owl nest box in the tree in the center of the photograph.

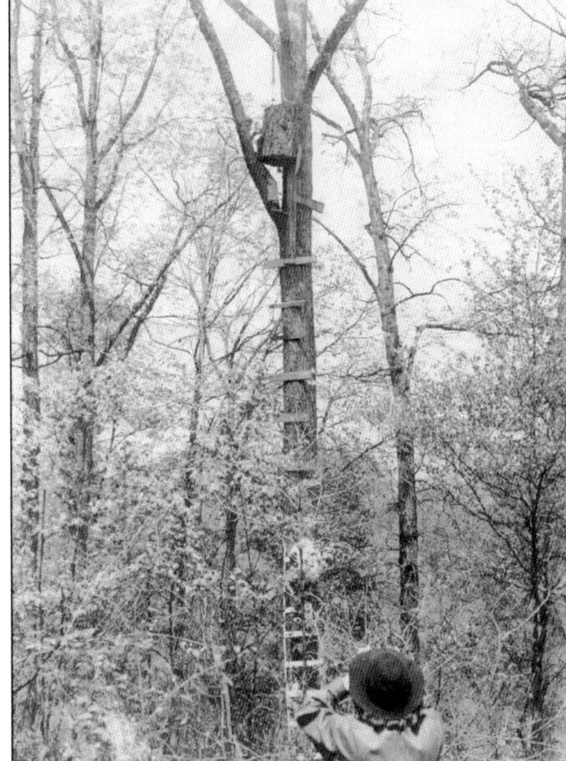

A female member of the bird club gets a close view through binoculars at the nest box, which, although barely noticeable, is being inspected by a fellow birder at the top of the ladder.

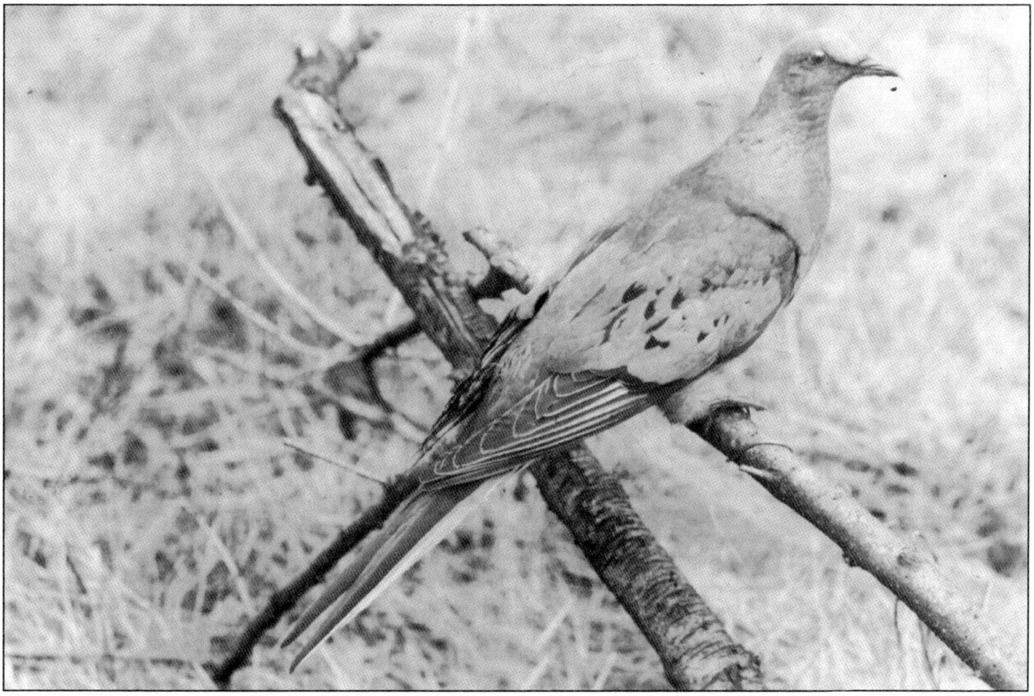

In 1928, H. P. Ijams purchased a collection of mounted birds containing a passenger pigeon that had originally been collected by Gen. Benjamin Cheatham near Nashville around 1856. At the time it was taken, the species was well known throughout East Tennessee for huge congregations that roosted along the Pigeon River, giving name in part to one of Tennessee's most famous towns, Pigeon Forge.

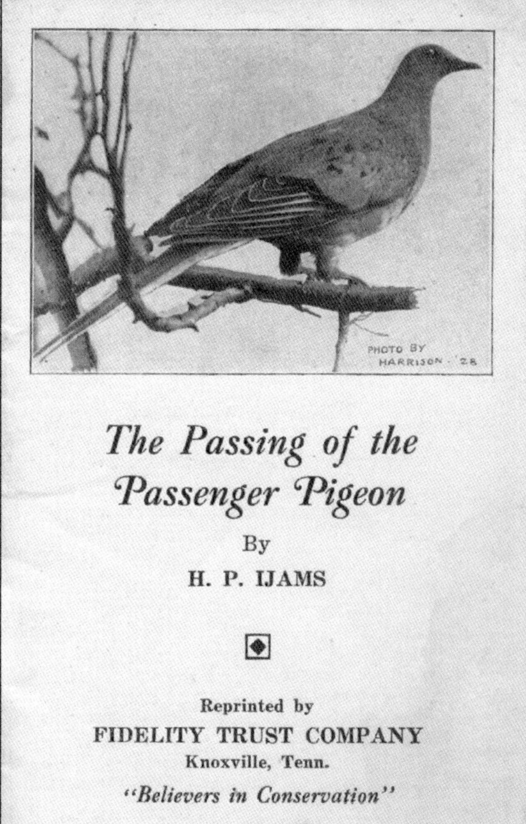

PHOTO BY HARRISON '28

The Passing of the Passenger Pigeon

By

H. P. IJAMS

Reprinted by

FIDELITY TRUST COMPANY

Knoxville, Tenn.

"Believers in Conservation"

Fascinated by the species, H. P. Ijams wrote and produced a booklet in 1928 entitled *The Passing of the Passenger Pigeon*. This reprint from the following year included additional graphics and was sponsored by the Fidelity Trust Company, where Ijams's fellow birder and taxidermist S. Arthur Ogden worked.

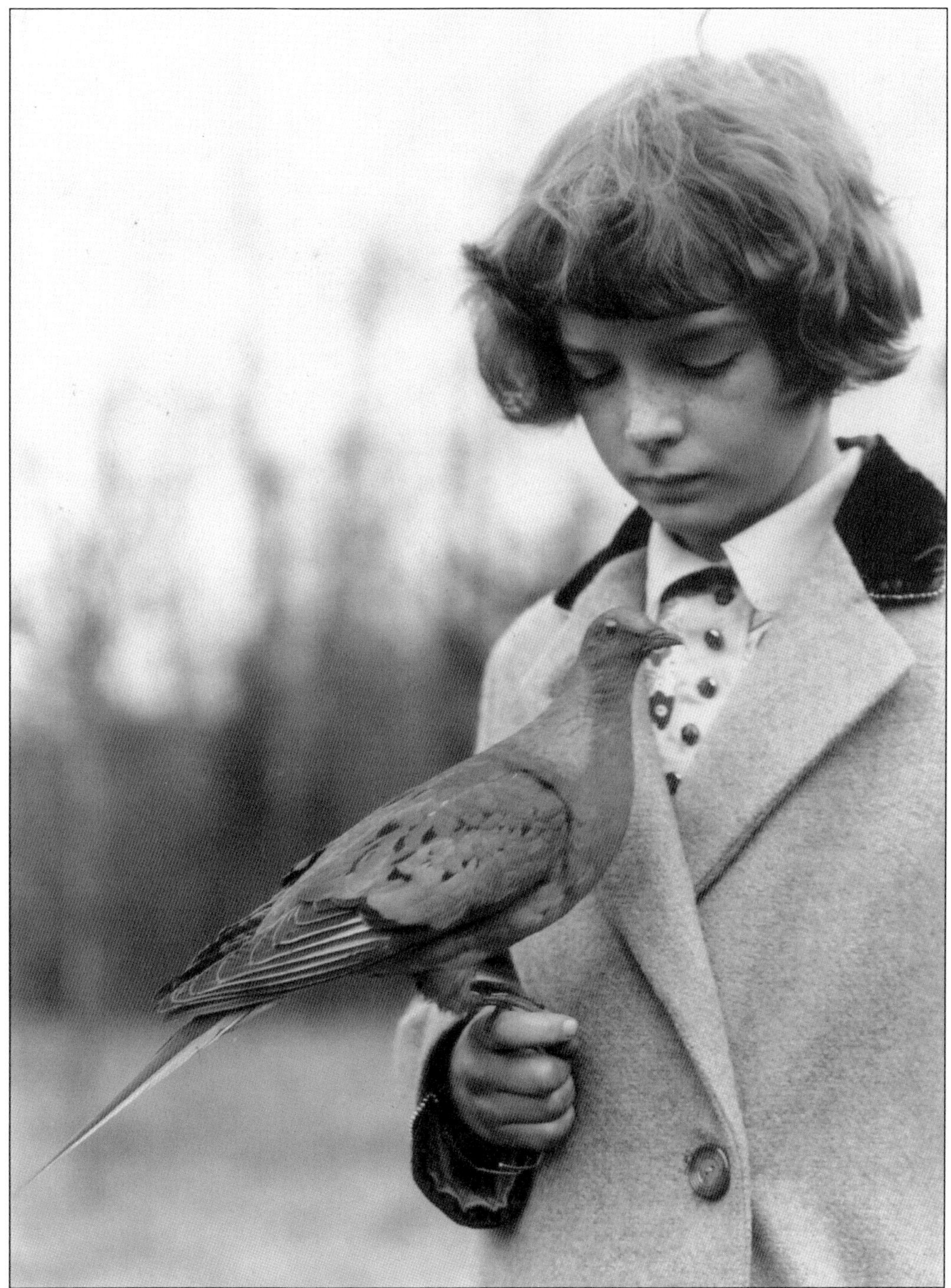

A young Martha Ijams poses for Knoxville photographer Russell Harrison (Brockway Crouch's brother-in-law) with her father's passenger pigeon. This mounted specimen was H. P.'s prize possession. Late in life, he wrote a note to his son-in-law, Frank Lovingood, that in the case of a fire, the pigeon was to be the first item removed from the house, as "it can never be replaced." Martha donated the pigeon to the National Park Service in 1987.

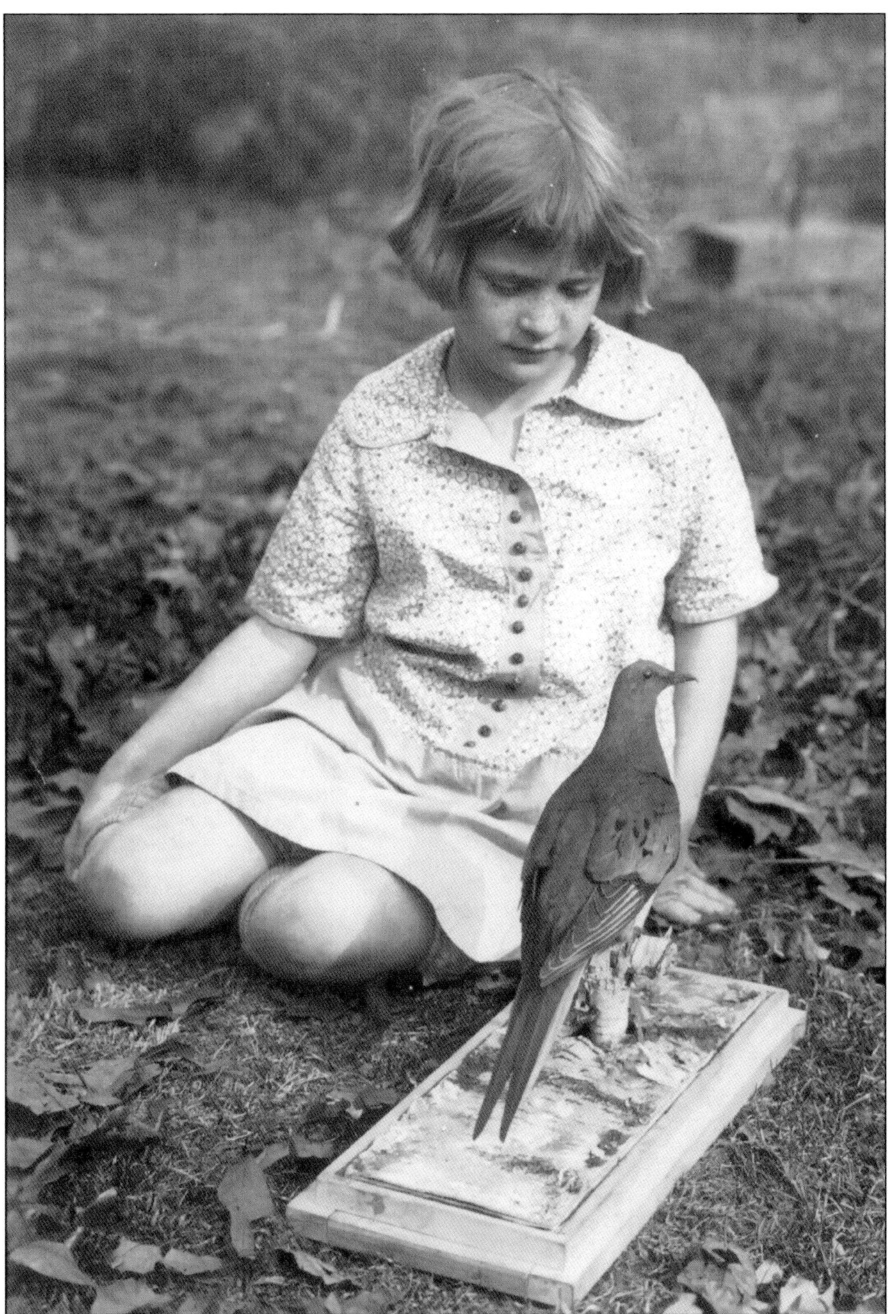

Martha Ijams ponders the fate of the extinct passenger pigeon, which may have been the most numerous bird species ever to live on earth. Once thriving in the billions, enormous flocks of passenger pigeons migrated in search of food from the Gulf of Mexico to the southern ranges of Canada. Russell Harrison, who took this photograph in February 1928, visited Cincinnati in 1913 to see another Martha, the very last passenger pigeon, which lived in a pagoda-style aviary at Cincinnati Zoo. Martha passed away a year later, on September 1, 1914, and her body was encased in a block of ice before being shipped to the Smithsonian Museum of Natural History for mounting and display in the bird collection.

Albert Ganier, a founding member of the Tennessee Ornithological Society, frequently camped at the Ijams place and often accompanied H. P. Ijams on birding trips in the Smokies. When H. P. passed away in 1954, Ganier asked a number of fellow birders to contribute to Ijams's obituary in the *Migrant*.

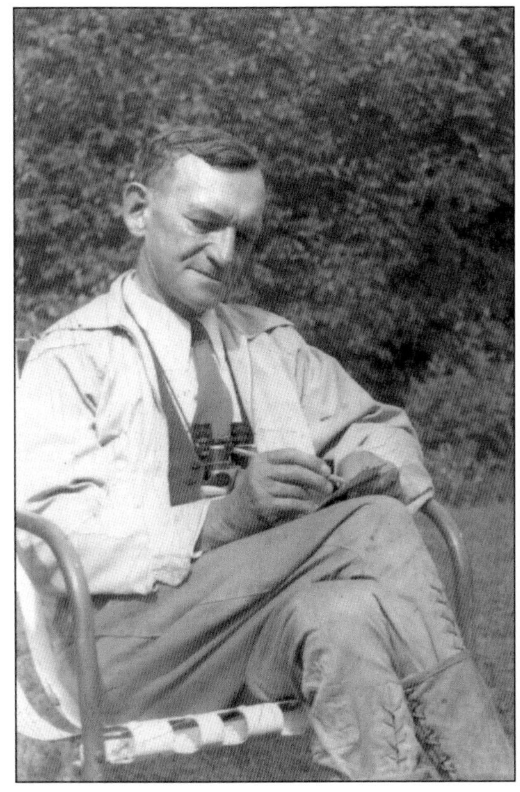

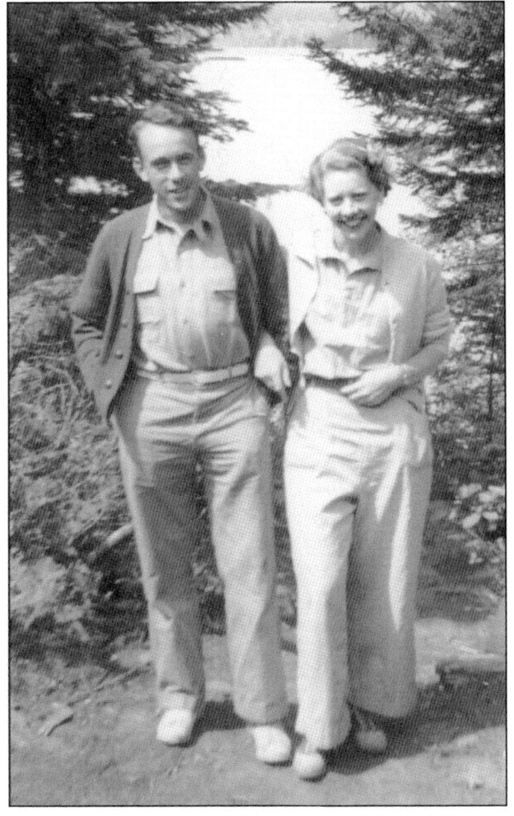

Nancy Tanner, here with husband Dr. James Tanner, was a longtime volunteer naturalist at Ijams Nature Center, leading groups of schoolchildren on the trails. The Tanners were once birding across the street at the disused Mead's Quarry site, before it came part of the nature center, when a young lad fell into the water across the lake. Jim took off his shoes, dove into the water, and was able to save the youngster's life.

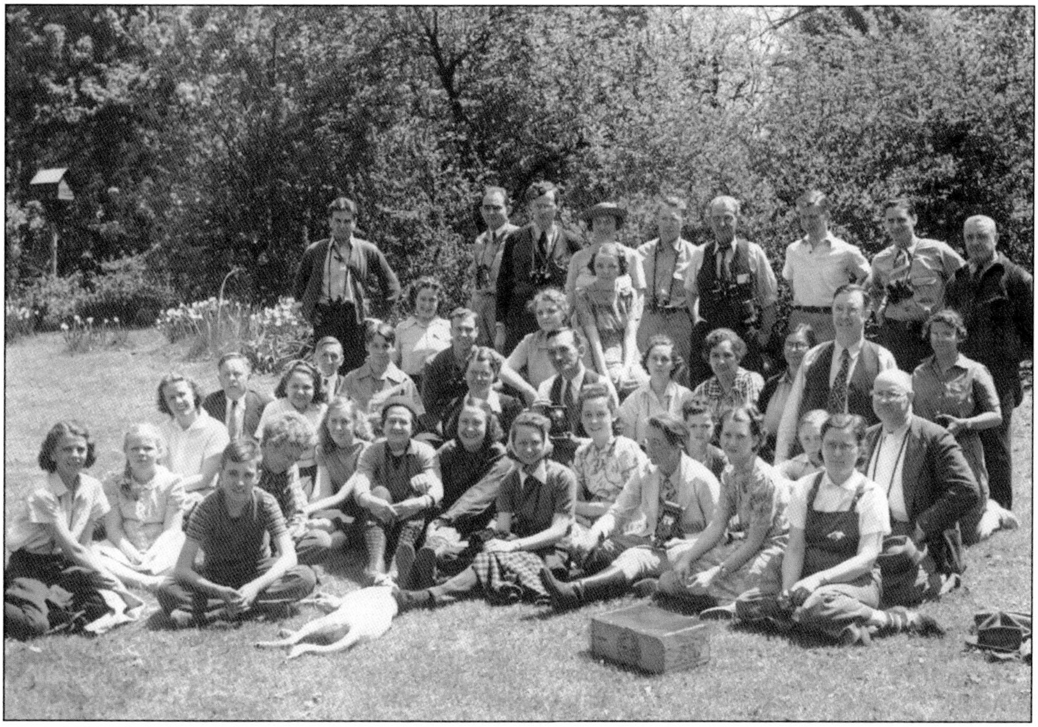

Knoxville dentist Earl O. Henry (standing second from left with binoculars) joins other members of the East Tennessee Ornithological Society around 1940. Dr. Henry frequently used his artistic skills when he gave lectures to students about birds. Drawing the birds he discussed using white chalk on a blackboard, Henry colored them in as he went, resulting in a fine series of drawings by the end of class.

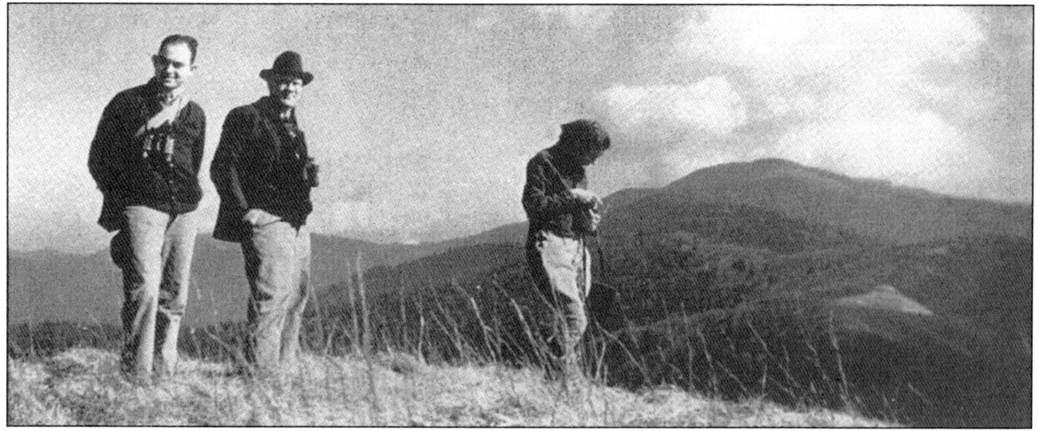

Throughout the 1920s and 1930s, Knoxville ornithologists made frequent trips to the Smokies. Here, Earl O. Henry (left), Brockway Crouch (center), and a Miss Robinson look for birds on Siler's Bald in December 1938 during a Christmas bird count. Arthur Stupka, the Smokies' first naturalist, credited Henry with the only high-altitude record of a great horned owl, along the Appalachian Trail between Clingman's Dome and Siler's Bald. (The *Migrant*, Tennessee Ornithological Society.)

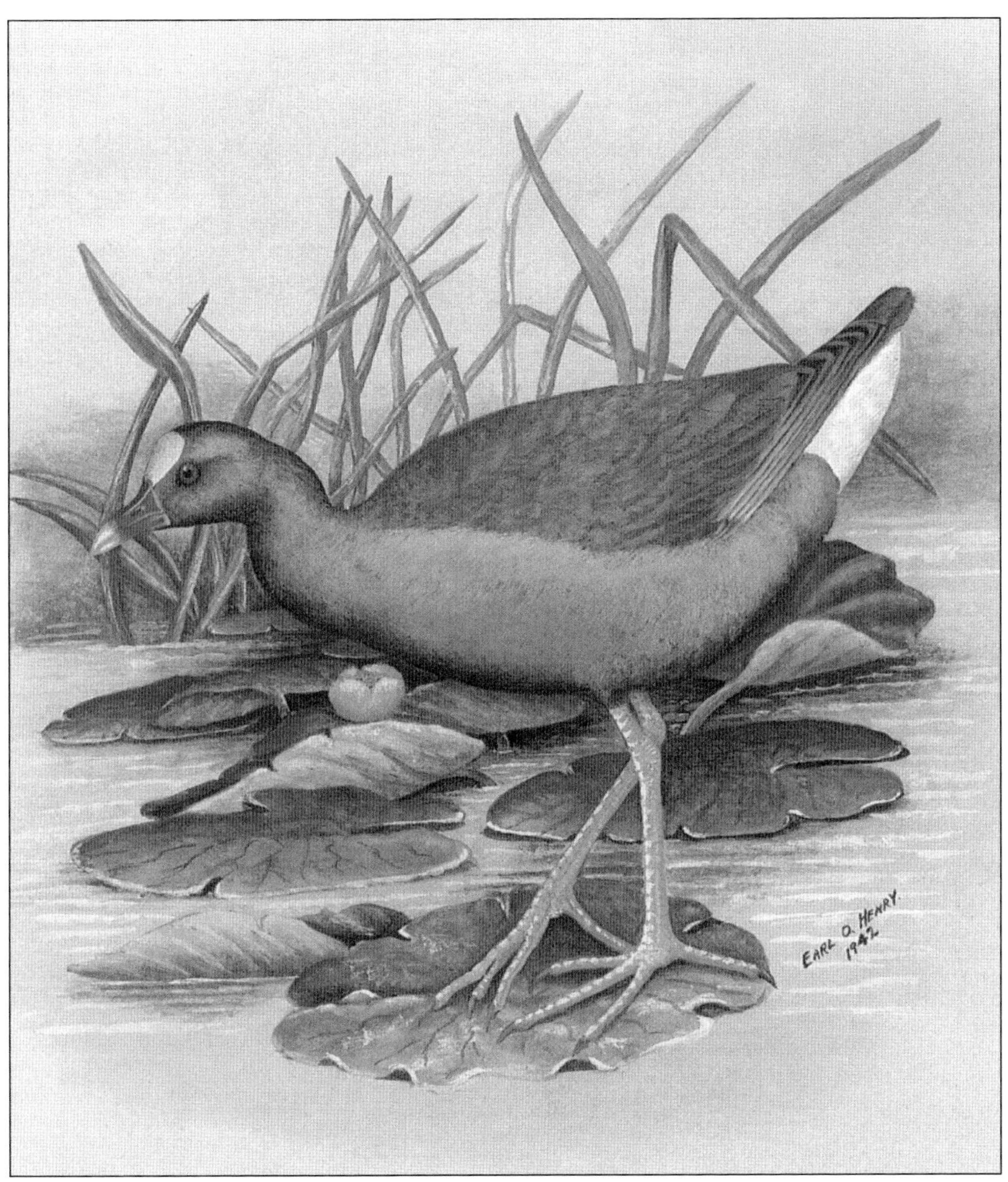

Lt. Comdr. Earl O. Henry painted this gallinule in 1942 before he departed for the Pacific from the Naval Academy in World War II. Like many others of the day, Henry became interested in birds as a boy after collecting small bird cards from Arm and Hammer baking soda boxes. Later, in the navy, Henry became known as "the bird guy" and frequently stopped to get out of a car to rush down a grassy bank to spot a new bird with his binoculars. Henry left behind an impressive collection of bird paintings before his tragic death on the USS *Indianapolis* on July 30, 1945. (Earl Henry Jr.)

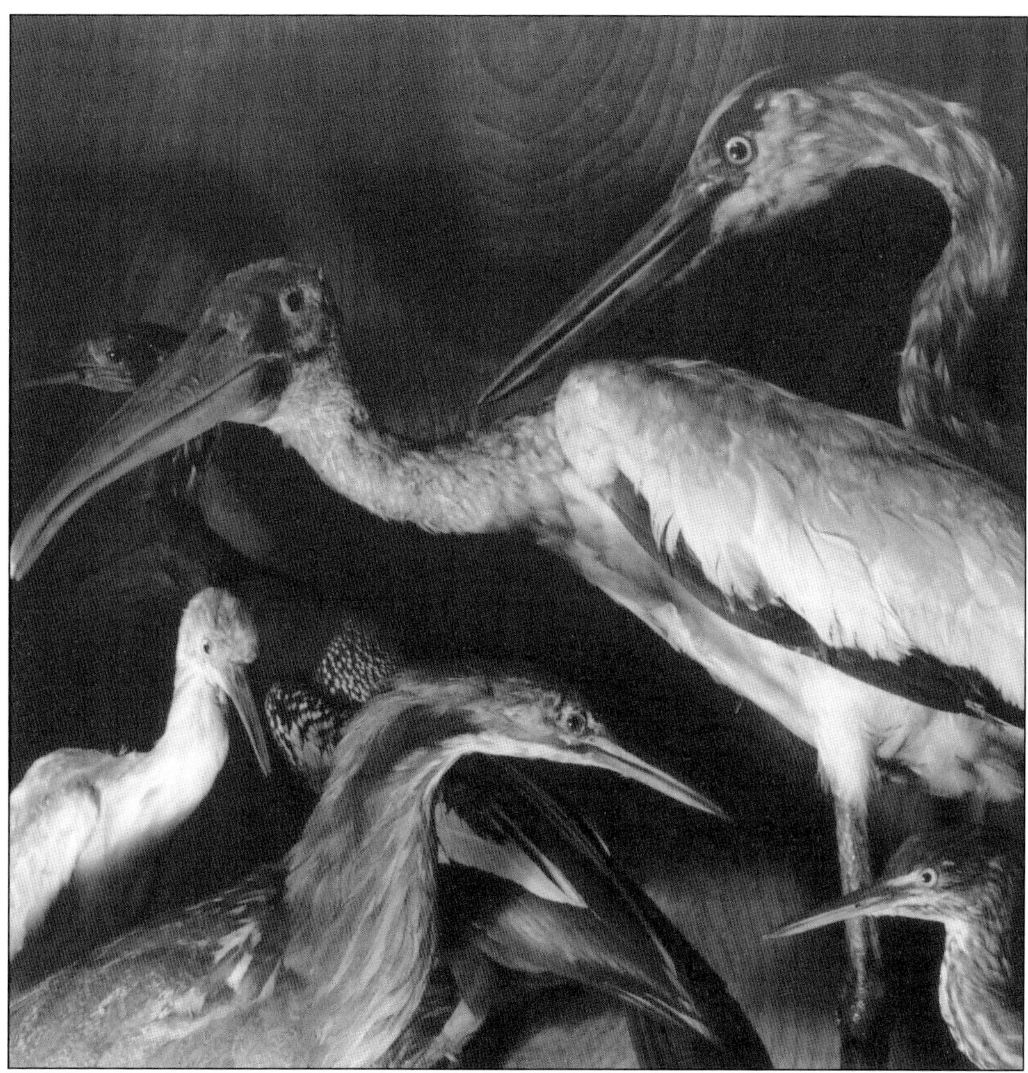

As well as being a talented artist, Dr. Earl Henry was also a skilled taxidermist. These wading bird specimens, including the wood stork (center), were taken some time during the late 1930s. Henry's bird collection first resided with him at his home off Island Home Boulevard before being moved after his death to his son's house in Nashville. The collection would make almost the same return journey when it was donated by Earl Henry Jr. to Ijams Nature Center when the new visitor center opened in 1997. The collection includes a fascinating array of species, including a peregrine falcon taken near Alum Cave in the Smoky Mountains in the early 1930s, when the species was very rare. Since Dr. Henry's death, Knoxville's Second District Dental Society has held an educational event, the Earl Henry Memorial Clinic, every year in his memory. (K. Heinzman.)

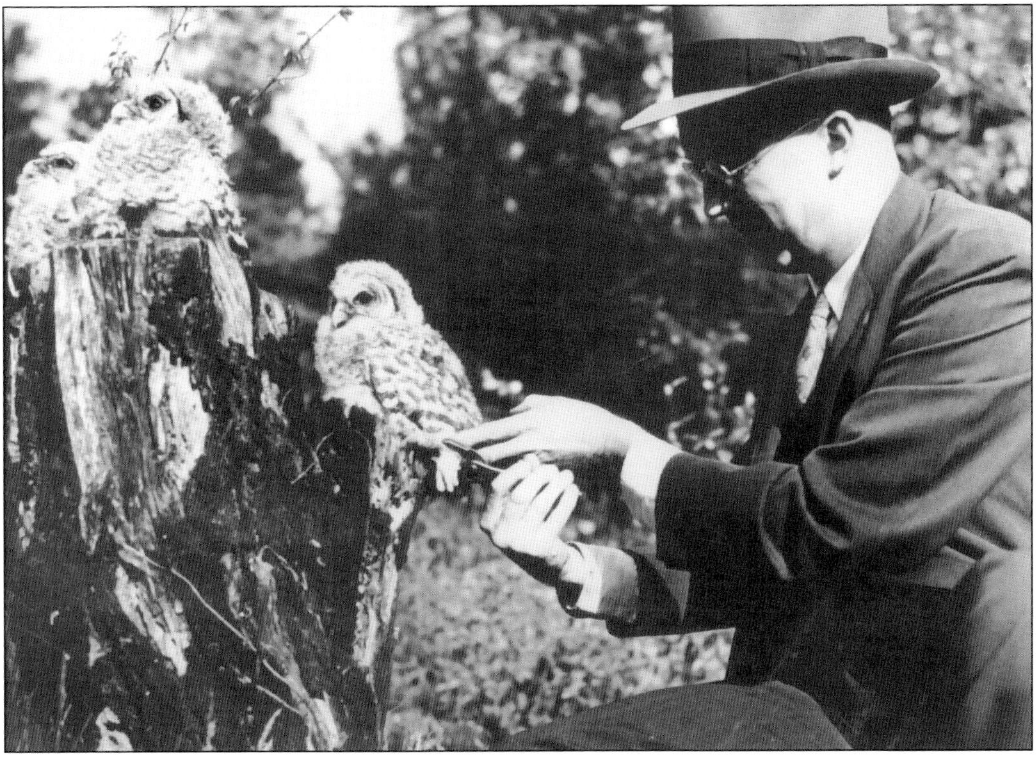

Brockway Crouch bands a trio of young barred owls raised by H. P. Ijams at the Ijams Bird Sanctuary in 1940. Although a nocturnal species, barred owls are regularly seen and heard during the daytime at Ijams Nature Center near the Lotus Pond and along the Discovery Trail.

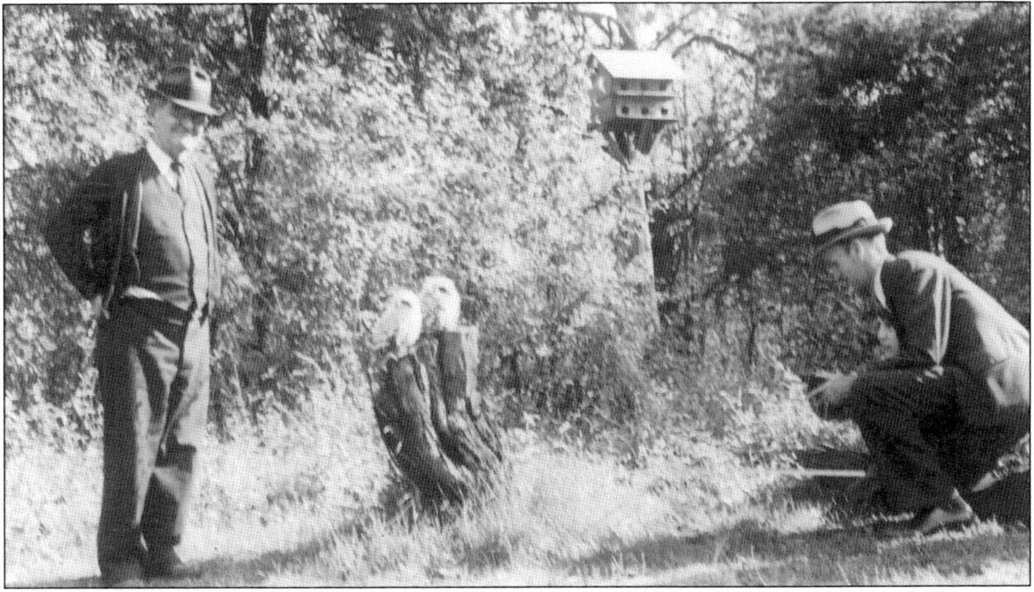

H. P. Ijams (left) has his photograph taken with the owls. Note the young face peering behind the unidentified man on the right with the camera.

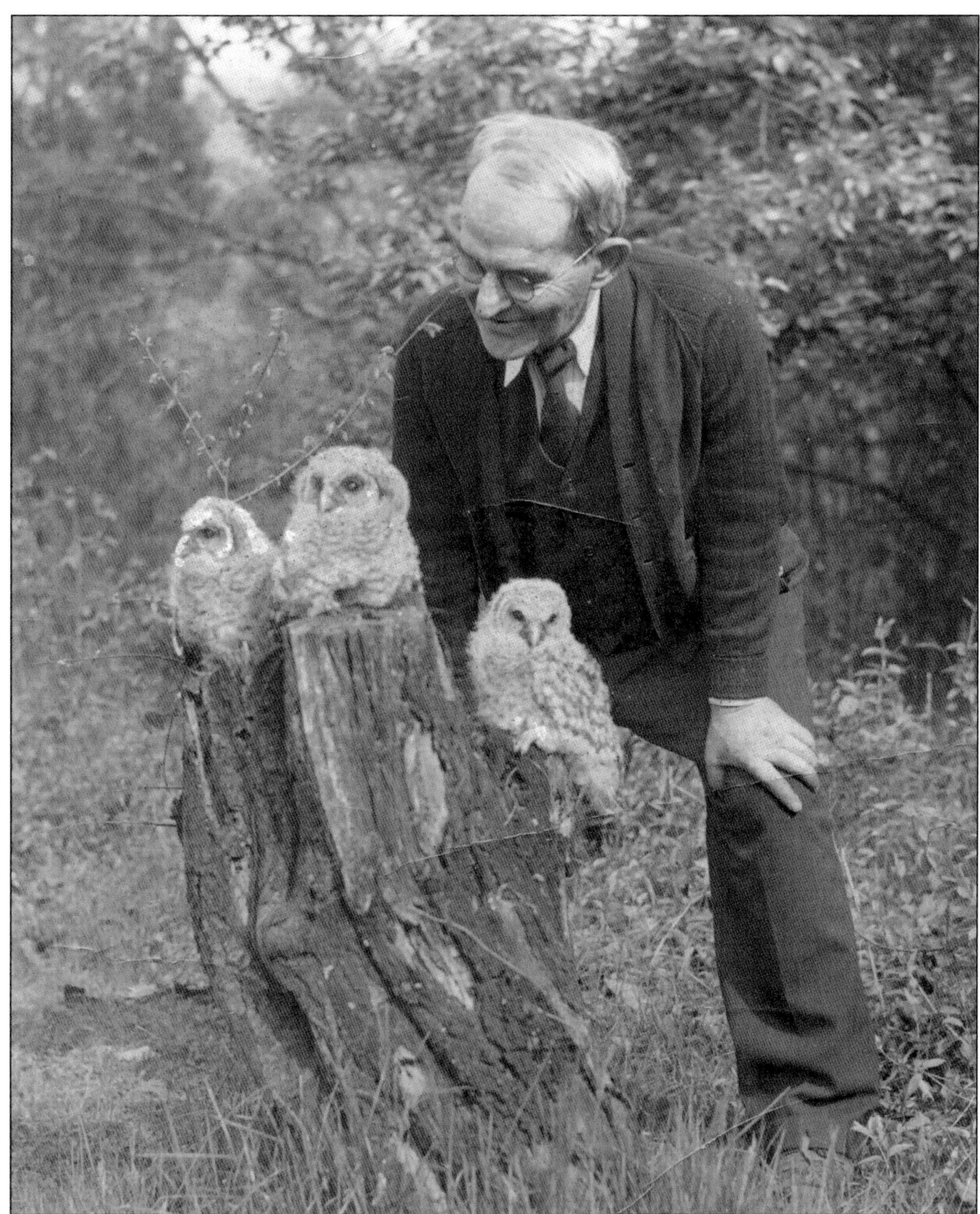

When Albert Ganier asked fellow birders to write a few words about H. P. after his death in 1954, Mrs. Robert A. Monroe wrote the following eulogy: "The Ijams' sanctuary welcomed friends and visitors, Scouts and students, as well as birds. Entering it, one felt removed spiritually, as well as physically, from the busy routine of life. For beyond Mr. Ijams' interest in ornithology was a great love for the birds themselves." H. P.'s great friend Brockway Crouch added, "Harry Ijams was the authority through whom those interested in nature in the Knoxville area checked their lore and made many acquaintances of kindred spirits. Even before I knew him personally, I felt his influence, for whether making trips across the mountains or canoeing to Chattanooga, I found I was following trails blazed by him and Arthur Ogden years before."

Seven

Creating a Public Nature Park

In the 1950s, Jo Ijams Kern moved back to the Ijams place with her family and cared for the gardens that her parents had created. During the same period, she became an active member of the Knoxville Garden Club, which conceived the idea of preserving the Ijams property as a public nature park. The timing was certainly right, tying in with the emergence of the Dogwoods Arts Festival and urban renewal. In 1963, the Knoxville Garden Club established a special conservation project that forged a citywide campaign also involving the Knox County Council of Garden Clubs and the City of Knoxville, which would ultimately own the property and provide maintenance.

Under the leadership of landscape architect Mrs. Hobart Dunlap (Elizabeth), the Knoxville Garden Club pursued a federal open space grant, while local attorney and outdoors enthusiast Lindsey Young made the first donation to the project in December 1963. In early 1964, the Knox County Council of Garden Clubs contributed towards the renovation of the now-aging Ijams house. Mrs. Dunlap continued to court Mayor John Duncan and other city officials who, after much discussion, finally agreed to purchase the property. The Ijams heirs, Elizabeth, Jo, and Martha, each made generous donations. Other funds for the Ijams Park came from both traditional and unusual sources, including proceeds from ticket sales to see an animated miniature circus at Miller's Store on Gay Street. The circus, produced by Dunn Brothers, was used in the movie *The Greatest Show on Earth*. Other donations came from fashion parades as well as memorial gifts following the death of Alice Ijams in October 1964.

The funds to purchase the Ijams property were finally secured in 1965. At the ribbon cutting, presided over by Mrs. James L. Wilbanks, president of the council, special appreciation was lauded upon Mrs. Hobart Dunlap and Ivan Racheff of Knoxville Iron Works (who had donated his carpentry skills inside the house) for their outstanding contributions to the project. Following the restoration of the house and facilities, including outdoor restrooms and a new parking lot for visitors, the new 16-acre Ijams Nature Park was officially dedicated on April 18, 1968.

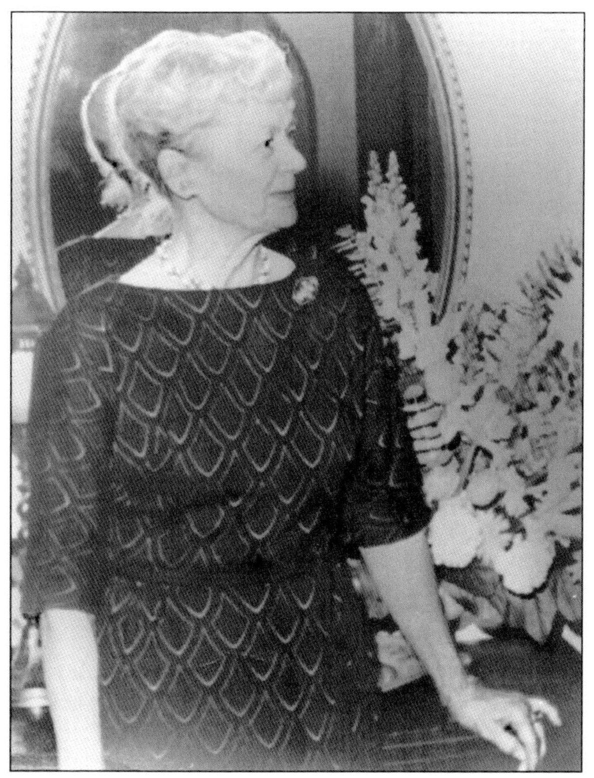

Elizabeth Dunlap, a landscape architect and conservation chairwoman of the Knoxville Garden Club, led efforts to turn the Ijams home into a public nature park. Upon the opening of the new Ijams Nature Park, Dunlap commented, "A botanical garden, a nature park, an arboretum—call it what you will, but [it is] a place to be used for all citizens, not as a playground, but for the study of trees and flowers, birds and animals."

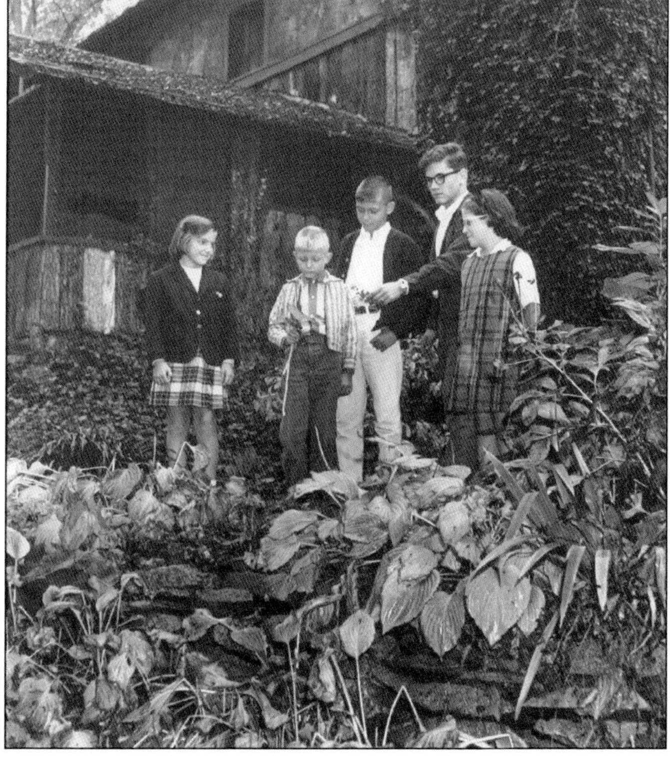

Children of garden club members enjoy a visit to the proposed nature park behind the Ijams house in November 1964, before restoration activities commenced. From left to right are Margaret Traver, Danny White, Steve White, Chip Miller, and Anne Davidson.

As their mother grew older, the three Ijams daughters decided that the Ijams Bird Sanctuary would make a perfect nature park to continue the family legacy of sustainable living, education, and bird-watching. Elizabeth (left), Martha (center), and Jo Ijams all contributed financially to the project.

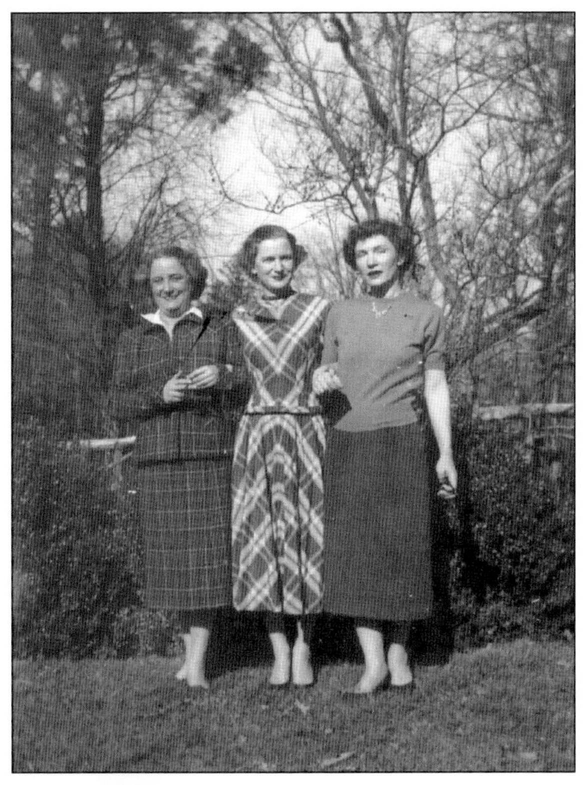

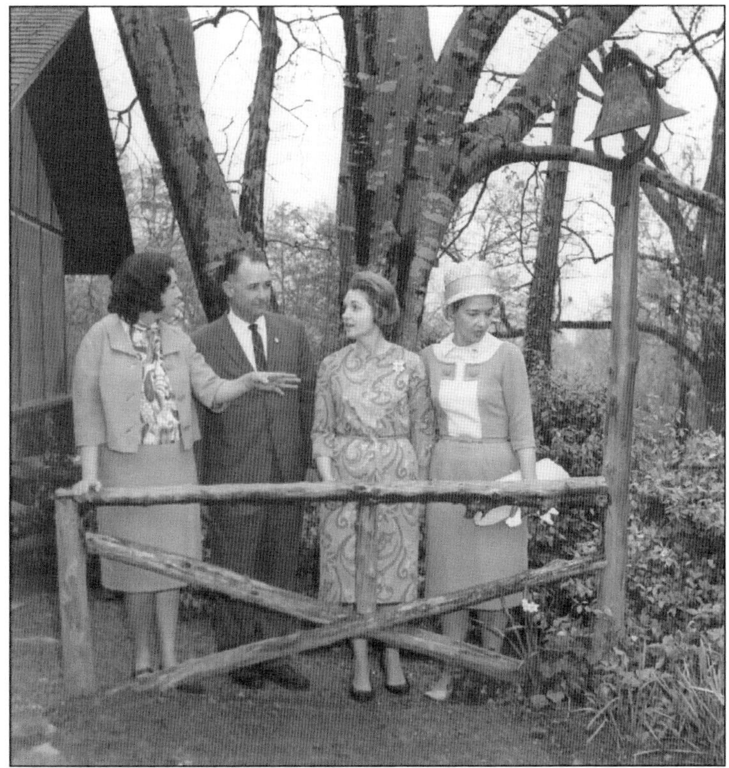

City of Knoxville mayor Leonard Rogers discusses the virtues and potential of the Ijams Nature Park with officers of the Knox County Council of Garden Clubs. From left to right are Mrs. E. J. Frederick, Mayor Rogers, Mrs. Charles Lee, and Mrs. Porter Taylor.

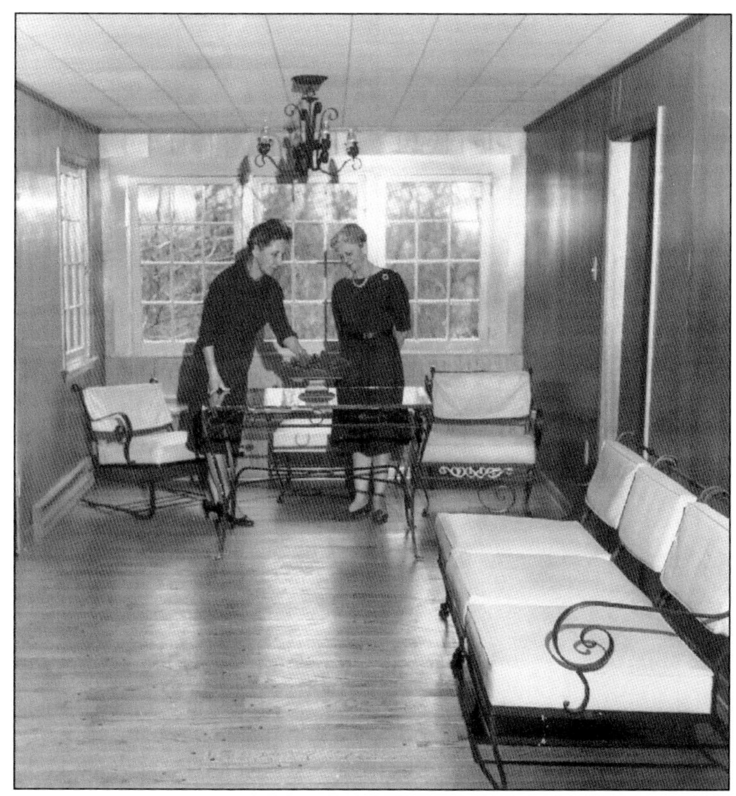

Mrs. Martin Baker (left), incoming president of the Knoxville Garden Club, and Elizabeth Dunlap make final adjustments to the furniture inside the main assembly room of the restored Ijams home in 1965. Dunlap also planned the renovations to the second story, which provided living space for a graduate student who also served park visitors. Ivan Racheff of Knoxville Iron Walks donated carpentry services.

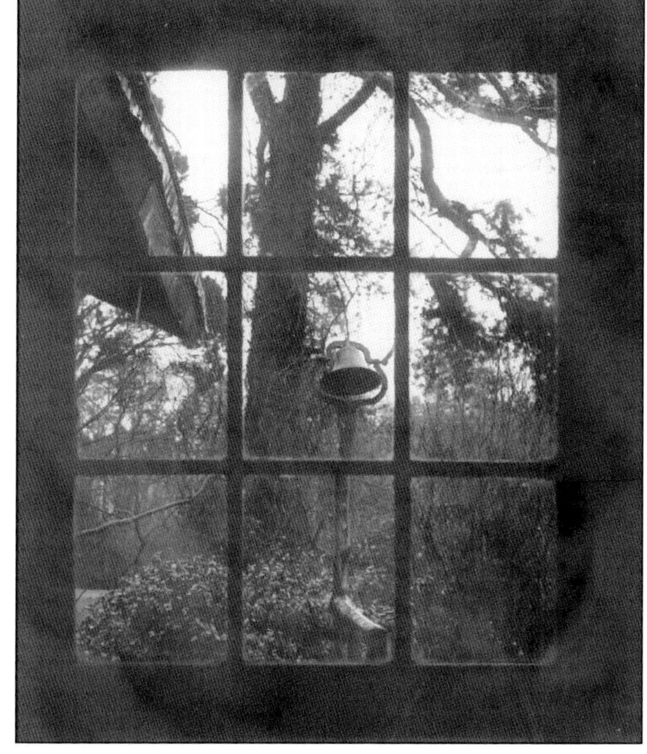

This photograph shows the view of the grounds from inside the restored Ijams home during the 1960s. The Ijams Memorial Nature Park Committee included representatives from the Knoxville Garden Club and the Knox County Council of Garden Clubs, as well as a landscape architect, representatives from the Girl Scouts, and the Akima Club.

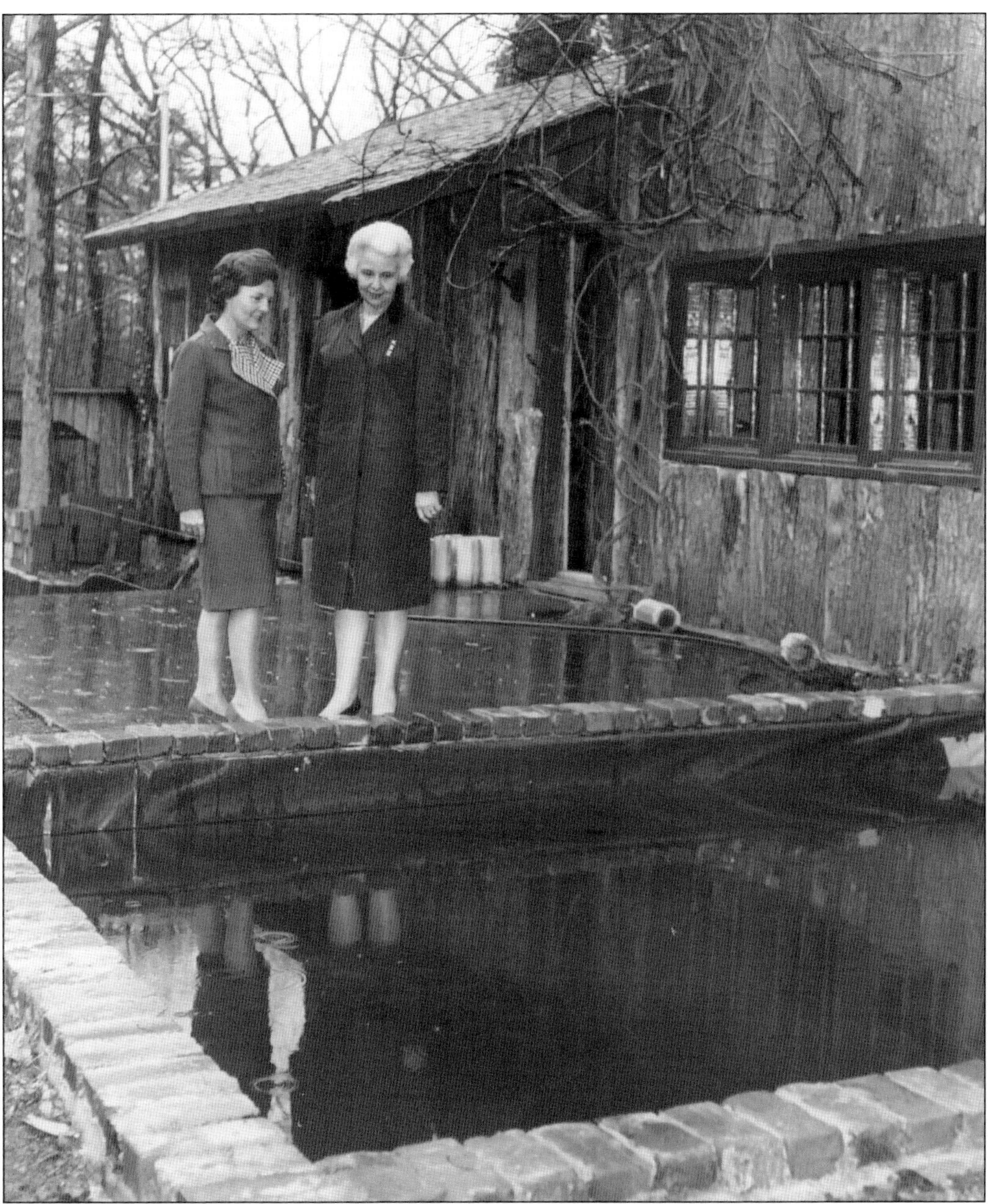

City and county beautification chairwoman Mrs. Lamar Knight (Mary Beth, left) and Mrs. Fred V. Brown (Ruth), president of the Knox County Council of Garden Club, share a reflective moment by the lily pond while the Ijams house and front terrace undergoes restoration. When the photograph appeared in the *Knoxville News Sentinel* on March 3, 1966, an article described the ongoing project: "The restoration is faithful to the rustic theme, with bark matched to bark for the main of the exterior, and trimming kept to the green of the forest. A terrace is now going in, a replacement for the greenhouse at front." The influence of the garden clubs still persists at Ijams Nature Center today. Both organizations, as well as the City of Knoxville, have permanent appointee representatives on Ijams's board of directors.

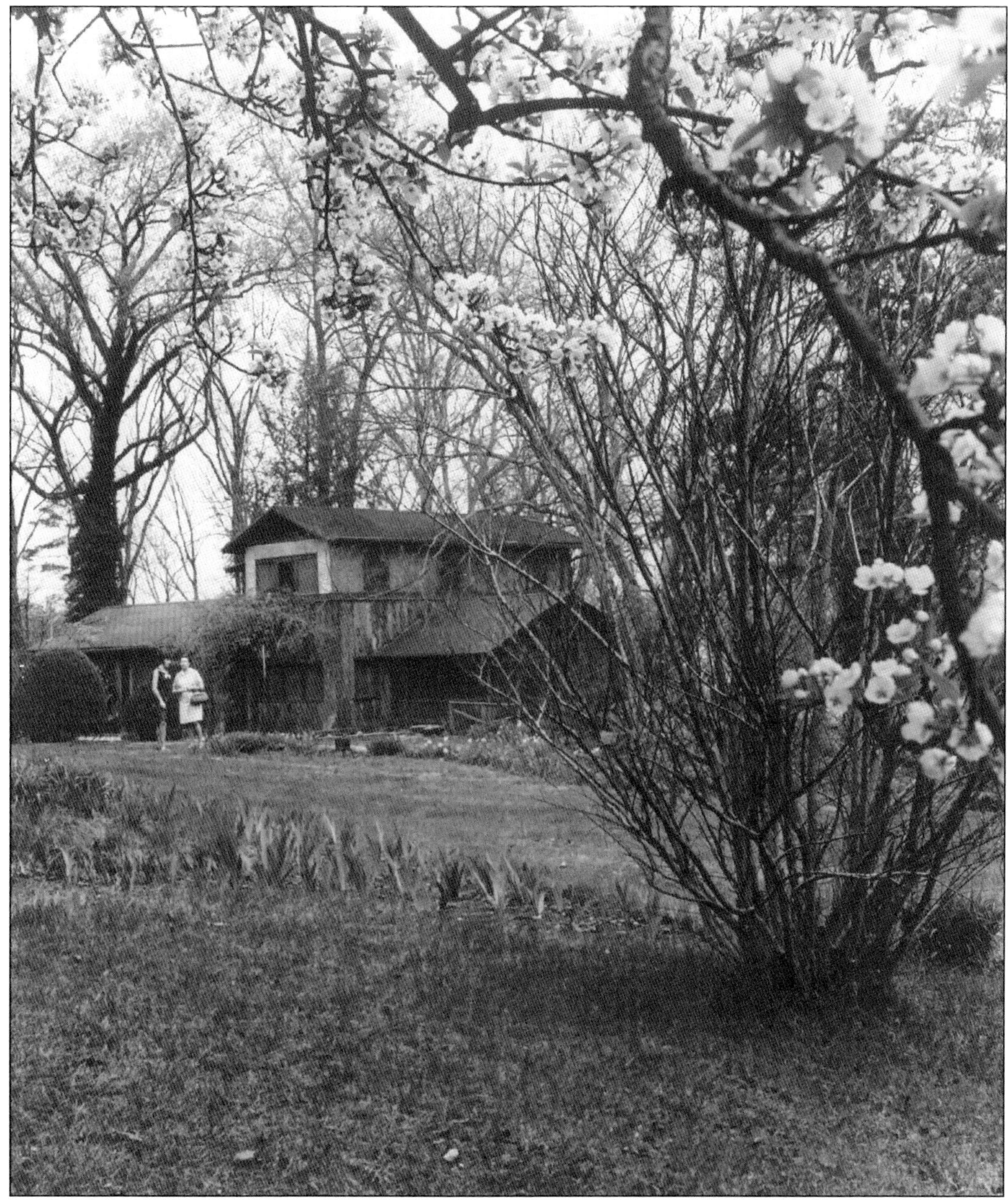

This photograph shows the house from a distance during the mid-1960s, when restoration efforts were still continuing. Even 40 years after H. P. Ijams renovated the original log cabin, the house still maintained a picturesque setting. Mary Fleury, a leading member of the Knoxville Garden Club, complimented H. P. Ijams on his lifetime's work: "Mr. Ijams was a professional artist and his layout of the grounds is excellent. The house, rustic in design, is an adaptation to, rather than an intrusion on, the setting. The entrance is flanked by a lily pool and large boxwoods, and at the rear is a terrace edged by huge boxwoods and a rock wall planted with alpines."

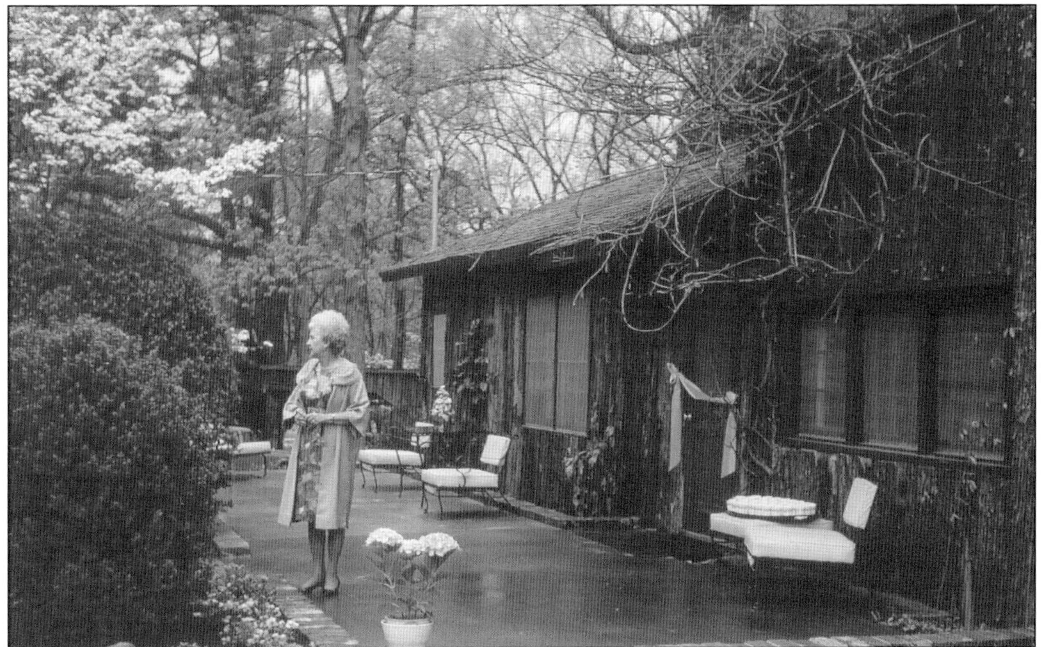

Mrs. Fred A. Hoeke (Eve), vice president of the Knox County Council of Garden Clubs, awaits fellow members to celebrate the ribbon cutting on the Ijams clubhouse. In the years following the opening of the new park, many plants and trees were labeled, and a self-guided trail guide was produced by landscape architect Roger B. Thompson, with a cover designed by Jo Ijams Kern.

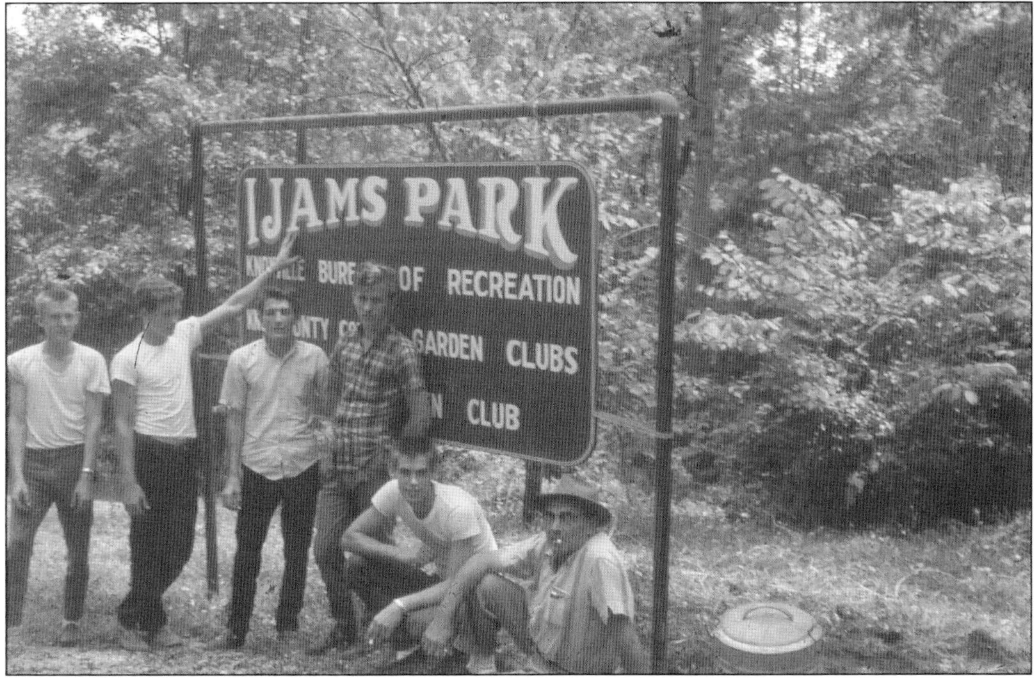

Partially obscured by a group of job corps volunteers, a new entrance sign recognizes the Knoxville Bureau of Recreation, Knox County Council of Garden Clubs, and Knoxville Garden Club for their efforts in creating and maintaining the new Ijams Park in 1966.

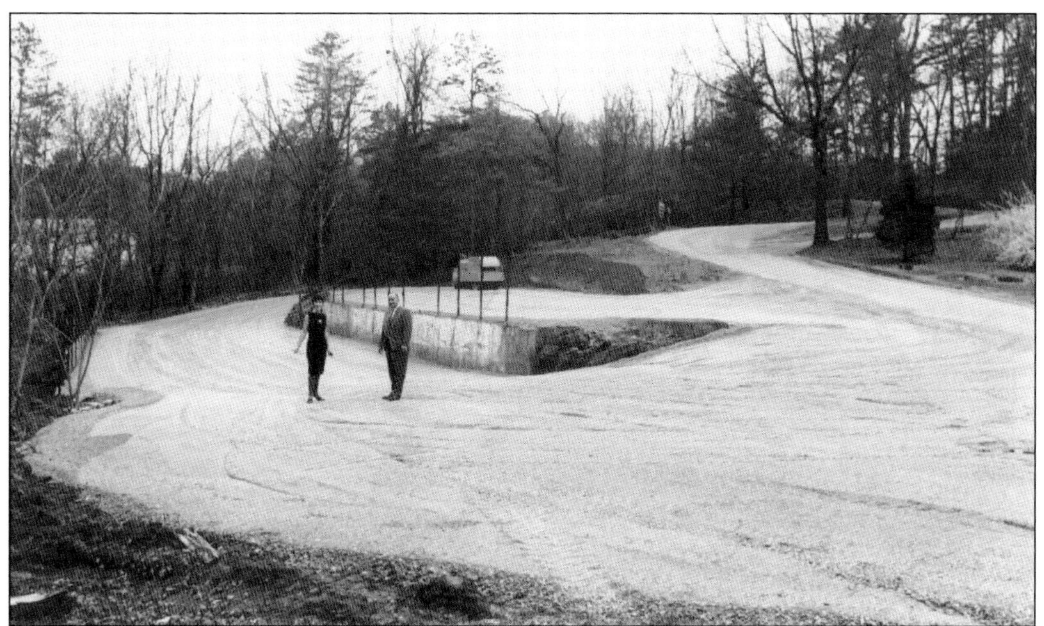

In March 1968, Mrs. L. E. Broyles (Ijams Park cochair) and Maynard Glen (city recreation director) check on the progress of the new parking facility where Alice Ijams's greenhouses once stood. Following the restoration of the house, the city also invested in park infrastructure, including restroom facilities and an underground water system.

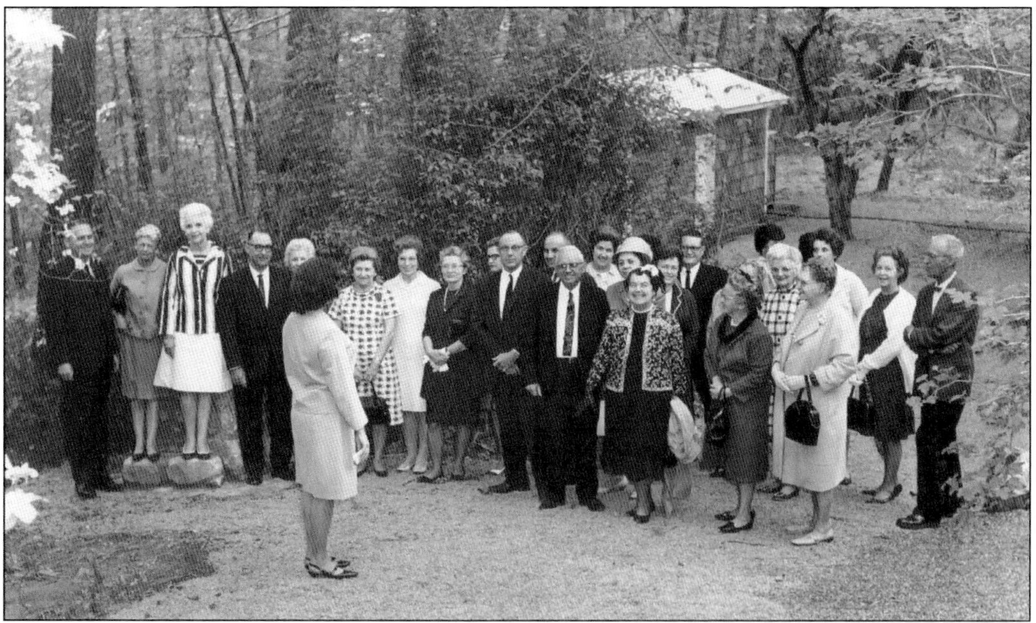

On the eve of the Dogwood Arts Festival on April 18, 1968, Mayor Leonard Rogers, Rep. John Duncan, and William McCammon, director of Metropolitan Planning Commission (front row center), pose with representatives from the Knoxville Garden Club and the Knox County Council of Garden Clubs to dedicate the new Ijams Park. Elizabeth Dunlap is pictured second from left, and Jo Ijams Kern, Ijams Park cochair, is eighth from left. Landscape architect Roger B. Thompson is on the far right. (*Knoxville News Sentinel.*)

Eight

An Emerging Nature Center

During the late 1960s and early 1970s, the Ijams Nature Park continued the philosophy of the Ijams family by offering volunteer-led nature and wildlife education programs to the public. As momentum gathered among board members and supporters such as Mary Fleury and Dr. Paul Wishart, the organization began to attract greater numbers of visitors and program participants. In 1976, Ijams Nature Center, Inc., was created as a formal nonprofit organization with the ability to raise revenue to expand programs and improve facilities. Shortly afterwards, the Knoxville Garden Club funded a two-year position for a part-time director, Harry Riley, who resided at the house, developed programs, and added benches, kiosks, and signage. The Knoxville Audubon Chapter renewed its interest in Ijams and created a friends club to support operations, including new trail guides, brochures, and a checklist of birds.

Over recent decades, a succession of full-time directors—Doris Gove, Sally Mirick, Bo Townsend, Diane Madison, and Paul James—and dedicated staff have built upon the foundations laid by the Ijams family, local garden clubs, and volunteers. In 1990, an adjacent 63-acre tract was acquired and funded by the City of Knoxville and a State of Tennessee land grant. This expansion inspired plans to develop a series of additional trails and build a new visitor center. A $5-million capital campaign launched in the early 1990s and chaired by Sherri P. Lee and Bill Miller attracted major support from the City of Knoxville, the Tennessee Valley Authority, and many corporate and individual donors. Ground-breaking occurred in 1995, with the visitor center officially opening to the public in May 1997.

During recent years, a number of significant projects have expanded the impact and scope of Ijams Nature Center. The addition of the former Mead's and John Ross marble quarries has extended the park far beyond the dreams of the Ijams family. In addition, a river boardwalk, raptor enclosure, and numerous interpretive exhibits, along with traditional science discovery programs, Scout workshops, and new education initiatives such as Living Clean and Green, Ijams Recycles, and First Child in the Woods have all contributed to Ijams's reputation as a leading wildlife sanctuary and environmental learning center.

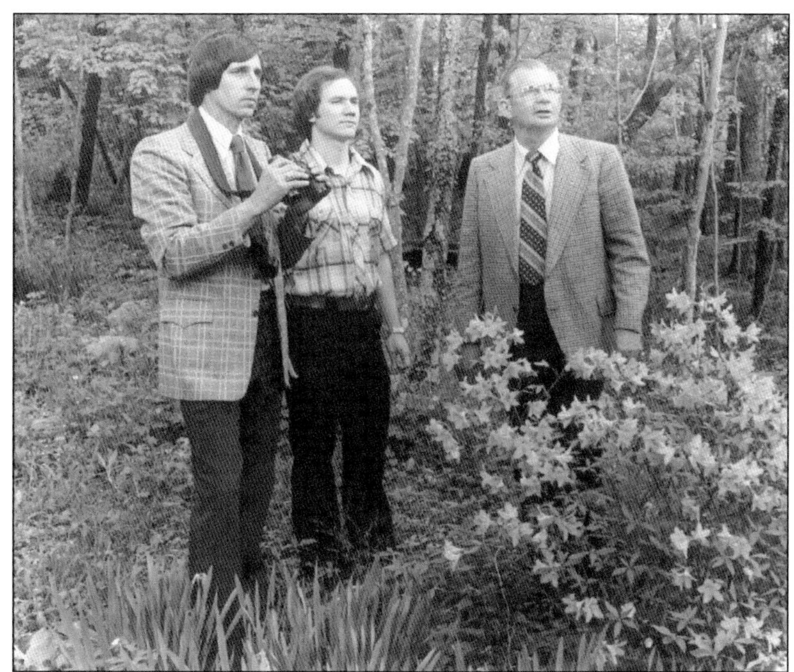

Ijams Nature Center was officially incorporated in 1976 as a nonprofit organization. The staff and board began preparing a new facilities plan and sought expert advice from other established nature centers. Paul Knoop (left), director of Aullwood Audubon Nature Center in Dayton, Ohio, looks for birdlife with Ijams director Harry Riley (center) and city councilman Howard Temple in April 1978.

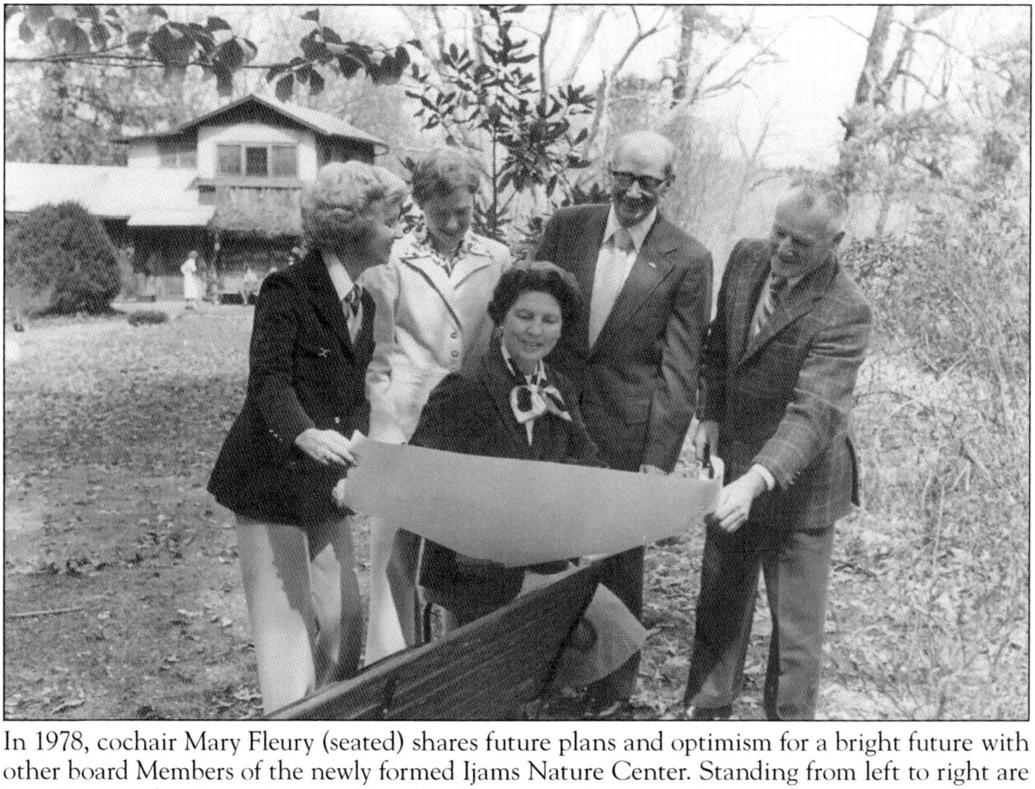

In 1978, cochair Mary Fleury (seated) shares future plans and optimism for a bright future with other board Members of the newly formed Ijams Nature Center. Standing from left to right are Mrs. Raymond F. Evans, Mrs. Gale Hedrick, Carson Chapin, and Harry Nacey Jr.

Ijams Nature Center board members take a stroll along the Discovery Trail overlooking the Tennessee River on March 27, 1978. The small island below, previously dubbed "Toehead Island" by the Ijams girls, has been known in recent years as Otter Island due to sightings of the aquatic mammals there. As a result, the island is rarely visited to protect undisturbed habitat. Pictured are treasurer Marilyn Dick (left) and cochairs Hugh Neil and Mrs. J. L. Greene.

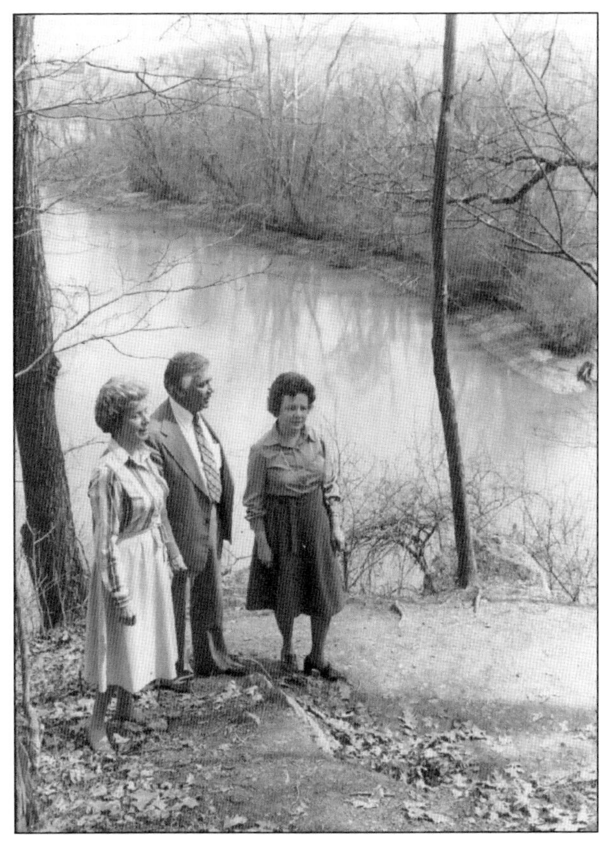

Around 1992, Ijams director Bo Townsend holds a planning meeting regarding the new visitor center at the former Ijams home, which served as park headquarters for many years. From left to right are Todd Witcher, Pam Petko-Seus, Jackie Lane, Debbie Godwin Kinnard, Lynda Ridgel, Jean Terry, and Bo Townsend.

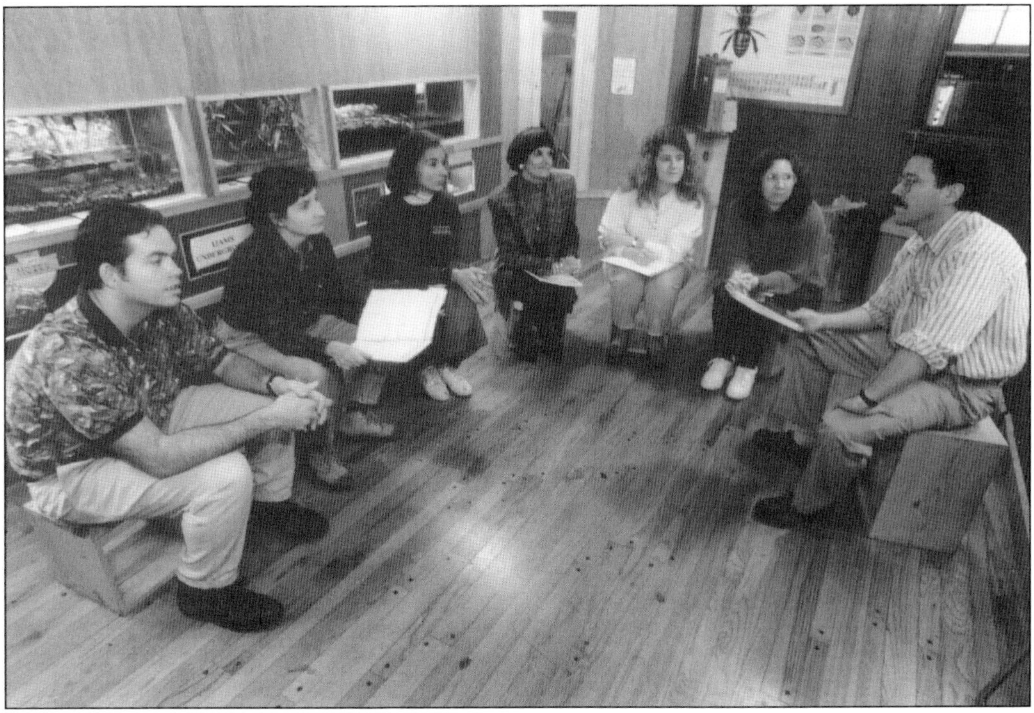

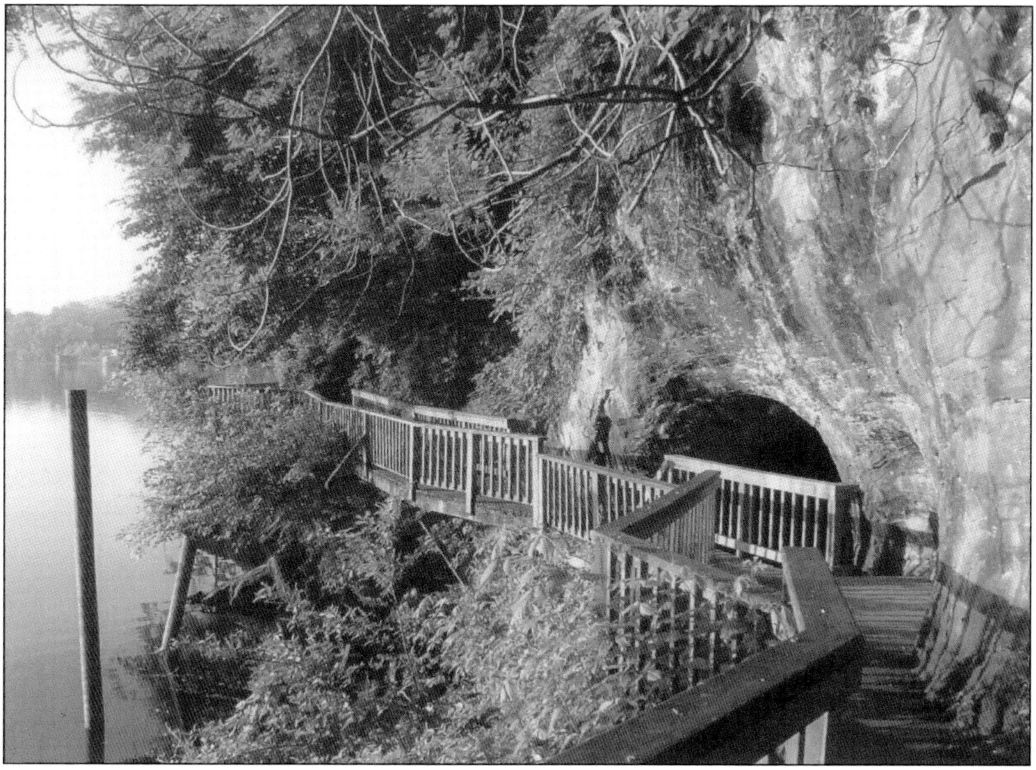

In 1998, Ijams opened up a previously inaccessible section of the wildlife sanctuary along the river bluff. The new River Trail featured an extensive boardwalk along the Tennessee River. Don Niday, Paul Forsyth, and others used all their craftsmanship and ingenuity to create the structure by rappelling from the rocks and working from below on floating platforms. The boardwalk has since become one of the most popular destination points for Ijams visitors.

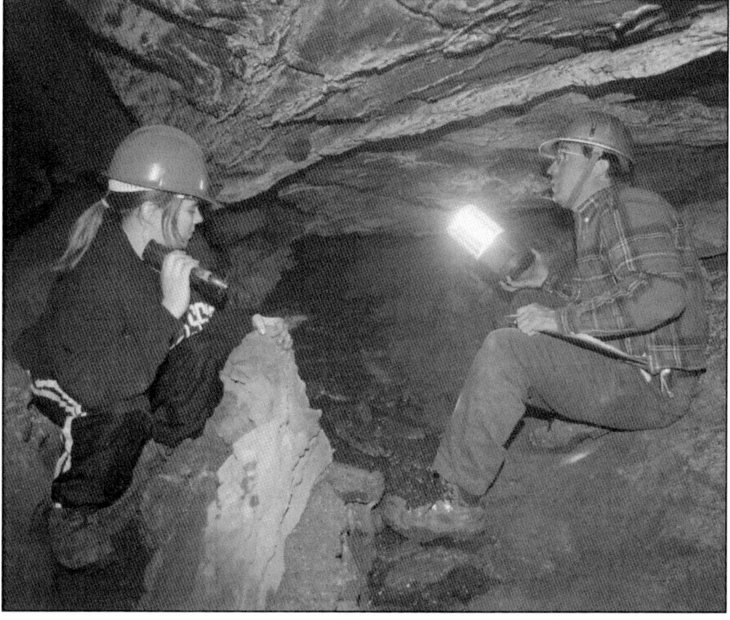

Park manager Ed Yost assists student Tracy Williams in documenting natural findings in the cave on the Tennessee River boardwalk. The cave was gated in 1997 by the nation's leading cave gate expert, Roy Powers, to act as a safety precaution for visitors and also to protect a resident bat population. Since the cave is only accessed once or twice a year by small controlled groups, the wildlife habitat and populations of cave life have dramatically increased.

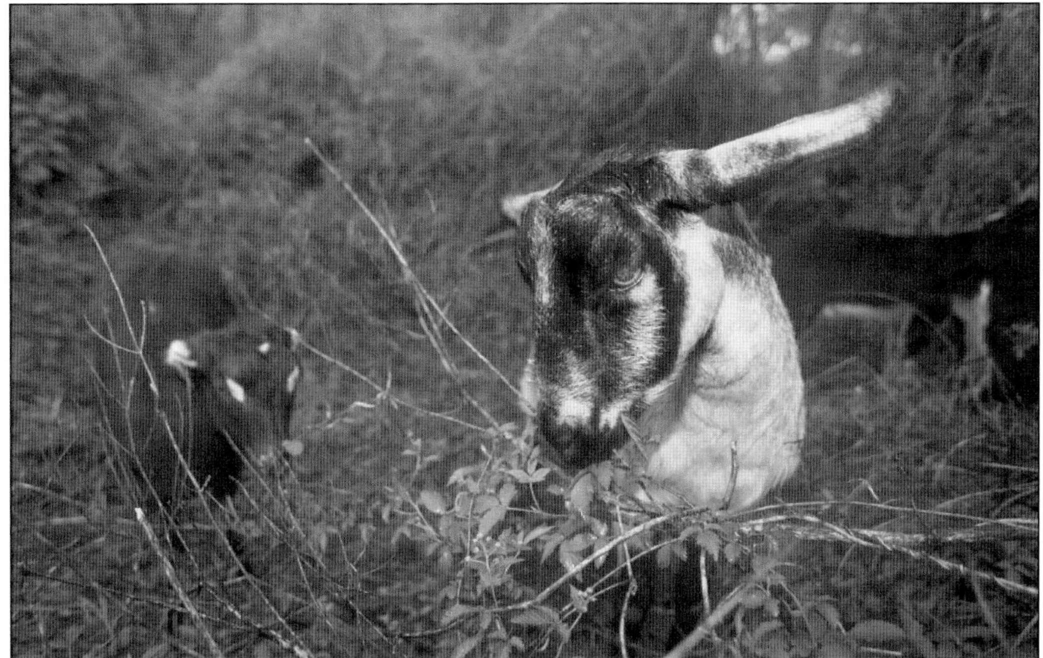

In 1997, this charming goat named Hans was brought in from the Blount County 4-H Club along with four others to help contain invasive, non-native plants spreading throughout the park. A kudzu field once covered the area where the visitor center is now located, and while invasive plants such as privet and Japanese honeysuckle remain a constant threat, willing volunteers of all ages generously share their time and efforts every year to make a huge contribution to the management of the wildlife sanctuary. (*Knoxville News Sentinel.*)

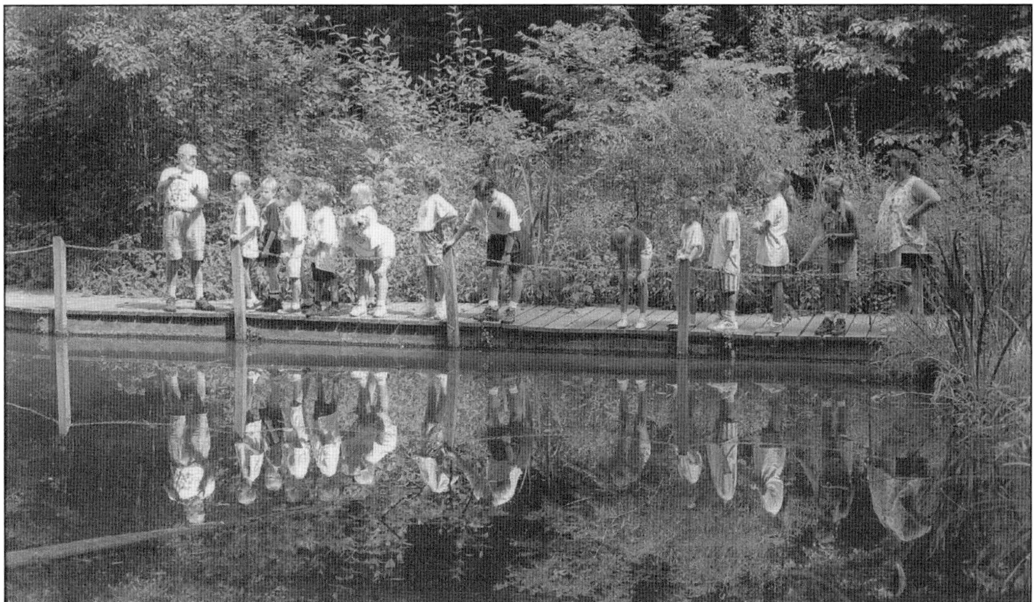

Almost 90 years after H. P. Ijams dammed up a spring-fed pond to form a pool for his daughters, the Lotus Pond is a frequent station for all age groups on nature hikes. Here the late Dr. Bob Harris, a volunteer naturalist, explains the intricacies of a pond ecosystem to a group of youngsters.

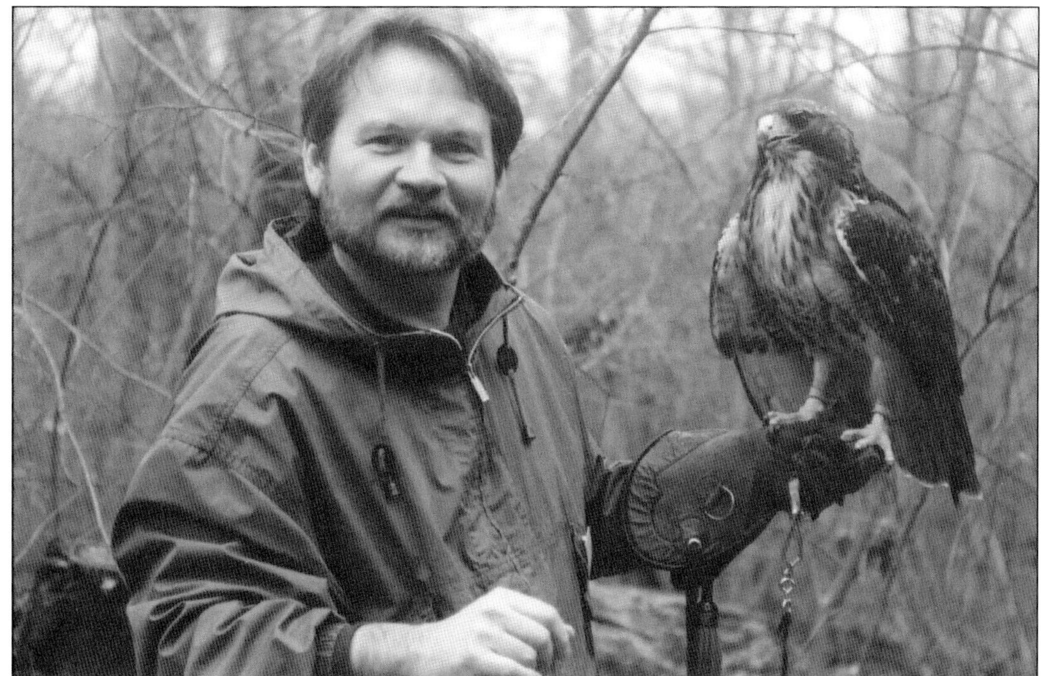

Ijams's non-releasable birds of prey form a powerful component throughout many of Ijams Nature Center's educational programs. Before joining the staff, Lyn Bales worked as a volunteer for two years, spending countless hours getting to know Ijams's resident red-tailed hawk. Over the years, staff and experienced volunteers have racked up thousands of hours showing educational hawks, owls, and snakes to people of all ages.

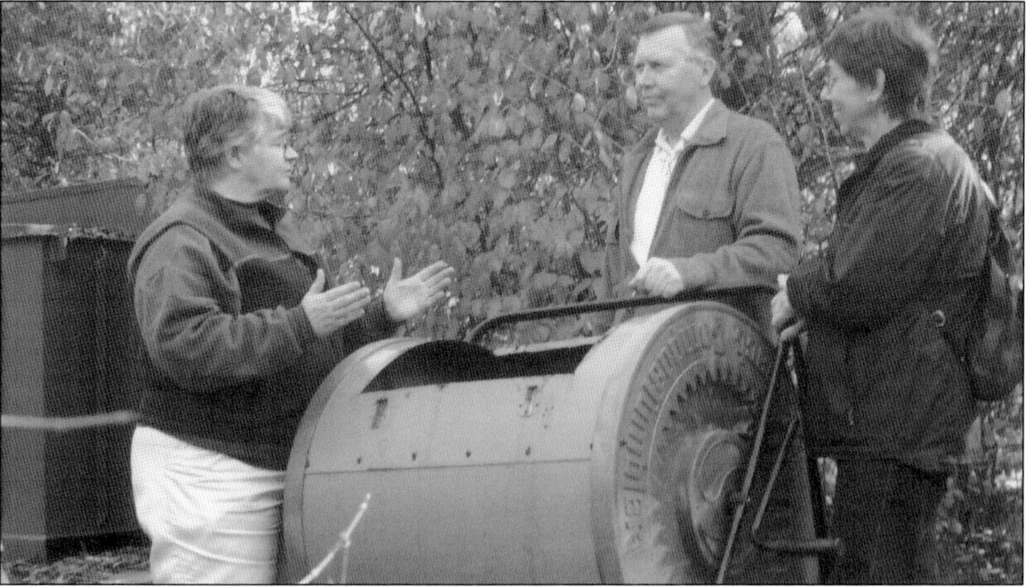

Educator Peg Beute leads a composting demonstration during a workshop, part of the Living Clean and Green educational series created in 2002 in partnership with Knoxville Utilities Board. In its first seven years, the series engaged more than 26,000 program participants through almost 1,000 programs at Ijams and throughout the community.

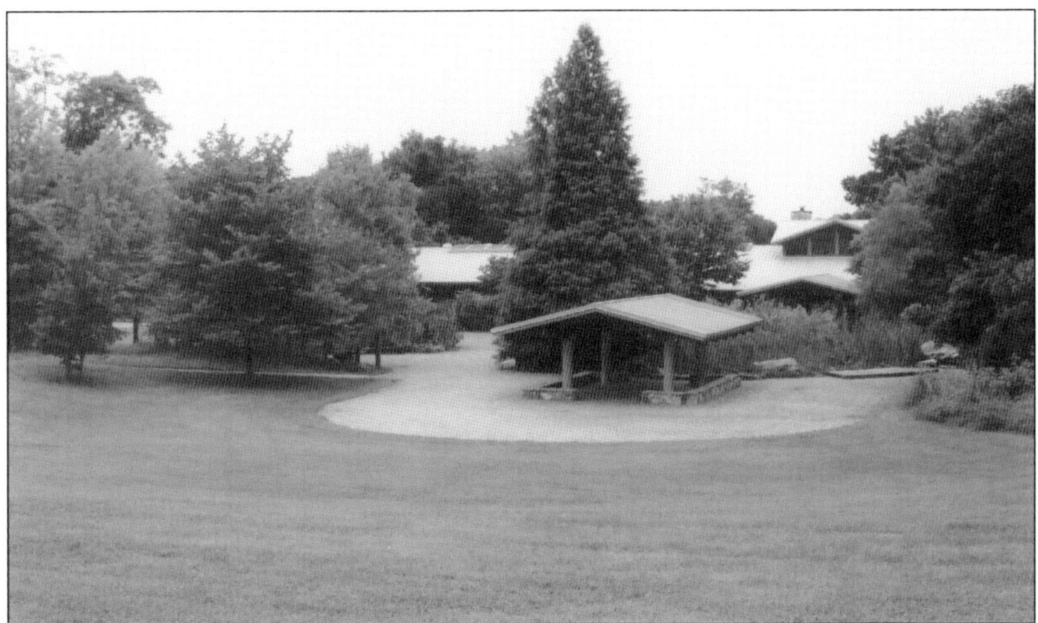

Where invasive kudzu once sprawled, the visitor center nestles seamlessly within its natural surroundings. The native landscaping has significantly matured since the new site opened in 1997, and the Universal Pond in front of the building is a popular learning station for Nature Preschoolers and students on science discovery expeditions.

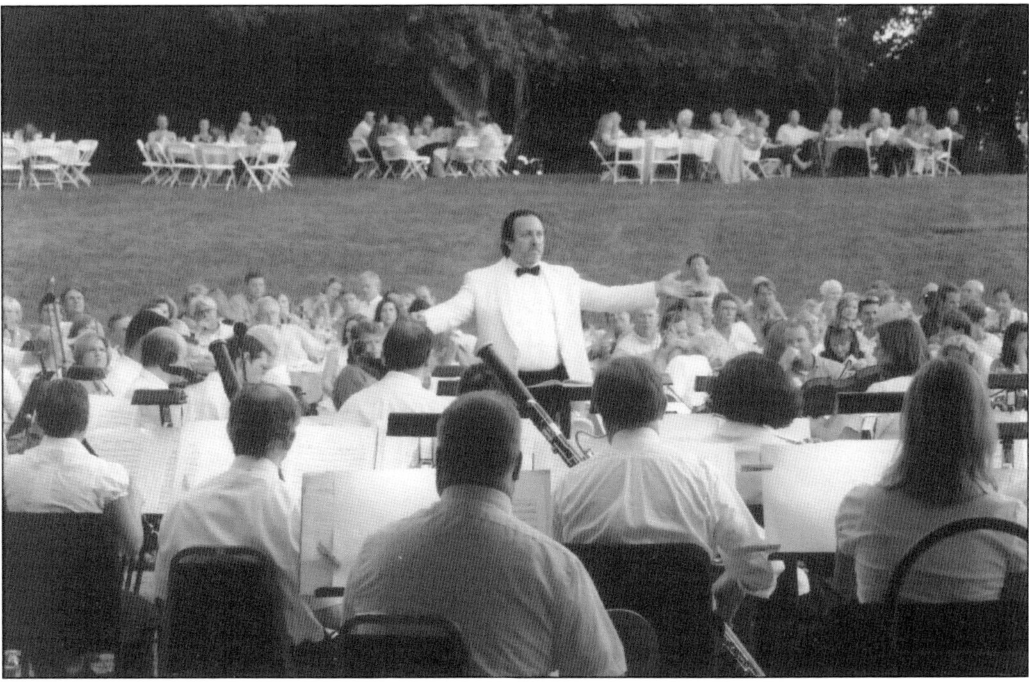

Created by Sherri P. Lee in 1986, the annual Symphony in the Park event is Ijams Nature Center's largest and most successful fund-raising event. Each September, the Knoxville Symphony Orchestra, here led by Maestro Lucas Richman, performs a memorable musical program in the twilight of a fall evening.

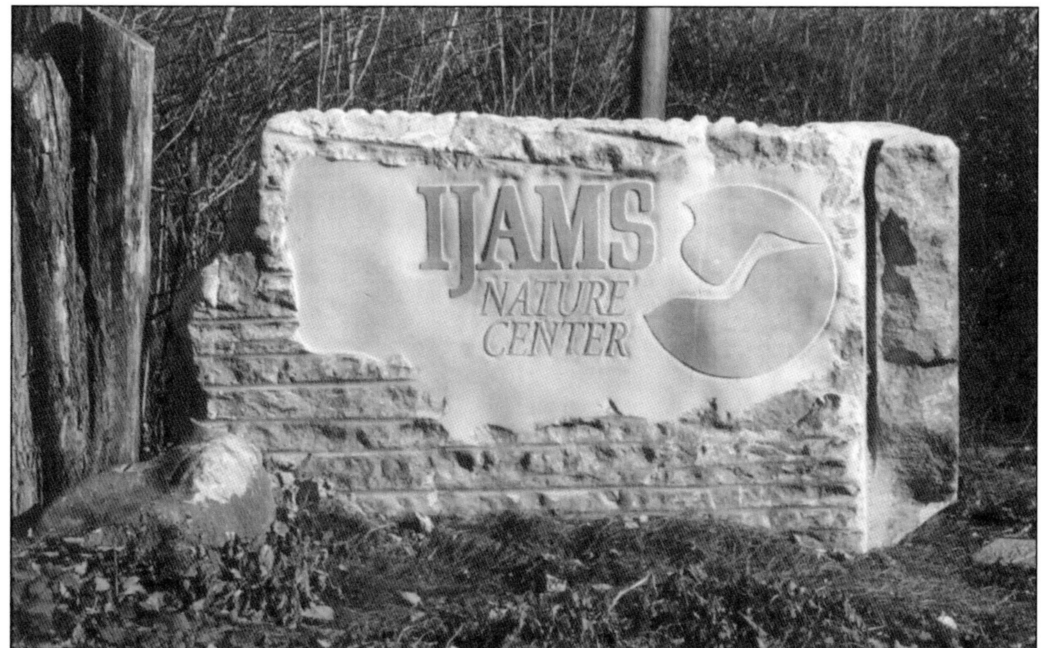

Abandoned blocks of Tennessee marble made unique entrance stones to Ijams Nature Center's main site and Mead's Quarry site. The stones were carved on site by Bruce Bennett's crew at Custom Marble and Design, who also work out of studios at the former Candoro Marble Company in Vestal, South Knoxville.

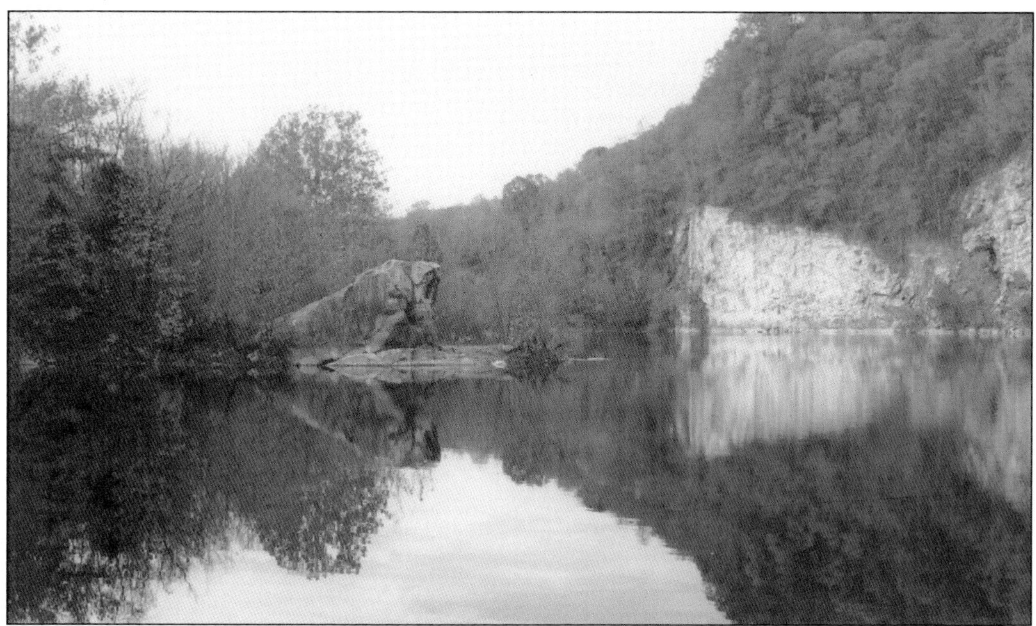

Despite Mead's Quarry being used as an illegal dump for many years, the water quality in the lake is remarkable, as evidenced by sightings of freshwater jellyfish. Nature is slowly but surely reclaiming the site, and the lake provides wildlife habitat for turtles, coots, Canada geese, and many other species. In 2008, a rare sighting of a diving duck showed the North American redhead pausing and enjoying a brief rest on the water before migrating south.

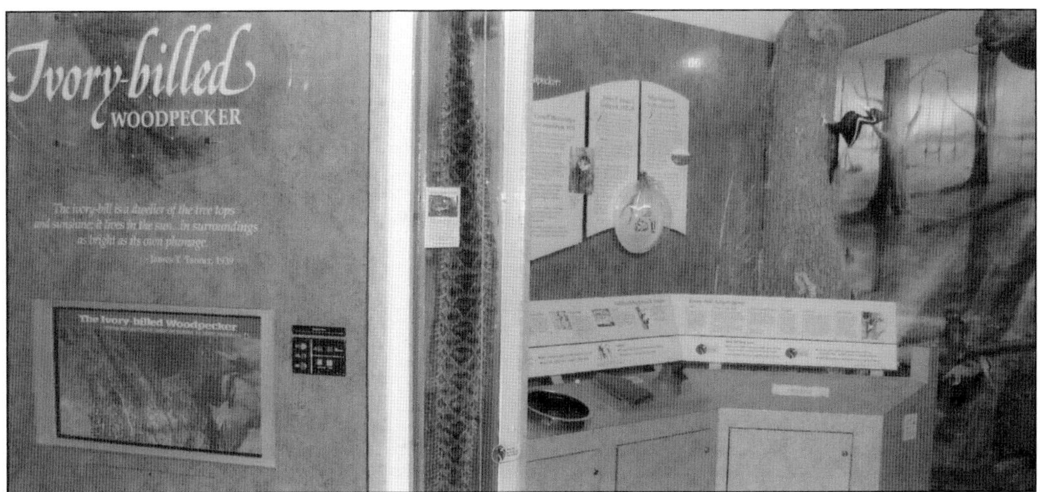

In 2006, a Lost Species exhibit was installed featuring original artworks and carvings by Randal Martin, Midori Barstow, Gene Canning, and others. Accompanying the stories of the extinct passenger pigeon and ivory-billed woodpecker, as told through the words of H. P. Ijams and Dr. James Tanner, is an interactive media kiosk featuring rare footage and photographs taken by Tanner during the legendary 1935 Cornell expedition.

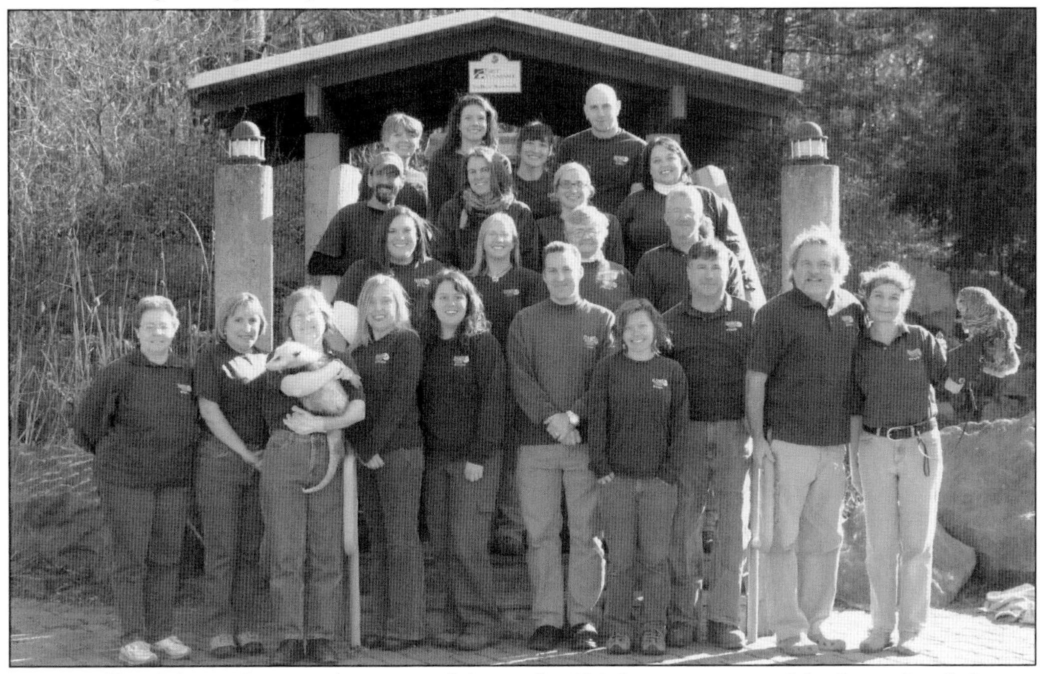

Ijams staff and AmeriCorps volunteers celebrate the 100th anniversary of the Ijams family legacy in 2010. Pictured from left to right are (first row) Sheila Goforth, Sally Judiscak, Louise Conrad (with opossum), Sabrina DeVault, Jennifer Ugolino (AmeriCorps), Paul James, Emily Boves, Ed Yost, Lyn Bales, and Pam Petko-Seus (with barred owl); (second row) Meredith Hess (AmeriCorps), Sarah Brobst, Peg Beute, and Paul Forsyth; (third row): Ben Nanny, Kimberly Womack, Kara Remington, and Jennifer Moore; (fourth row) Marielle Robertson, Kristy Keel (AmeriCorps), Jennifer Teagarden (AmeriCorps), and Travis Williams (AmeriCorps). Not pictured are Rachel Plausche and Ryan Worden.

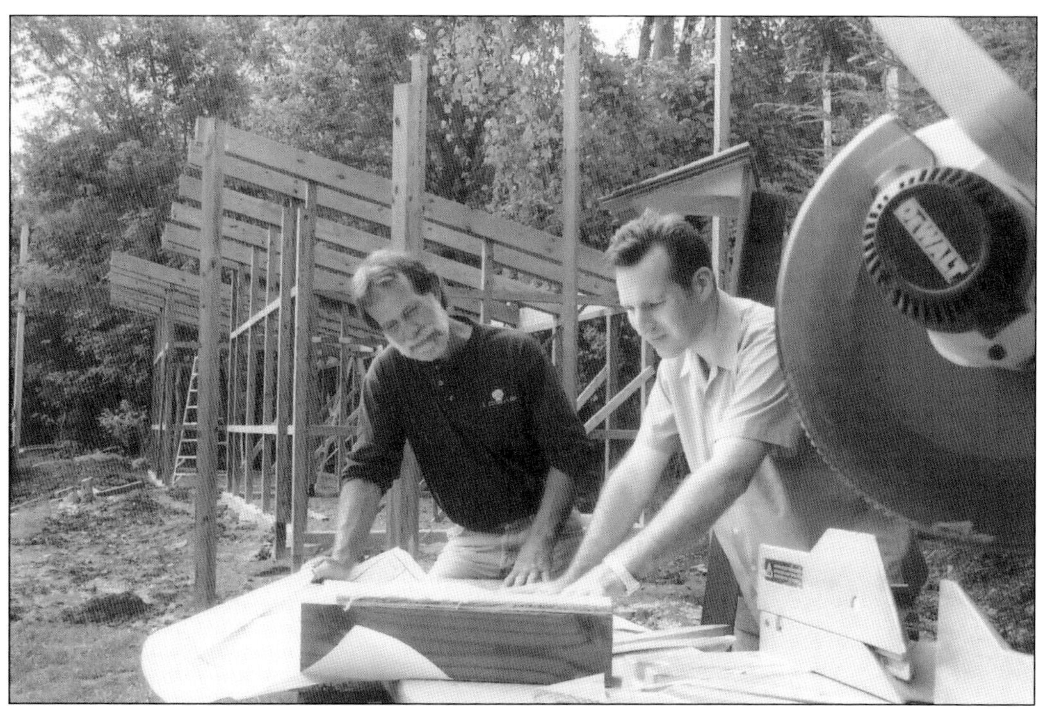

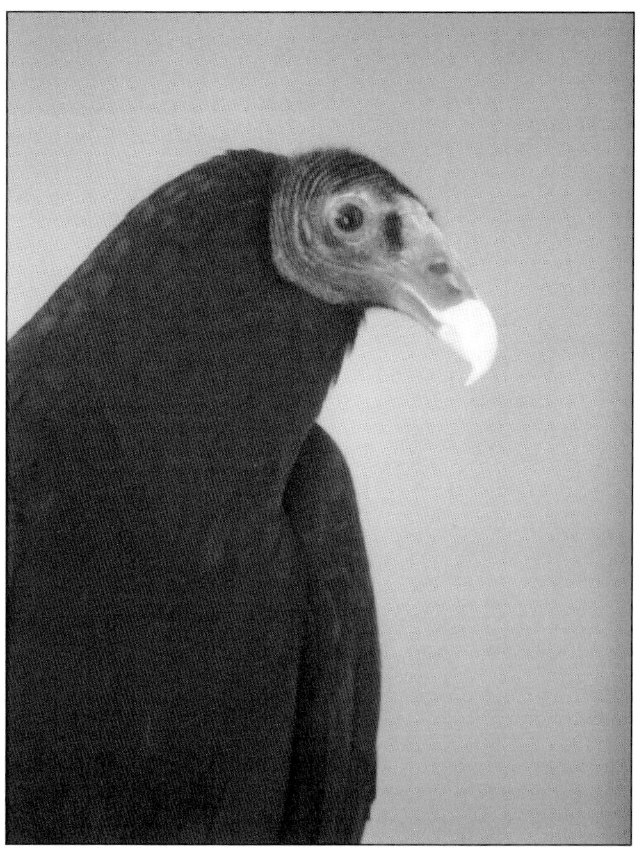

Don Niday was the creative force behind a number of capital improvements during recent years, including the Tennessee River boardwalk, the staircase and viewing platform at Mead's Quarry, and cabinetry for the Lost Species exhibits. Here Niday (left) and executive director Paul James review plans for the new raptor enclosure. The enclosure was built in 2004 to house non-releasable birds of prey.

The first birds to move into the raptor enclosure in 2004 included a red-tailed hawk and a turkey vulture supplied by the American Eagle Foundation. The vulture was found as an immature bird by the side of a road and fed by humans long enough to be considered "imprinted," a term used to describe behavioral learning early in life. Despite its reputation as a gloomy scavenger, the vulture plays a vital role as a member of nature's cleanup crew.

Nine

Tennessee Marble Quarries

Known as the "Marble City" in the 19th century, Knoxville has a long history of marble quarrying, with two active quarries adjacent to Ijams Nature Center. In 1881, the Ross Marble Company paid $100 for a plot of land on Island Home Pike and opened a new quarry to extract Tennessee marble. In 1892, the Ross Marble Company merged with the Republic Marble Company, becoming locally known as Mead's Quarry in honor of Frank S. Mead, the new company's first president. However, the quarry should be correctly known as "Island Home Quarry." At the peak of operations, the quarry produced between 25,000 and 35,000 cubic feet of marble per year and employed more than 100 workers, many of whom lived on site and patronized the company store. Adjacent to Mead's Quarry, further back towards Sevierville Pike, is another quarry formerly known as the John M. Ross Quarry, which was operated by the Knoxville Marble Company. However, by the Great Depression, demand for Tennessee marble had declined markedly, and both quarrying operations hit hard times.

In 1945, the Williams Limestone Company took over both operations to produce agricultural lime by baking small chunks of limestone in kilns. This continued until the late 1970s. However, a dark cloud hung over Mead's Quarry the last quarter of the 20th century, as the defunct operation and its isolated setting attracted illegal dumping and other crimes. Throughout the years, efforts by members of the local community, led by Minnie Tharp, encouraged local government and Ijams Nature Center to clean up the site and turn it into a park. Tharp's vision became a reality when Knox County purchased Mead's Quarry in 2001, and Ijams Nature Center opened the site to the public in 2005. The former John M. Ross Quarry, adjacent to Mead's, was donated by Imerys, Inc., in 2007 and incorporated into the Ijams wildlife sanctuary during Ijams's 100th anniversary year in 2010; it is now known as the Ross Marble Quarry.

With the help of many volunteers, the transformed quarries are now an extension of the Ijams wildlife sanctuary, complete with looped trails, overlooks, and observation points. Once again, the South Knoxville landmarks are appreciated for their natural resources, although in a more sustainable way and for the benefit of all people.

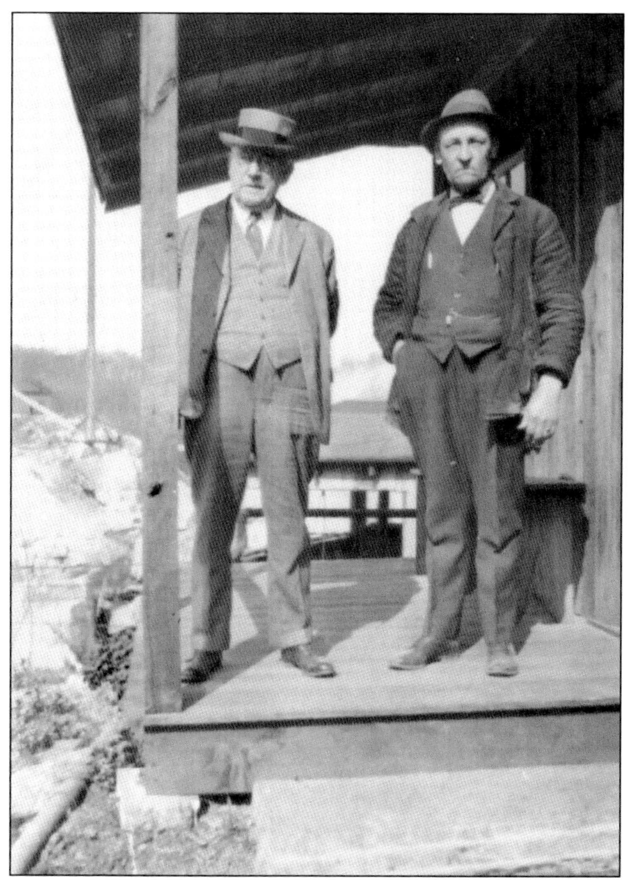

Mead's Quarry is named after Frank S. Mead (left), the first president of the Ross and Republic Marble Company, which originally opened in 1881. Mead also managed a similar quarry in Luttrell, Tennessee, before taking over operations on Island Home Pike. The gentleman to the right is a Mr. Harmon, although his title and function are unknown. (Knox County Two Centuries Photograph Project, McClung Historical Collection.)

The rough blocks of Tennessee marble extracted from the quarry face were taken to the mill, where they were cut and prepared for market. The facility also included a coal-burning furnace, which generated steam to power the channeling machines used to extract large blocks of marble. (Calvin M. McClung Historical Collection.)

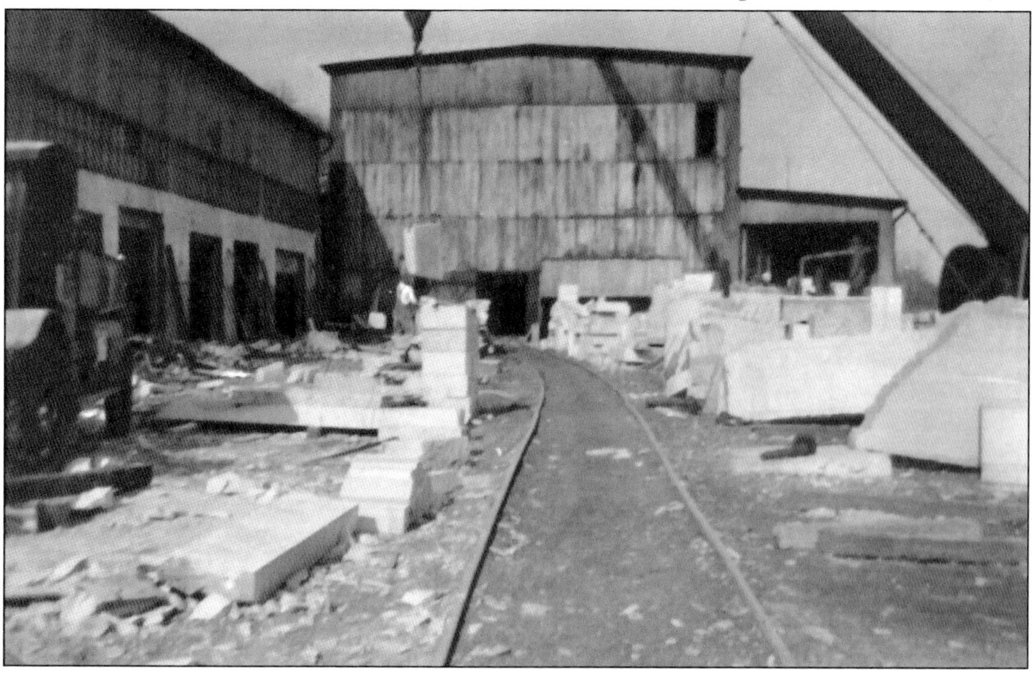

The quarrying operation, including these blacksmiths, often employed more than 100 men who earned 40¢ per hour during a 10-hour workday, which was reasonable pay back then. Cota Tharp, a quarry worker who lived most of his life near Mead's Quarry, once recalled, "That's the price of an eight-pound bucket of lard back then. You could send your kid to town on the trolley to the movies and he'd come back with change." (Knox County Two Centuries Photograph Project, McClung Historical Collection.)

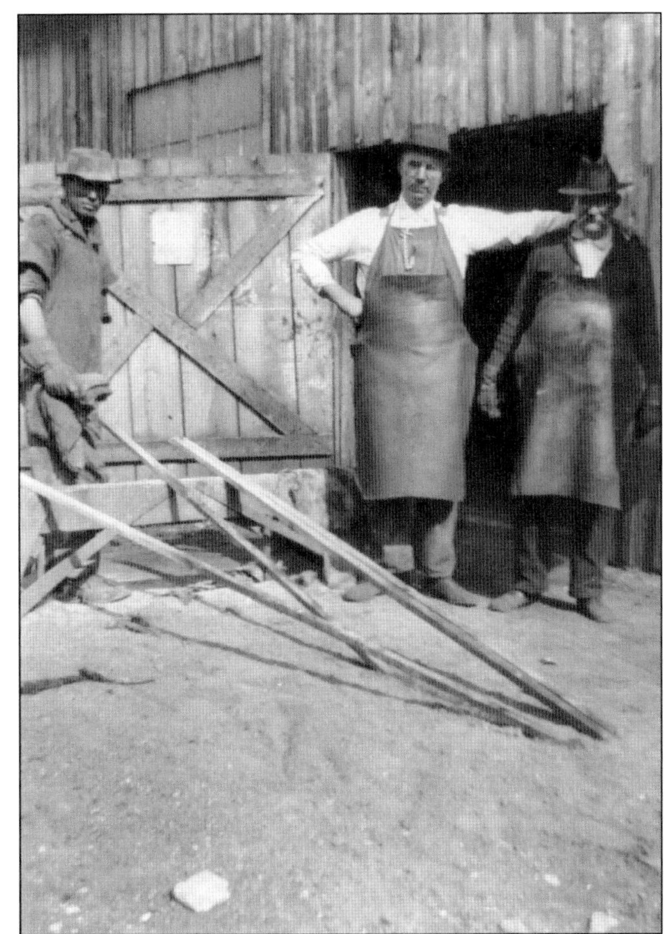

Log cabins and residences were provided for workers by the Ross and Republic Marble Company, which also ran a company commissary onsite. Workers' children were also sent to the three-room Mead's School, just along the road towards downtown on Island Home Avenue. (Knox County Two Centuries Photograph Project, McClung Historical Collection.)

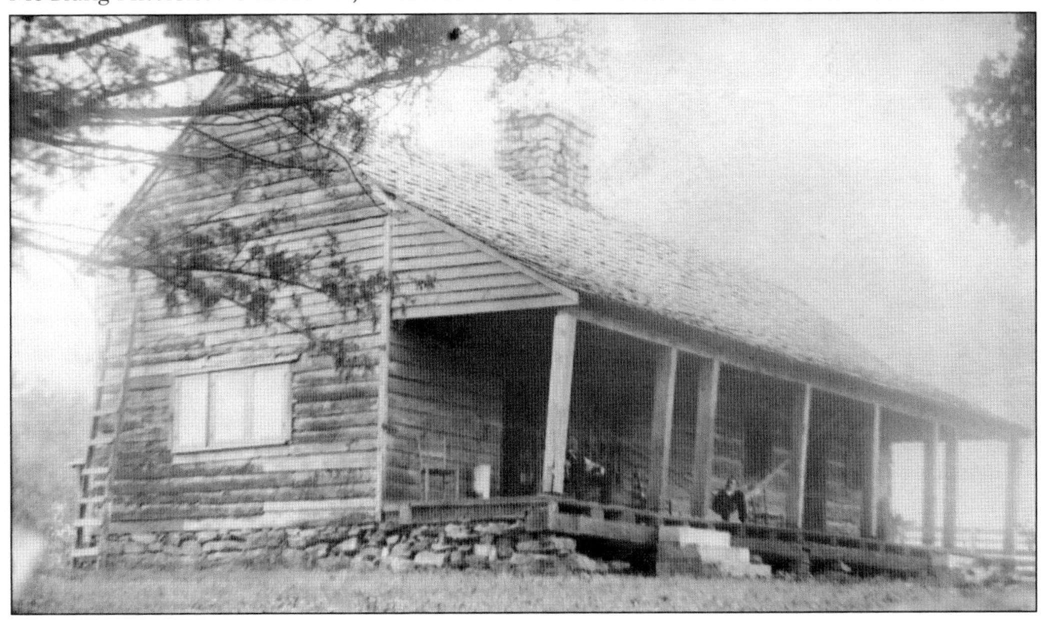

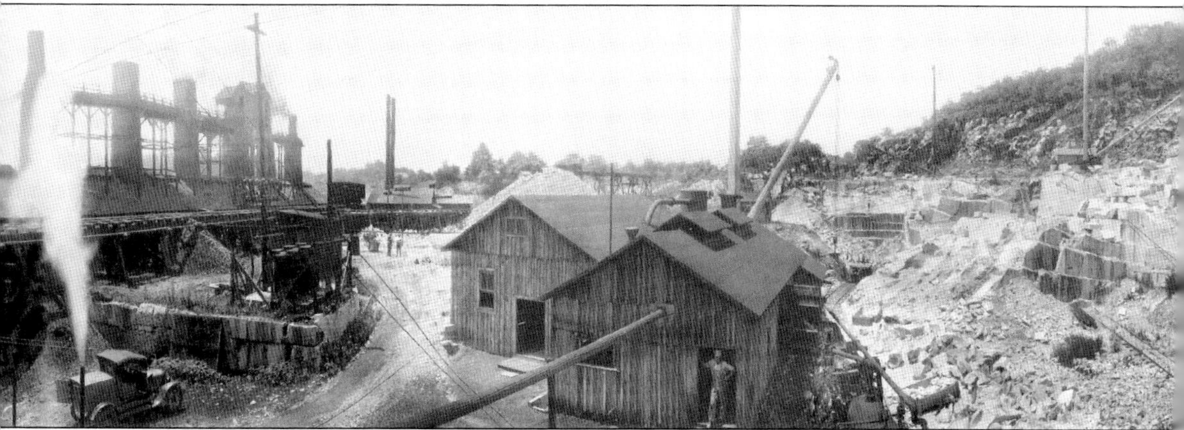

Jim or Robin Thompson, Knoxville's most famous photographers, captured this spectacular panoramic snapshot of operations at Mead's Quarry in the late 1920s. The quarry face is only partially excavated at this point, and rough cuts of Tennessee marble can clearly be seen near the railroad tracks to the right, waiting to be transported to the mill. Today the observation point at the

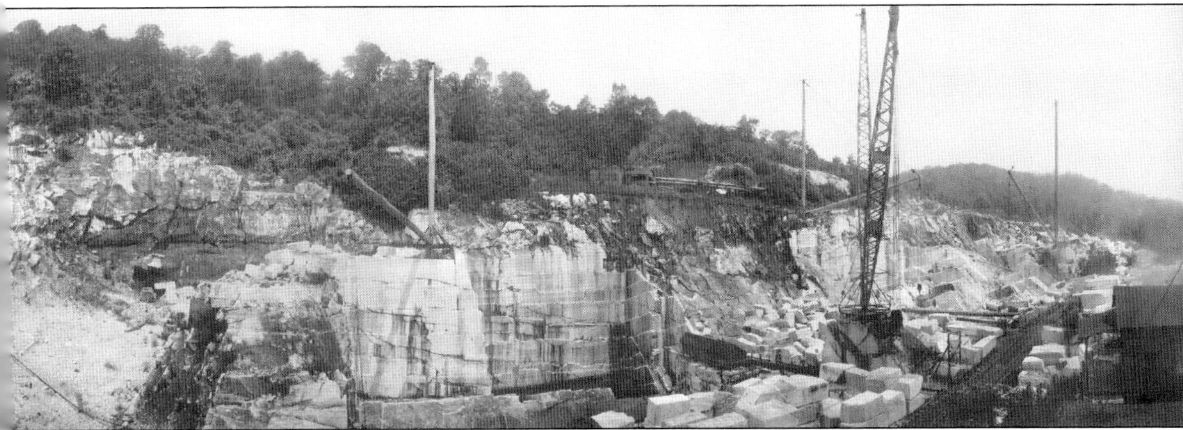

Interpretive Plaza overlooking the lake is situated where the first cabin on the left is shown. The derrick platform immediately to the right of the limekilns is now a picnic shelter. Overlooks at the far end of the lake and along the Tharp Trace loop trail afford spectacular views of the property and, on a clear day, a glimpse of Mount LeConte in the distance. (Thompson Photograph Collection.)

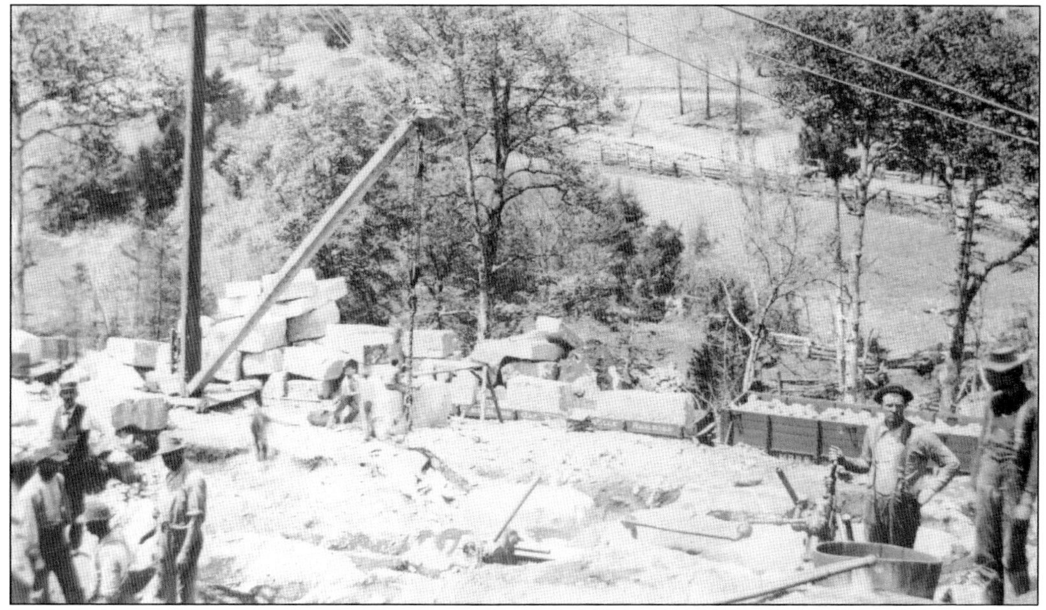

This scene shows a multidimensional view of the quarry operation, with workers hooking rough-cut marble blocks onto a crane winch before loading onto railcars, which are adorned with a sign for the Cumberland Gap and Knoxville Railroad. In the background, rustic fences mark the site's transition with the South Knoxville rural landscape. (Knox County Two Centuries Photograph Project, McClung Historical Collection.)

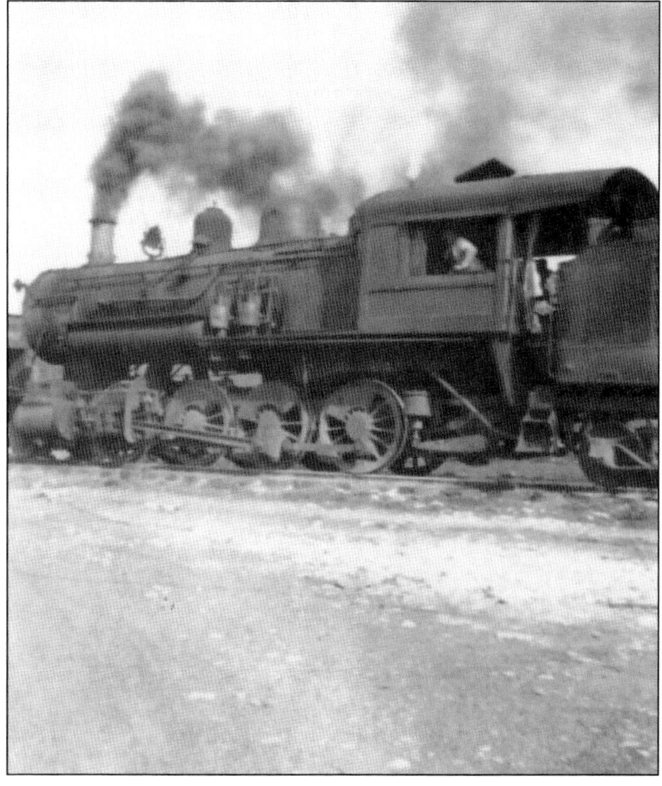

Steam trains filled with blocks of Tennessee marble hauled their loads to the bank of the Tennessee River just a short distance away. The blocks were then transferred to barges and floated downriver to Knoxville or other market destinations. When built in the early 1940s, the National Gallery of Art in Washington, D.C., required 800 railcars of Tennessee marble from Mead's and other local quarries. (Knox County Two Centuries Photograph Project, McClung Historical Collection.)

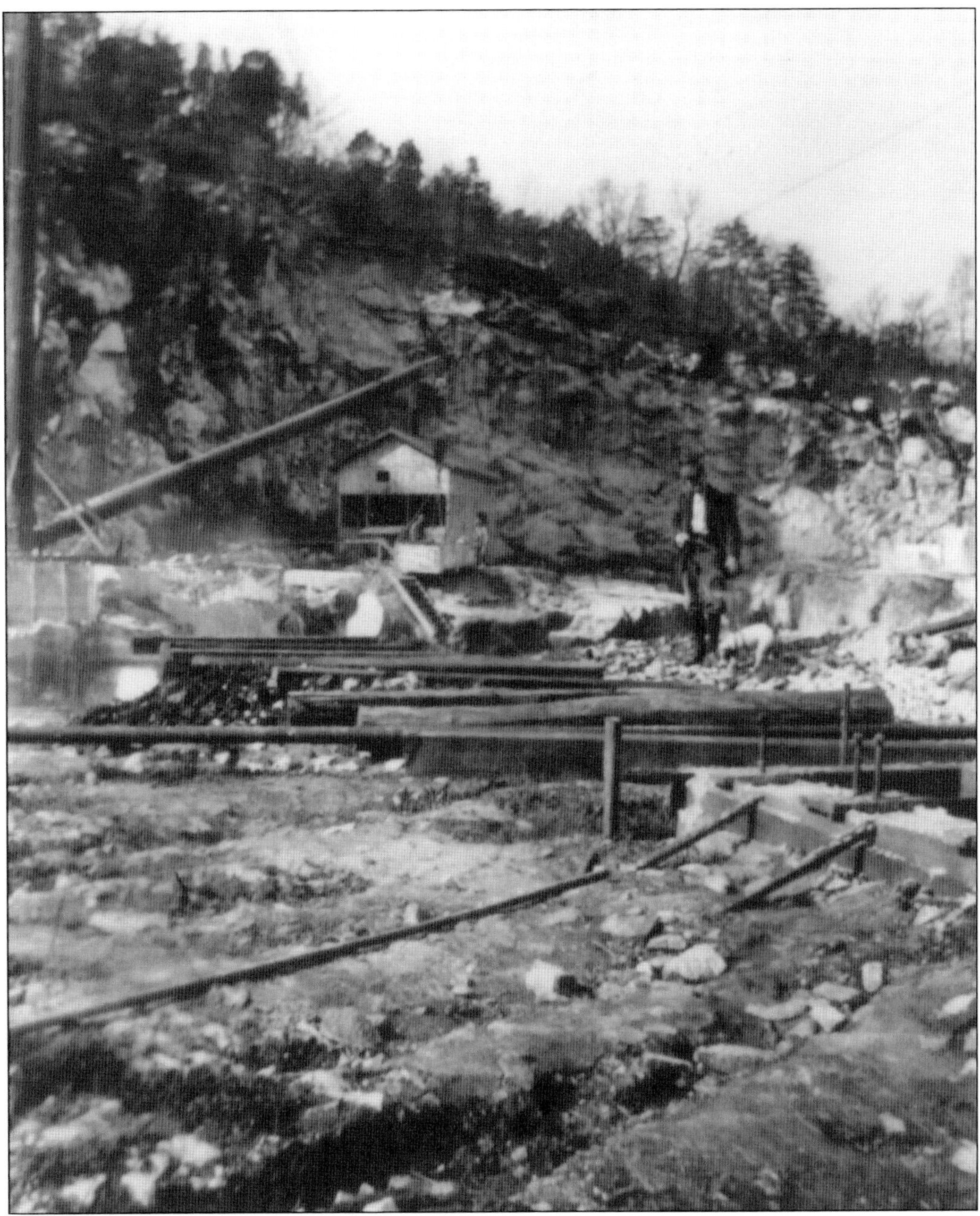

This photograph shows operations down in the quarry pit, which is now submerged. The unidentified man taking a leisurely stroll seems in stark contrast to the industrial milieu that occurred almost daily during the quarry's heyday. In the intervening years, the vegetation on top of the bluff has matured, and healthy woodland now envelops the Tharp Trace Trail, which traverses Mead's Quarry at Ijams Nature Center. (Knox County Two Centuries Photograph Project, McClung Historical Collection.)

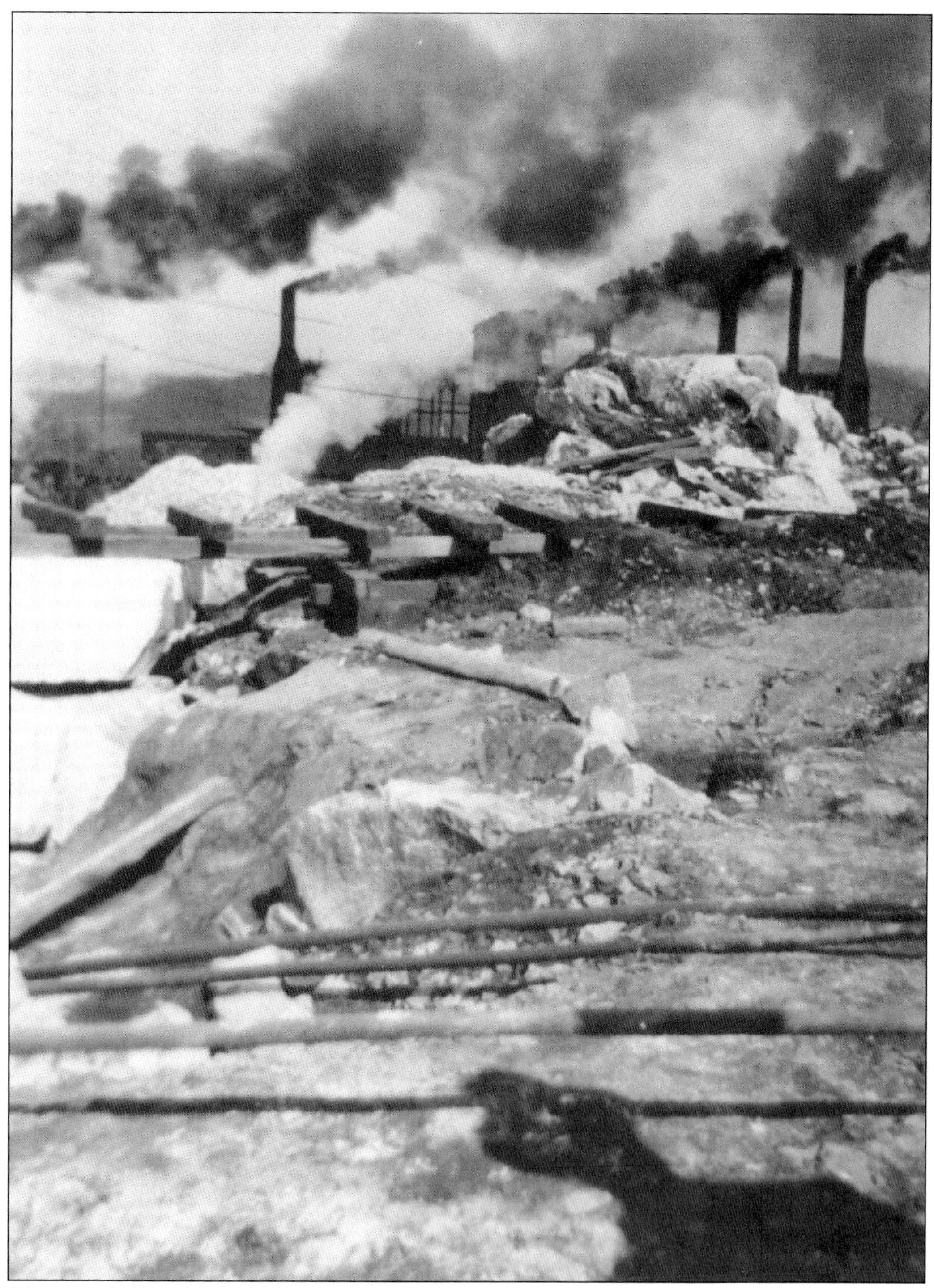

Chimneys billow thick black smoke during intensive operations at Mead's Quarry during the 1920s. Given the neighboring environment, it was truly a visionary act for Harry and Alice Ijams to develop a bird sanctuary on the adjacent property at the same time. (Knox County Two Centuries Photograph Project, McClung Historical Collection.)

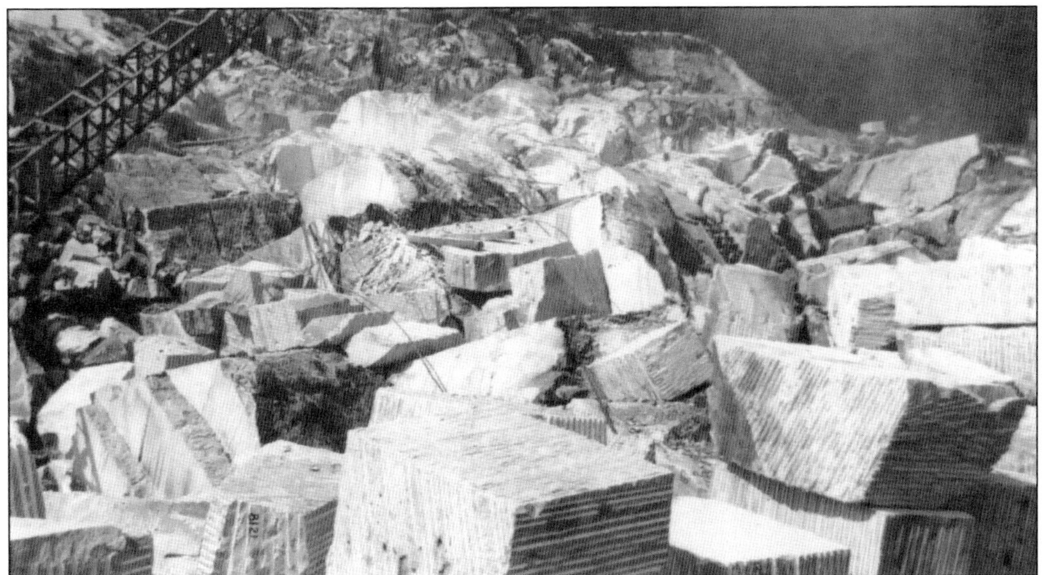

Piles of rough-cut blocks of Tennessee marble lay scattered in the quarry pit. In the foreground, parallel gorges on the blocks highlight where drilled holes formed a line along which the strain forces in the rock caused it to crack. This method prevented further cracking of the rock, resulting in better marble blocks for building purposes. (Knox County Two Centuries Photograph Project, McClung Historical Collection.)

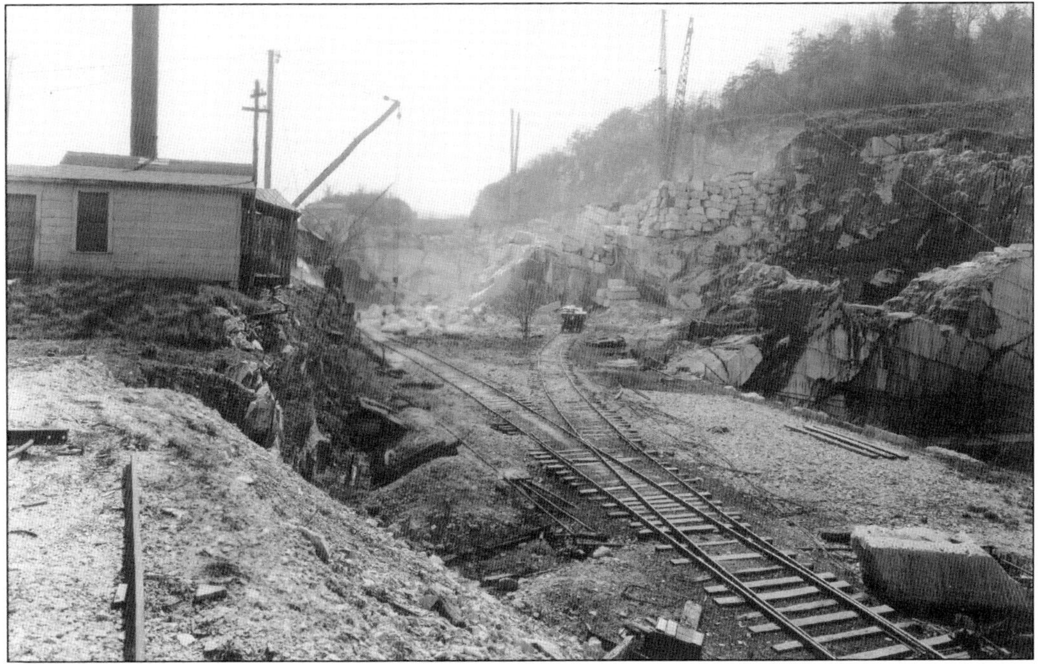

Railroad tracks leading directly into the quarry pit give some sense of the scale of activities at Mead's Quarry. During later operations, the water table was struck, and it was necessary to run pumps night and day to prevent the quarry from flooding. Nowadays, such a landscape forms the bottom of the quarry lake, which is approximately 80–100 feet deep in places. (Thompson Photograph Collection, McClung Historical Collection.)

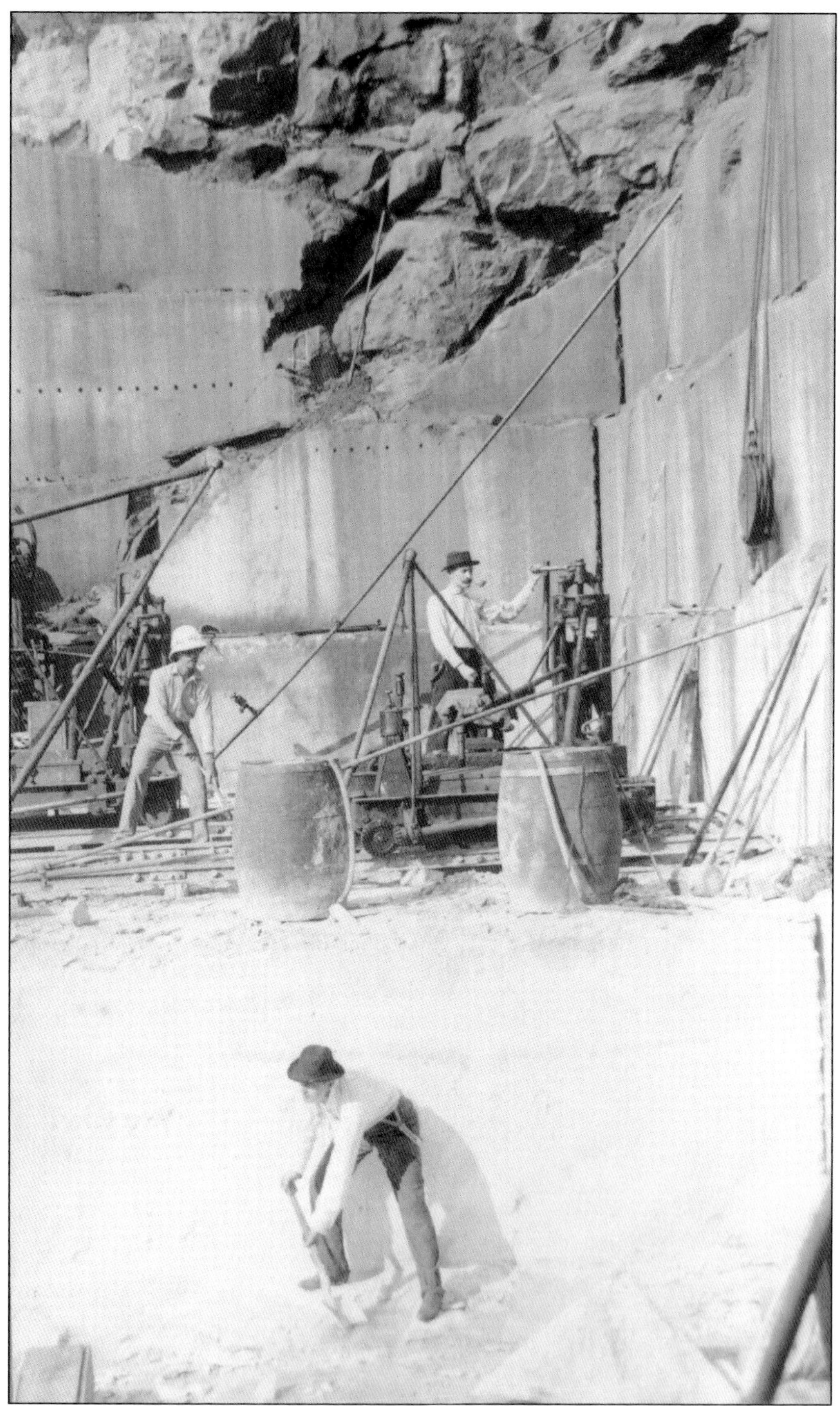

This photograph captures the quarrying operation, where machinery and hard labor went hand-in-hand to extract large blocks of stone. The smooth sides of the quarry face indicate that the operator seen on the right was highly skilled in the science and art of marble extraction. (Knox County Two Centuries Photograph Project, McClung Historical Collection.)

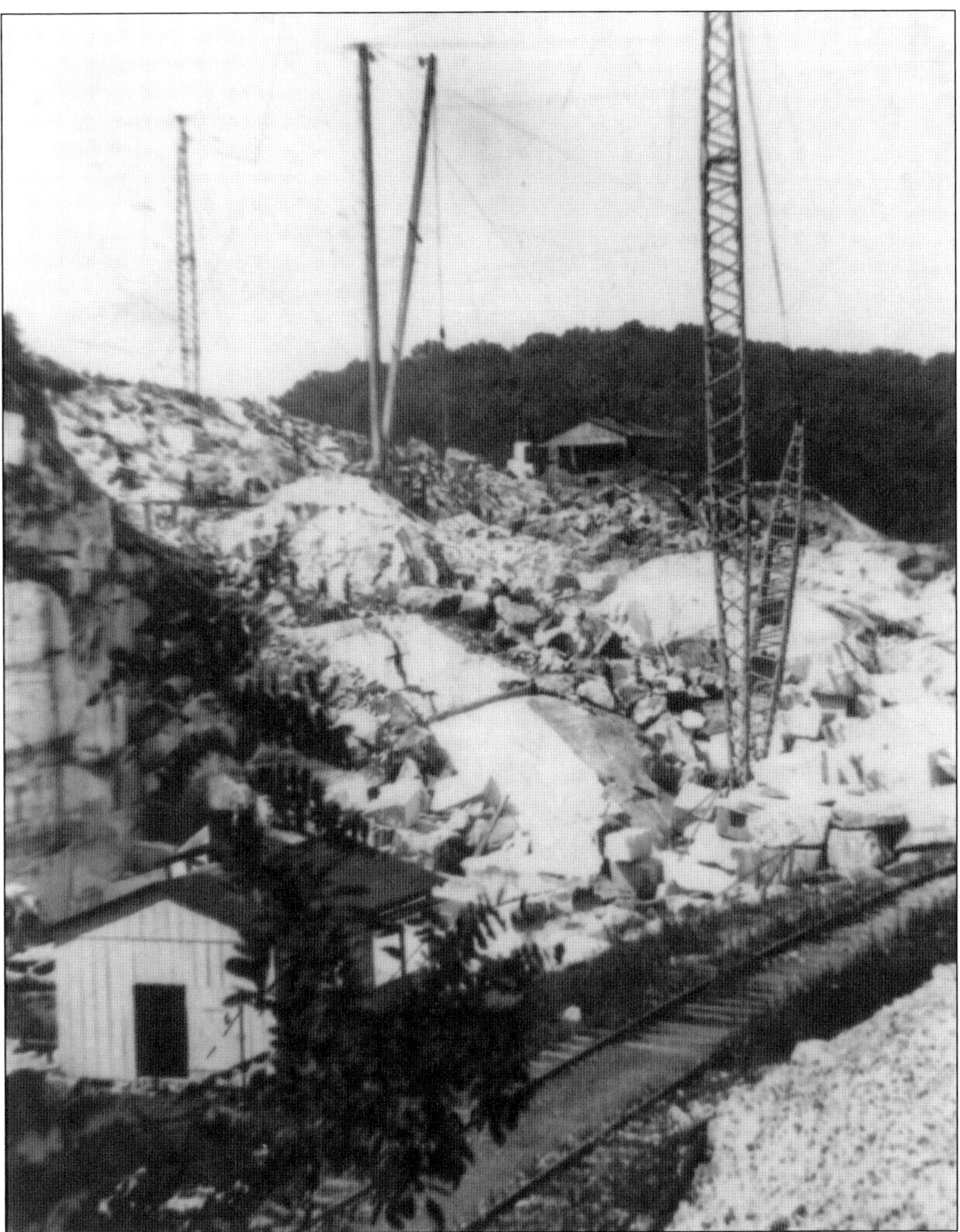

Steel derricks situated around the quarry pit made easier work of moving the marble blocks from the quarry face to the mill or straight on to a railcar. However, as quarrying progressed, lower levels of marble were often fractured or too low in quality to be usable. During the limestone-manufacturing era, marble was blasted using dynamite and transferred to a crusher by crane. It was then heated in the limekilns to remove moisture to make lime. (Knox County Two Centuries Photograph Project, McClung Historical Collection.)

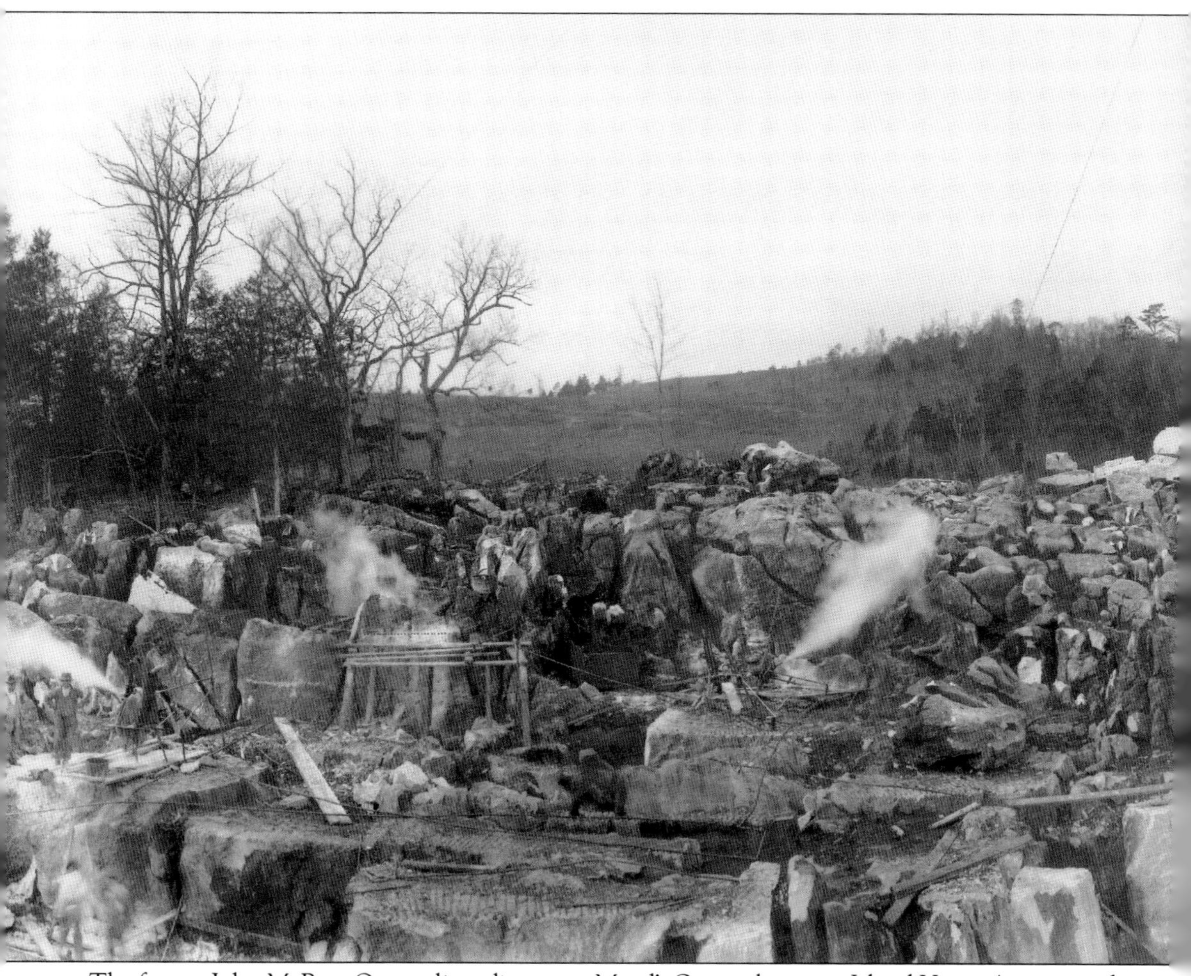

The former John M. Ross Quarry lies adjacent to Mead's Quarry between Island Home Avenue and Sevierville Pike. Unlike Mead's Quarry, the quarry gorge is dry and adds another topographical dimension to the Ijams wildlife sanctuary. The property features several natural cave formations, which have been gated for visitor safety and to protect critical habitat for the Berry cave salamander, a rare and threatened species in Tennessee. Although not a true marble, the rock originally

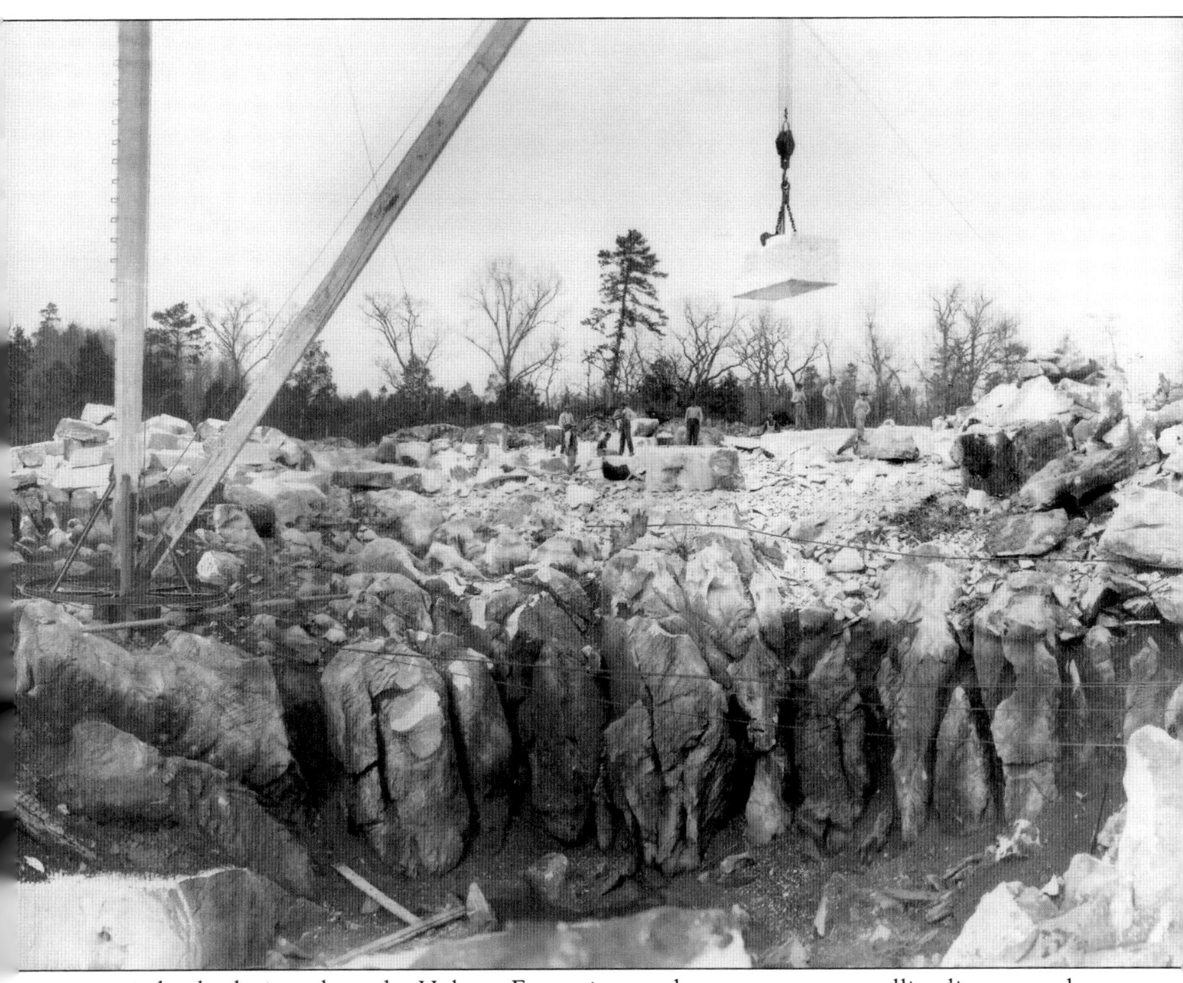

quarried at both sites along the Holston Formation produces a coarse-crystalline limestone that is easily polished, producing an attractive, decorative stone. The Holston Formation, high in calcium carbonate, is an accumulation of sediments from an ancient reef complex believed to be 500 million years old. (Thompson Photograph Collection.)

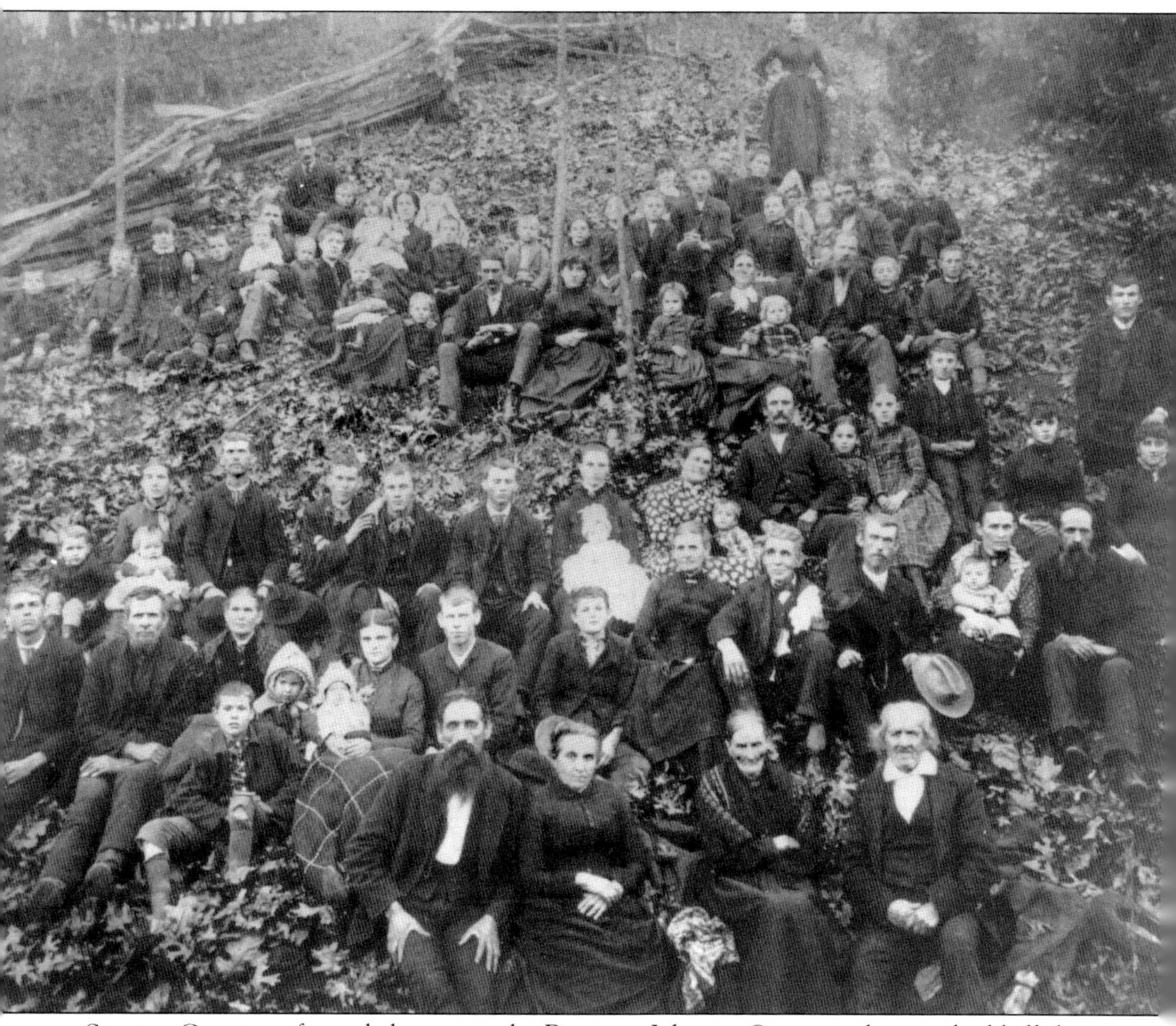

Stanton Cemetery, formerly known as the Dempsey Johnson Cemetery, lies on the bluff above Mead's Quarry. The name changed when the site evolved into a community cemetery. The photograph shows a Johnson family reunion in 1880, with Dempsey Johnson sitting on the front row at far left. The graves of Dempsey and Mary Johnson face east and west; they were laid to rest head-to-head because they were divorced in life. It is likely that many of the men pictured here worked at Mead's Quarry. (Mary Farmer.)

About the Author

Paul James is executive director for Ijams Nature Center, a 275-acre wildlife sanctuary and environmental learning center providing community-wide connections and experiences through education, conservation, recreation, and responsible environmental stewardship for all people.

A native of Great Britain, James joined Ijams as development director in 2000 before assuming a leadership role in 2004. Prior to joining Ijams, James worked in New York and Atlanta with CARE USA and at the University of Derby in the United Kingdom. He has a bachelor's of science in organization management, a higher national diploma in business and finance, and a diploma in management. He has served on a number of Knoxville community boards, including as chair of Knox County Parks and Recreation Advisory Board and chair of Dow Chemical Company Community Advisory Panel, and he is an ex-officio board member of Legacy Parks Foundation. He graduated from Leadership Knoxville in 2006.

James has written a series of articles for the *Tennessee Conservationist* magazine as well as the guide for Ijams's Lost Species exhibit. He is a regular speaker on extinct species and the history of Ijams Nature Center throughout the community and at the acclaimed annual Wilderness Wildlife Week in Pigeon Forge.

Author royalties from sales of this book directly support Ijams Nature Center. To learn more about Ijams Nature Center, please visit www.ijams.org.

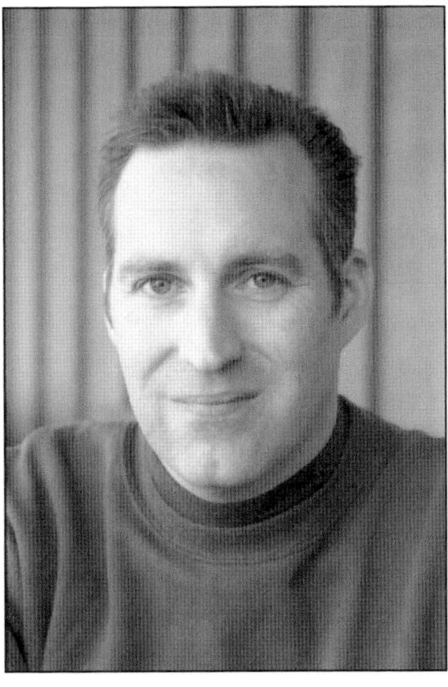

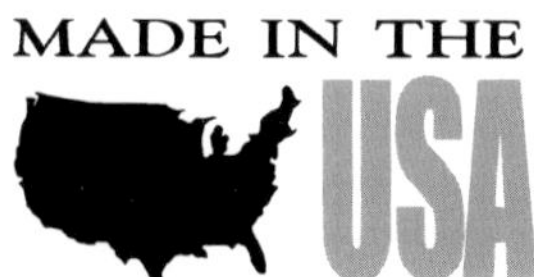

MADE IN THE
USA